AF600342

DISQUALIFICATION OF ELECTORS IN ECCLESIASTICAL ELECTIONS

THE CATHOLIC UNIVERSITY OF AMERICA
CANON LAW STUDIES
No. 365

Disqualification of Electors in Ecclesiastical Elections

A DISSERTATION

SUBMITTED TO THE FACULTY OF THE SCHOOL OF CANON LAW OF THE CATHOLIC UNIVERSITY OF AMERICA IN PARTIAL FULFILLMENT OF THE REQUIREMENTS FOR THE DEGREE OF DOCTOR OF CANON LAW

BY

TIMOTHY MOCK

PRIEST OF THE CONGREGATION OF MARIANNHILL MISSIONARIES

THE CATHOLIC UNIVERSITY OF AMERICA PRESS
WASHINGTON, D.C.
1958

IMPRIMI POTEST:
WILLEHAD K. KRAUSE, C.M.M.
Superior Regionalis
Dearborn, Michigan, May 9, 1955

NIHIL OBSTAT:
EDWARD G. ROELKER, S.T.D., J.C.D.
Censor Deputatus
Washington, D.C., May 25, 1955

IMPRIMATUR:
✠ PATRICK A. O'BOYLE
Archiepiscopus Washingtonensis

Washington, D.C., May 25, 1955

Printed by The Abbey Press, St. Meinrad, Indiana, U.S.A.

FOREWORD

In her solicitude for the spiritual welfare of the souls entrusted to her by her Spouse, Holy Mother Church has always been concerned about securing worthy and competent superiors to rule the faithful. Since Christ himself did not determine the method of selecting persons to fill the various positions of authority, the task has fallen to the Church. She has used diverse methods at different times, using whatever method, in view of circumstances, best insured the choice of qualified persons. Among the methods used are election, presentation, postulation, and direct appointment.

Election, as a means of selecting ecclesiastical officials, has its definite advantages. It precludes the danger of forcing a superior on unwilling subjects. An election evinces the choice of the many, not of the few. Where communication with higher superiors is difficult, the local community usually knows the qualities of the candidates better than do the distant superiors. Election has, on the other hand, its disadvantages. A group of electors may sometimes be swayed by very superficial qualities and accordingly elect the one who pleases rather than the one who is best qualified for the task. It is also a fact of history that those who are most in need of reform are the ones least likely to do anything to bring it about. Thus the members of a lax community will probably elect as superior a person who is indulgent and easygoing rather than one who will wield the rod that spares the soul.

The success of election as a means for selecting qualified officials will depend first of all on the obtaining of fit electors, and the excluding of those who are unfit. As an excellent brush in the hands of a second class painter does not produce first class works of art, so an election in the hands of unworthy electors does not lead to the obtaining of good officials. This dissertation will treat of the exclusion of unfit electors from ecclesiastical elections. Disqualifications in papal elections will not be treated, for such elections are governed by their own very particular set of rules.

Election was the most common means of filling ecclesiastical offices in the early Church. After the thirteenth century it was used less and less. After that time bishops were no longer elected but were appointed directly by the Holy See. New religious communities, such as the Society of Jesus, and the Congregations of simple vows which began to appear in the sixteenth century, were modeled along military lines and made much less use of elections than did the older religious orders. Elections have not, however, fallen into desuetude. They still play a role in the administration of the Church, especially in some religious communities. The historical part of this dissertation is of considerable importance, for indeed most of our present legislation in this matter was developed long before the promulgation of the Code of Canon Law. The study of its history will help us understand the present legislation.

In the canonical commentary the writer has sought to give a composite picture of the elements which effect the disqualification of electors. The origin, nature, effects, and cessation of disqualifications have been treated. The pre-Code history with reference to disqualifications has opened the door to the solution of many of the difficulties which arose in connection with the task of interpreting the canons of the Code.

The writer wishes to take this opportunity to acknowledge his sincere appreciation to his former Regional Superior, the Very Reverend Joseph Reiner, C.M.M., for extending the opportunity to undertake graduate study in Canon Law, and to his former Regional Superior, the Very Reverend Willehad Krause, C.M.M., for granting the further opportunity to complete his studies. The writer is deeply grateful to the members of the Faculty of the School of Canon Law of the Catholic University of America not only for the generous and considerate assistance they have given him in the preparation of this dissertation, but also for having given him some insight into the meaning and wisdom of the laws of Holy Mother Church.

TABLE OF CONTENTS

PART TWO

CANONICAL COMMENTARY

PART ONE

HISTORICAL SYNOPSIS

CHAPTER I

PRELIMINARY CONCEPTS

ARTICLE I. THE CONCEPT OF ELECTION

Election, says Cardinal Hostiensis (d. 1271) in his *Summa Aurea,* is a term which can be used in various senses. In the widest sense, election denotes any selection, as for example, choosing one apple out of a basketful. In a narrower sense, it means any choosing of a person for an office, and includes nomination and postulation. In the strictest sense, election can be defined as the canonical call of a qualified person to a dignity (office) or to membership in a fraternal society.[1]

To be canonical the call had to be made according to the form prescribed by the twenty-fourth chapter of the IV General Council of the Lateran (1215).[2] This form gave detailed instructions for voting by scrutiny, but allowed a simpler method of election *per compromissarios.* It also admitted the possibility of election *quasi per inspirationem,* that is, by unanimous and spontaneous consent of all the electors without the usual procedure of balloting. In the present work only election in the strict sense, excluding nomination and postulation, will be considered.

The terms "*electio*" and "*nominatio*" had somewhat different significations at the time of the Decretals than these words have at the present time. Nomination, in connection with election, did not mean the proposing of a person as a candidate to be voted on, but it meant the casting of one's ballot for a candidate. Nomination was called "private election" later in the decretalist period. In the eyes of the medieval canonists the balloting by the electors (nomina-

[1] Hostiensis (Henricus de Segusio), *Summa Aurea* (Venetiis, 1570), *de electione et electi potestate* (I, 6), § *Quid sit electio,* 27, a. r.

[2] Labbeus-Cossartius, *Sacrosancta Concilia* (17 vols. in 18, Parisiis, 1672), XI, par I, 176 (hereafter cited Labbeus); Mansi, *Sacrorum Conciliorum Nova et Amplissima Collectio* (53 vols. in 60, Parisiis, 1907-1927), XXII, 1011 (hereafter cited Mansi).

tion or private election) did not constitute the true act of election. The true election consisted in the "common or capitular election." This capitular election was performed after the balloting had taken place and after the votes had been counted and the results published. One member of the electoral college, in the name of the majority who had voted for a certain candidate, proclaimed, "I, N. N., in my own name (provided he had voted for the successful candidate), and in the name of all those who are in agreement with me, elect N. N. as Bishop (or Abbot, Archdeacon, etc.), and I pronounce him as elected, in the name of the Father, and of the Son, and of the Holy Ghost." If the speaker had not voted for the successful candidate, he said, "In the name of all who agreed upon this man, etc." This act, which seems rather superfluous to us moderns, was considered as the essence of the election. This resulted from the strong idea that the election was a capitular or common act. The individual ballots were, in the opinion of the decretalists, so many distinct and individual acts, and not the act of the voting chapter as a whole.[3] Sometimes a minority of the electors would object to the candidate elected by the majority, and proceed to have one of the electors elect the candidate of their choice. The dispute between the candidate elected by the majority and the candidate elected by the minority often came to the Holy See for settlement, and much of the Decretal Law consists of the decisions of such cases.

Article II. The Concept of Disqualification

Section 1. Invalidity

A disqualifying law in the strict technical sense may be defined as a law which deprives a person who posseses the *natural* capacity to act validly, of his *juridic* capacity to act

[3] Cf. *Casus* ad c. 56, X, *de electione et electi potestate*, I, 6; Reiffenstuel, *Ius Canonicum Universum* (4 vols., Venetiis, 1735), Lib. I, tit. 6, nn. 283-294 (hereafter cited Reiffenstuel); Hostiensis, *Summa Aurea, de electione et electi potestate* (I, 6), § *Ubi fieri debet*, 26 b. r.

validly.[4] According to this definition, laws which declare a person incapable of acting validly because of the lack of natural requirements are not disqualifying laws.[5] In a wider sense, such laws may be called natural laws of disqualification, and they will be so considered in this dissertation.

Disqualifying laws which render contrary acts null and void *ipso facto* are disqualifying in the fullest sense of the word. Those laws which do not render contrary acts automatically void, but render them only voidable through the sentence of a judge or of a superior, are disqualifying in a lesser degree. Laws which prohibit certain acts, with or without threatening a penalty, but which render contrary acts neither void nor voidable, are not disqualifying laws; they are merely prohibitory laws.[6]

It is clear from the whole of title six, *de electione et electi potestate,* of the Decretals of Pope Gregory IX (1227-1241) that the Decretal laws which excluded certain persons from voting were true laws of disqualification and not merely prohibitory laws. The various chapters of the title, which are, for the most part, decisions of cases, deal not with the question of licitness but with that of validity. One does not find any simple prohibitory laws in connection with elections till the advent of the Code.

Not only were the disqualifications of the Decretals truly disqualifying, but they were disqualifying in the fullest sense. Votes cast by voters who were disqualified were not merely voidable but were void *ipso facto.* This can be seen by the wording of the various laws. Such expressions as "*eligendi ea vice potestate priventur,*" "*eligendi tunc potestate*

[4] Cf. Cicognani, *Canon Law* (Westminster: The Newman Press, 1949), p. 558; Vermeersch-Creusen, *Epitome Iuris Canonici* (Vol. I, 7. ed., 1949, Vol. II, 6. ed., 1940, Vol. III, 6. ed., 1946, Mechliniae-Romae: H. Dessain), I, 103-104 (hereafter cited *Epitome*); Beste, *Introductio in Codicem* (3. ed., Collegeville: St. John's Abbey Press, 1946), pp. 68-69.

[5] Cf. Vermeersch-Creusen, *Epitome,* I, 104.

[6] Beste, *Introductio in Codicem,* pp. 68-69; Vermeersch-Creusen, *Epitome,* I, 104-105.

privati," and "*eligendi potestate careant*" are used.[7] These expressions do not merely threaten a future sentence of nullification, but indicate that the person does not have the *power* to vote validly. The phrase "*nullam obtineat firmitatem*" is used as regards an election conducted with laymen taking part.[8] This expressive phrase demonstrates clearly that the election was invalid *ab initio*. The clearest proof of all is contained in the *glossa ordinaria* to c. 16, X, *de electione et electi potestate,* I, 6. The gloss, in commenting on the word *cassata,* stated, "*id est cassa nunciata, quia suspensi eligere non possunt.*"[9] This shows that the sentence was not condemnatory but simply declaratory.[10] The contention that the votes of disqualified electors were invalid *ipso facto* is supported by the commentary of Pope Innocent IV (1243-1254). The Pope, in giving rules to decide whether an election is valid even though an earlier election had taken place, wrote:

> Melius credimus quod si electio [prima] est nulla propter eligentes, nullam habent nec habuerunt potestatem eligendi, quia tunc tenet secunda electio . . . vel habuerunt quidem potestatem eligendi, sed amiserunt, ut quia sunt excommunicati . . . quia *semper* nulla est electio prima, et secunda tenet.[11]

SECTION 2. IGNORANCE

According to the Code of Canon Law, an act performed by a person laboring under a disqualification is invalid even

[7] Cf., e.g., c. 6, 25, 41, 43, 50, X, *de electione et electi potestate,* I, 6.

[8] C. 56, X, *de electione et electi potestate,* I, 6.

[9] Cf. also Hostiensis, *In Libros Decretalium Commentaria* (6 vols. in 4, Venetiis, 1581), ad c. 16, X, *de electione et electi potestate,* I, 6, s. v. *cassata,* I, 45 b. v., n. 16 (hereafter cited *Commentaria*).

[10] Cf. *glossa ordinaria* ad c. 37, X, *de electione et electi potestate,* I, 6, s. v. *irritare;* c. 43, 53, 55, X, *de electione et electi potestate,* I, 6.

[11] Innocentius IV (Sinibaldo de' Fieschi), *In V Libros Decretalium Commentaria* (Venetiis, 1570), ad c. 10, X, *de electione et electi potestate,* I, 6, p. 55, n. 3 (hereafter cited *Commentaria*).

though the person is unaware of his disability, unless the law expressly disposes otherwise.[12] As today, so at the time of the Decretals, ignorance did not save one from the invalidating effects of a disqualification. Thus, impediments to marriage did not cease to bind because of ignorance.[13] Hostiensis taught that a person cannot allege ignorance as an excuse when a legate of the Holy Father had laid down the requirement of sacred orders for voters in a clerical chapter.[14] Pope Innocent IV did not admit ignorance of law or ignorance of fact as an excuse to save an election from invalidity if the voters were disqualified or if some other violation of the law made the election void or voidable.[15]

It may be pointed out that, although ignorance did not undo the invalidating effects of a disqualification already incurred, it did sometimes excuse from the *incurring* of the disqualification.[16]

[12] Can. 16, § 1.

[13] C. 3, X, *de clandestina desponsatione*, IV, 3.

[14] *Summa Aurea, de electione et electi potestate*, (I, 6), § *Et qui nullo*, 28 a. r.

[15] "... Nec valent excusari, quod ex ignorantia iuris vel facti deliquerunt, sive scienter sive ignoranter contra praedicta fecerint; electio est nulla vel annullanda ..."—*Commenaria*, ad. c. 10, X, *de electione et electi potestate*, I, 6, p. 55, n. 2.

[16] Cf. c. 25, X, *de electione et electi potestate*, I, 6; et *glossa* ad idem, s.v. *scienter*.

CHAPTER II

DISQUALIFICATIONS BY REASON OF DEFECTS

ARTICLE I. NON-MEMBERS

It was a principle of the Decretal law that the election of prelates belonged to the respective collegiate chapters. The election of other ecclesiastical officials was usually determined by custom. The right to choose minor officials could be the joint right of the chapter and the Ordinary, the right of the chapter alone, or the right of the Ordinary, with or without the obligation of consulting the advice of his cathedral chapter.[1]

SECTION 1. ELECTION OF BISHOPS

The exclusive right of the cathedral chapter to elect the Bishop for the diocese was well established by the time of Pope Gregory IX. Innocent III, in deciding a case, stated: "*. . . secundum statuta canonica electiones episcoporum ad cathedralium ecclesiarum clericos regulariter pertinere noscantur.*"[2] This rule excluded monks.[3] At an earlier time they had been admitted to give advice and to give their approval of the candidate chosen, but not to elect.[4]

Secular clerics who did not belong to the chapter were also excluded.[5] Even suffragan bishops were excluded from the election of a metropolitan bishop, unless they had acquired the right by ancient custom.[6]

[1] *Hostiensis, Summa Aurea, de electione et electi potestate* (I, 6), § *Quis possit eligere,* 27 b. r.—28 a. r.

[2] C. 3, X, *de causis possessionis et proprietatis,* II, 12.

[3] *Loc. cit.*

[4] ". . . ad eligendum episcopum sufficiat ecclesiae matricis arbitrium." —*Dictum* ad c. 35, D. LXIII.

[5] C. 50, X, *de electione et electi potestate,* I, 6.

[6] ". . . requisito suffraganeorum assensu *si* esset de antiqua et approbata consuetudine requirendus."—C. 4, X, *de postulatione praelatorum,* I, 5.

SECTION 2. ELECTION OF ABBOTS

Pope Gregory I (590-604) in the III Council of the Lateran (601), guaranteed monks freedom from intereference from outsiders in their monastic elections.[7] This decree of the III Council of the Lateran corresponds almost word for word with an epistle of Pope Gregory, written in April of the year 598.[8] This law is found also in the *Decretum* and in the *Panormia* of Ivo of Chartres (d. 1117).[9] It is found incorporated in the *Decretum* of Gratian.[10]

C. 43, C. XVI, q. 7, reiterating the legislation contained in the eighteenth chapter of the Council of Mainz (847), forbade the bishop of the diocese to appoint an abbot against the will of the monks of the abbey.[11] Pope Innocent III stated it to be the common law that the election of the abbot belonged to the monks of the abbey.[12] Not only secular clerics were excluded, but also the monks from other abbeys.[13]

[7] Labbeus, V, 1607; cf. Hardouin, *Acta Conciliorum et Epistolae Decretales ac Constitutiones Summorum Pontificum* (12 vols., Romae, 1714-1715), III, 538-539 (hereafter cited Hardouin); Hefele-Leclercq, *Histoire des Conciles* (11 vols. in 21, Paris: Letouzey et Ané, 1901-1952), III, 239.

[8] *Gregorii I Papae Registrum Epistolarum* (2 vols. in 5, ed. P. Ewald et L. M. Hartmann, Berolini, 1891-1899), II prima pars, 19; Jaffé, *Regesta Pontificum Romanorum ab condita Ecclesia ad Annum post Christum natum MCXCVIII* (2. ed. by F. Kaltenbrunner [—to the year 590], P. Ewald [590-882], and S. Löwenfeld [882-1198], and referred to as JK, JE, JL), n. 1504.

[9] *Decretum,* VII, c. 24—Migne (1800-1875), *Patrologiae Cursus Completus,* Series Latina (221 vols., Parisiis, 1844-1864), CLXI, 551 (hereafter cited *MPL*); *Decretum,* VII, 11—*MPL,* CLXI, 547; *Panormia,* III, 181—*MPL,* CLXI, 1173.

[10] C. 4, C. XVIII, q. 2.

[11] Cf. Burchard of Worms (d. 1025), *Decretum,* VIII, 86—*MPL,* CXL, 809; Ivo, *Decretum,* VIII, 104—*MPL,* CLXI, 568.

[12] C. 8, X, *de consuetudine,* I, 4.

[13] *Loc. cit.;* c. 47, X, *de electione et electi potestate,* I, 6. In the latter canon Pope Honorius III (1216-1227) denied two abbots the right of participating in an election in the monastery to which they had belonged before they became abbots.

SECTION 3. ADMISSION OF NON-MEMBERS

The law of the exclusive right of the chapters to elect their own prelates was overgrown with various contrary customs and Apostolic indults.[14] If, however, anyone claimed the right to participate in an election by reason of a privilege, custom, or prescription, he had to prove his claim. To prove his rightful dependence on a custom, he had to show a *iustus titulus* and continued possession.[15] If a non-member's right to be present was challenged by any of the electors, he was admitted under the "protest" or proclamation that only the votes of those who had the right to be present would be valid. This "protest" put the burden of proof on the non-member. If he failed to prove his right, his vote was invalid.[16] Both the non-member and the chapter had to agree to this "protest."[17] The commentators did not indicate how much time was given to a person within which to prove his right. It seems that the matter was referred to the competent higher superior for decision whenever the vote of such a non-member played a vital role in the outcome of the election. The "protest" prevented easy admission of a non-member to an election. It also prevented the election from being invalid by reason of lay interference *(abusus saecularis potestatis)* in case a layman who actually lacked the right to be present was admitted, for the layman did not intrude himself into the election by force or fraud, nor did the chapter willingly admit a non-qualified layman.[18] If the "protest" was not asked or given, the vote

[14] C. 50, X, *de electione et electi potestate,* I, 6; c. 4, X, *de postulatione praelatorum,* I, 5; c. 3, X, *de causis possessionis et proprietatis,* II, 12; c. 8, X, *de consuetudine,* I, 4; cf. Hostiensis, *Summa Aurea, de electione et electi potestate* (I, 6), § *Qui potest eligere,* 27 b. r.

[15] Hostiensis, *loc. cit.;* c. 8, X, *de consuetudine,* I, 4; c. 17, X, *de praescriptionibus,* II, 26.

[16] Hostiensis, *loc. cit.;* c. 50, X, *de electione et electi potestate,* I, 6; *glossa ordinaria* ad idem c., s. v. *protestatione.*

[17] Hostiensis, *Commentaria,* ad c. 50, X, *de electione et electi potestate,* I, 6, s. v. *sub huiusmodi protestatione,* I, 71 b. v., ante n. 1.

[18] *Glossa* ad c. 43, X, *de electione et electi potestate,* I, 6, s. v.

of anyone who had quasi-possession of the right to vote was valid.[19]

According to the teaching of the commentators, the electoral chapter could admit a non-member to participate in an election, provided that the non-member was a cleric.[20] The commentators argued that, inasmuch as the chapter could entrust the entire election to non-members in an election *per compromissarios*, it could also bestow part of the election (namely, the right to vote) on non-members.[21] Unanimous consent of the electors was required when there was to be granted to an outsider the right to vote, because this was a matter affecting each voter, inasmuch as the worth of his vote was depreciated by the admission of other voters.[22] The chapter could not give a non-member the permanent right to vote, but could grant the right only *per modum actus*. This, no doubt, was due to the fact that the right to elect in future elections belonged to the members who were to constitute the chapter at that later time. The consent of each of those future members, who might be different from the earlier members, was required to give a non-member the right to vote in the later election, just as the consent of the earlier members was required when there was to be given to a non-member the right to vote in the earlier election.

abusum; Hostiensis, *loc. cit.;* Innocentius IV, *Commentaria,* ad. c. 50, X, *de electione et electi potestate,* I, 6, s. v. *protestatione,* p. 93, n. 1.

[19] *Glossa* ad c. 50, X, *de electione et electi potestate,* I, 6, s. v. *protestatione.*

[20] Cf. Panormitanus (Nicholaus de 'Tudeschi, Abbas Siculus), *Omnia quae extant Commentaria* (8 vols., Venetiis, 1588), ad c. 40, X, *de electione et electi potestate,* I, 6, I, 426, n. 3 (hereafter cited *Commentaria*); Innocentius IV, *Commentaria,* ad c. 25, X, *de electione et electi potestate,* I, 6, p. 69, n. 4; Hostiensis, *Commentaria,* ad. c. 25, X, *de electione et electi potestate,* I, 6, s. v. *admittendos,* 53 b. r., nn. 6 & 7.

[21] Cf. Panormitanus, *op. cit., loc. cit.*

[22] Panormitanus, *op. cit.,* ad c. 25, X, *de electione et electi potestate,* I, 6, I, 378, nn. 3 & 4; Reg. 29, R. J., in VI°.

Article II. The Absent

Absent voters, as a general rule, could not vote in elections. Under certain conditions, however, it became possible for an absent voter to cast his ballot by proxy. The conditions under which one could vote by proxy were given in the twenty-fourth chapter of the IV Lateran Council.[23] If the absent voter was in a place in which he could receive the summons, and if he was impeded from attending the election by a real impediment, then he could commit his vote to one of the members of the electoral body. The absent voter had to be willing to verify the existence of the impediment under oath if necessary.[24]

A person did not need to be summoned if this could not be done without danger to any of the persons involved,[25] or if the person was too far distant. A person was considered to be too far distant if the distance could not be covered in two days' journeying.[26] The person was to be summoned even though it was obvious that he could not come personally, since possibly he could vote by proxy.[27] The law did not list what could be considered as lawful *(iustum)* impediments, but the gloss gave a few examples, such as fear of harm, sickness, and a summons to some higher tribunal.[28] There were, of course, many other reasons, but, as Hostiensis remarked, not all of them could be enumerated.[29] The oath concerning the existence of the impediment was taken by the proxy. For this he needed a special mandate from

[23] Labbeus, XI, pars 1, 176; Mansi, XXII, 1011; c. 42, X, *de electione et electi potestate,* I, 6.

[24] *Loc. cit.*

[25] C. 28, X, *de electione et electi potestate,* I, 6; *glossa* ad. c. 42, X, *de electione et electi potestate,* I, 6, s. v. *commode.*

[26] Hostiensis, *Commentaria,* ad c. 42, X, *de electione et electi potestate,* I, 6, s. v. *ne quis,* I, 67 b. r., n. 59.

[27] *Glossa* ad c. 42, X, *de electione et electi potestate,* I, 6, s. v. *venire.*

[28] *Loc. cit.;* cf. *glossa* ad c. 23, X, *de electione et electi potestate,* I, 6, s. v. *metuebant;* c. 1, C. V, q. 3.

[29] *Commentaria,* ad. c. 42, X, *de electione et electi potestate,* I, 6, s. v. *iustoque impedimento,* I, 68 b. v., n. 64.

the absent voter.[30] This oath had to express the belief of the absent voter that at the time of the election, without any fraud on his part, he was in a place where he had the right to receive the summons, and in which he was truly detained. Further, the oath had to express concrete facts, and was not to be taken according to a set stereotyped form.[31] When one reads c. 42, X, *de electione ėt electi potestate,* I, 6, one could be led to believe that the proxy had to be chosen from among the members of the chapter. Innocent IV was of this opinion.[32] Hostiensis, however, seemed uncertain about the matter, feeling that the choosing of one of the members of the chapter to act as proxy could indeed have been a requirement of the law, but it could also, perhaps, have been merely the customary way of doing it. The law, then, according to Hostiensis, was not necessarily laying down a prescription, but was simply saying that the customary voting by proxy was still permitted.[33] The problem was settled by Pope Boniface VIII (1294-1303). C. 46, *de electione et electi potestate,* I, 6, in VI°, reads: "...*nec ipse, nolente capitulo, extraneum valeat deputare.*" The chapter, then, could, if it wished, admit an outsider to act as proxy, but it was not obliged to do so. Panormitanus (1386-1453) explained that this rule was made for the purpose of safeguarding the secrets of the chapter, and of keeping the secrets from becoming known to those who did not belong to the chapter.[34] If one of the members of the

30 Hostiensis, *Commentaria,* ad c. 42, X, *de electione et electi potestate,* I, 6, s. v. *ne quis,* I, 68 a. v., n. 62; Innocentius IV, *Commentaria,* ad idem c., s. v. *illud,* p. 89, n. 11.

31 Hostiensis, *loc. cit.;* Innocentius IV, *loc. cit.;* Guido de Bayso (or Baysio, or Baisio), *In Decretorum Volumen Commentaria* (*Rosarium*) (Venetiis, 1577), ad c. 46, *de electione et electi potestate,* I, 6, in VI°, s. v. *iste procurator,* 40 a. b. (hereafter cited *Rosarium*).

32 "... haec procuratio [viz., per personam qui non est membrum collegii], quae est haec canone prohibente, pro nulla est habenda." —*loc. cit.*

33 *Commentaria,* ad. c. 42, X, *de electione et electi potestate,* I, 6, s. v. *de collegio,* I, 68 b. v., n. 65; *ibid.,* I, 65 b. r., n. 25.

34 *Commentaria,* ad. c. 42, X, *de electione et electi potestate,* I, 6, § *Illud,* s. v. *uni de collegio,* I, 441, n. 2.

chapter was chosen to act as proxy, the chapter had no choice but to admit him to vote as proxy.[35] No member of the chapter had to accept the office of acting as proxy for an absent voter.[36] If a member of the chapter accepted the task of acting as proxy, he had two votes, namely, his own and that of the absent member.[37] Thus it could happen that one voter cast votes for two different candidates. This could happen when the mandate commissioned the proxy to vote for a definite person. If the proxy felt that someone else was better qualified than the man named in the mandate, he could vote for the other man in his own name, and for the man named in the mandate in the name of the absent voter.[38] If, however, the mandate did not specify a definite candidate, the proxy could not vote for different persons, but had to cast both votes for the same candidate. The reason for this was that he was bound in conscience to vote for the person he believed to be best qualified for the vacant office.[39] If the proxy knew the person named in the mandate to be unworthy, he was morally bound to refuse to act as proxy.[40] If the absent voter died, the mandate ceased, unless the proxy did not know of his death. In the latter case the

[35] Ioannes Andreae, *In Titulum de Regulis Iuris Novella Commentaria* (Venetiis, 1581), reg. 79, § *septimo* (hereafter cited *Commentaria Novella*) ; *glossa* ad c. 42, X, *de electione et electi potestate,* I, 6, s. v. *venire.*

[36] "Invitus procurationem suscipere nemo cogitur..."—C. (2.12) 17; Inst. (3.26), § *mandatum; glossa* ad c. 46, *de electione et electi potestate,* I, 6, in VI°, s. v. *procurator.*

[37] Hostiensis, *Summa Aurea, de electione et electi potestate* (I, 6), § *Et qui nullo,* 29 a. r.; *Commentaria,* ad. c. 42, X, *de electione et electi potestate,* I, 6, s. v. *vicem suam,* I, 68 b. v., n. 65; Innocentius IV, *Commentaria,* ad idem c., s. v. *vicem suam,* p. 90, n. 14; c. 40, 53, X, *de electione et electi potestate,* I, 6; c. 12, X, *de sententia et re iudicata,* II, 27; c. 45, X, *de appellationibus,* II, 28.

[38] Hostiensis, *Summa Aurea, de electione et electi potestate* (I, 6), § *Et qui nullo,* 29 a. v.; Innocentius IV, *Commentaria,* ad. c. 42, X, *de electione et electi potestate,* I, 6, p. 90, n. 15.

[39] Innocentius IV, *loc. cit.*

[40] Hostiensis, *Summa Aurea, de electione et electi potestate* (I, 6), § *Et qui nullo,* 29 a. v.; cf. c. unic., X, *de scrutinio,* I, 12.

mandate and the vote cast were valid.[41]

The question of voting by letter was discussed by almost every commentator on the Decretals. The gloss ad c. 42, X, *de electione et electi potestate,* I, 6, s. v. *venire,* stated that an absent voter could vote by letter if no one in the chapter was willing to act as proxy for him. Hostiensis admitted that the opinion of Pope Innocent IV, namely, that the ballots cast by letter were invalid, was more in keeping with the strict sense of the wording of c. 42, X, *de electione et electi potestate,* I, 6, which required that the votes be cast secretly, singly, and *not before the scrutiny.* He thought, however, that if the sealed letter was opened only at the time of the scrutiny, then the requirements of the law were duly fulfilled. This interpretation was also more benign and equitable than the opposite opinion.[42] The stricter opinion of Pope Innocent IV prevailed, however, and became the law under Pope Boniface VIII.[43]

Article III. Laymen

The ecclesiastical discipline on the exclusion of the laity from ecclesiastical elections had developed gradually. The *Decretum* of Gratian marked the end of the participation of lay persons in ecclesiastical elections. The "*electio per clerum et populum,*" which had prevailed in earlier times, gave way to election by clerics alone. There are canons in the *Decretum* of Gratian which, indeed, seem mutually contradictory. The one canon treats of election by the clergy and the people, and another adverts to the exclusion of the laity.[44] Gratian resolved the difficulty by saying that the clerics were to do the actual electing, and the members of the laity

[41] *Rosarium,* ad c. 46, *de electione et electi potestate,* I, 6, in VI°, s. v. *iste procurator,* 40 a. r.

[42] *Commentaria,* ad c. 42, X, *de electione et electi potestate,* I, 6, s. v. *ne quis,* I, 68 a. r., n. 63.

[43] C. 46, *de electione et electi potestate,* I, 6, in VI°.

[44] Cf., e.g., c. 13, 20, 43, D. LXIII; c. 1, 2, D. LXII; c. 10, 11, 12, 26, D. LXIII.

were to approve the person elected.[45] The people, including temporal princes, were forbidden to meddle in the actual election.[46] Even the requirement of the approval by the laity was toned down by the author of the *glossa ordinaria* to the *Decretum* of Gratian (Ioannes Teutonicus), so that "the people were understood to consent if they did not object."[47] Refusal of the people to give consent did not automatically invalidate the election, but they could petition the competent superior to nullify it. It seems that such a petition was seldom made, and even more rarely granted. As the gloss points out, there were too many considerations militating against such a nullification.[48]

Although many canons in the *Decretum* forbade princes and emperors to participate in the election of clerics,[49] yet there are at least two canons which purported to give the Emperor the right to elect the Pope.[50] Gratian did not question the authenticity of these decrees. He explained that they were special privileges granted by the Pope in order to strengthen his position in his fight against heretics and schismatics. In the *dictum* to c. 33, D. LXIII, he claimed that this privilege was no longer in force because it had been surrendered by King Louis [V ?].

Gratian summed up his interpretation of the various laws on the participation of laymen in elections in his *dictum* before c. 25, D. LXIII, in these words:

> . . . liquido colligitur, laicos non esse excludendos ab electione, neque principes reiciendos ab ordinatione ecclesiarum. Sed quod populus iubetur electioni interesse, non praecipitur advocari ad electio-

[45] Cf. c. 1, 2, D. LXII; C. 10, 11, 12, 26, D. LXIII. Cf. also *dicta* and *glossa* ad haec capitula.

[46] C. 1, 2, 6, 8, D. LXIII.

[47] *Glossa* ad c. 1, D. LXII, s. v. *nec a plebibus*.

[48] *Loc. cit.*

[49] Cf., e.g., c. 1, 2, 3, 4, 5, 7, D. LXIII; c. 12-20, C. XVI, q. 7.

[50] C. 22, D. LXIII (cf. JE, n. 2406), which is the false decree attributed to Pope Hadrian I (772-795), supposedly granting Charlemagne and his successors the right of selecting the Pope; c. 23, D. LXIII (cf. JL, n. 3704), in which Pope Leo VIII (963-965) supposedly repeated the grant to Emperor Otto I (936-973).

> nem faciendum, sed consensum electioni adhibendum. Sacerdotum enim (ut in fine superioris capituli Stephanae Papae legitur) est electio; et fidelis populi est humiliter consentire.

The content of Gratian's *dictum* is embodied in various canons of the Decretals of Pope Gregory IX. To the Abbot of Cluny, Pope Gregory wrote that the right to elect in a collegiate church cannot fall to a layman. Any such practice was an infringement on the liberty of the Church and remained without binding force.[51] To the chapter of Massa (Italy) he wrote: *"Edicto perpetuo prohibemus ne per laicos cum canonicis Pontificis electio praesumatur. Quae si forte praesumpta fuerit, nullam obtineat firmitatem, non obstante contraria consuetudine, quae dici debet potius corruptela."*[52] The right, as Hostiensis insisted, could not be obtained by a layman except by way of a direct concession from the Holy Father.[53]

The patron of a collegiate church sometimes had the right to approve the elections conducted for that particular church. If, however, he withheld his approval, the election was not invalidated.[54] Hostiensis granted that a prince could be present to protect the clerics from oppression, and that the people could be present to give their approval to the election.[55] But all the canons, he added further, which allowed laymen to be present at an election were to be corrected, unless they were to be understood as simply allowing the laymen to be present after the election had been completed.[56]

Article IV. The Mentally Defective

The writer has not found any canon in the *Corpus Iuris Canonici* which expressly declares that the mentally defec-

[51] C. 51, X, *de electione et electi potestate*, I, 6.

[52] C. 56, X, *de electione et electi potestate*, I, 6.

[53] *Summa Aurea, de electione et electi potestate* (I, 6), § *Quis potest eligere*, 27 b. r.

[54] Hostiensis, *loc. cit.;* c. 14, X, *de electione et electi potestate*, I, 6.

[55] *Loc. cit.;* cf. c. 20, X, *de electione et electi potestate*, I, 6.

[56] Hostiensis, *loc. cit.;* cf. *supra*, p. 8.

tive are disqualified as voters. Perhaps this may be accounted for by the fact that the Roman law, under which the Church lived, had quite thoroughly treated of the legal incapacity of mental defectives.

The commentators on the *Corpus Iuris Canonici* did not treat the matter at great length, but they did make an occasional reference to it. Thus the author of the *glossa ordinaria* to the *Liber Sextus* [Ioannes Andreae (d. 1348)] stated that the insane cannot vote because, like children, they lack discretion.[57] In his *Commentaria Novella,* Ioannes Andreae taught that the insane cannot be admitted to elections, not even as proxies, for the same reason that minors cannot be admitted.[58] Hostiensis had earlier asserted that minors lacked the maturity of judgment necessary for voting and, therefore, were barred from elections.[59] His argument applied with even greater force to the demented. Indeed, the insane and the demented were mentioned along with minors in the *dictum* to D. (4.8) 27, and the *dictum* of Gratian to C. III, q. 7, which Hostiensis cited in support of his argument against the eligibility of minors.

In other places the commentators, while not mentioning elections specifically, stated that the mentally defective are incapable of human acts, that is, of the acts which flow from the intellect and the will. The *glossa ordinaria* to c. 2, C. XV, q. 1, s. v. *furiosus,* pointed out that the acts of the insane ought to be considered as accidents rather than as human acts. Elsewhere also it was stated that the insane cannot give consent.[60]

Article V. Persons Lacking the Requisite Age

Persons below the age of puberty were disqualified as

[57] *Glossa ordinaria* ad. c. 32, *de electione et electi potestate,* I, 6, in VI°, s. v. *discretione.*

[58] Reg. 67, § *Octavo;* cf. D. (3.3) 2.

[59] *Summa Aurea, de electione et electi potestate* (I, 6), § *Et qui nullo,* 28 a. r.

[60] *Glossa ordinaria* ad c. 3, *de haereticis,* V, 2, in VI°, s. v. *non sane;* c. 24, X, *de sponsalibus et matrimoniis,* IV, 1.

voters. Hostiensis argued from the Roman law in favor of their disqualification. He remarked that, inasmuch as persons below the age of *twenty-five* were not allowed to vote according to civil law, *a fortiori* persons below the *age of puberty* should not be allowed to vote in ecclesiastical elections.[61] This disqualification was considered as a *natural* disability, because youths of such tender years were regarded as lacking the discretion necessary for electing wisely.[62] The age of puberty was fourteen for boys and twelve for girls.[63]

In this matter of age, Hostiensis indeed required more than the age of puberty. It seemed, so he contended, that all below the age of eighteen could not vote, unless they had a dispensation from the Pope. His reason for taking this position was that a person younger than eighteen could not be delegated to act as judge except by the ruling prince;[64] therefore, by analogy, a person younger than eighteen could not vote (which in the opinion of Hostiensis seemed to require the same maturity of judgment), except with the consent of the supreme ruler of the Church.[65] The gloss to c. 2, *de aetate et qualitate,* I, 6, in Clem., s. v. *constitutus,* insisted that not only must a man be a subdeacon in order to qualify as an elector in a collegiate church, but he must also have attained the age of eighteen. The reasoning in this instance was that the legislator had demanded the subdiaconate as a requirement both because of the order and because of the minimum age required for that order, viz., eighteen. Therefore, if a man, by special dispensation, was ordained a subdeacon before eighteen, he was not allowed to exercise the

[61] *Summa Aurea, de electione et electi potestate* (I, 6), § *Et qui nullo,* 28 a. r.; cf. D. (50.2) 6.

[62] Hostiensis, *loc. cit.; dictum* ad C. III, q. 7; c. 32, *de electione et electi potestate,* I, 6, in VI°; D. (4.8) 27.

[63] C. 3, X, *de aetate et qualitate et ordine praeficiendorum,* I, 14; c. 32, 43, *de electione et electi potestate,* I, 6, in VI°.

[64] C. 41, X, *de officio et potestate iudicis delegati,* I, 29.

[65] *Summa Aurea, de electione et electi potestate* (I, 6), § *Et qui nullo,* 28 a. r.

voting rights attached to that order until he had reached the age of eighteen.[66] Panormitanus, following Paul de Liazariis (d. 1356), a commentator on the Clementine Constitutions, disagreed. He wrote: "*Paulus tamen ibi tenet contrarium, et forte hoc casu verius, quia hic non requiritur ordinis executio, ut habeat vocem, nec est ipse iure suspensus sed suspendus.*"[67] The discussion was not concerned with elections in convents of nuns. For such elections the age of puberty certainly sufficed.[68]

In computing the age of electors, commentators generally followed the rule of civil law, namely, that in favorable matters it sufficed to have begun the day or the year stated in the law, whereas in unfavorable matters the day or year had to be completed before the obligation began.[69] Panormitanus followed a different rule. The interpretation, so he claimed, depended on the grammatical case of the words used in the law. If the law used "in" with the ablative, it sufficed to have begun the year. If, however, the law used the possessive case, or "in" or "ad" with the accusative case, then the year had to be completed before the right or the obligation began.[70] It seems that Panormitanus stood quite alone in following this rule.

[66] Cf. c. 3, *de aetate et qualitate*, I, 6, in Clem.

[67] Panormitanus, *Commentaria in Clementinas Epistolas* [i.e., Constitutiones] (continetur in *Omnia quae extant Commentaria*, vol. 7, post *Commentaria in Quinque Libros*) (Venetiis, 1588), ad c. 1, *de aetate et qualitate*, I, 6, in Clem., 403 b. v., n. 8 (hereafter cited *In Clem.*); *ibid.*, ad c. 2, *de aetate et qualitate*, I, 6, in Clem., 404 a. r., n. 4.

[68] C. 48, *de electione et electi potestate*, I, 6, in VI°.

[69] *Glossa* ad D. (4.4) 3, § *Minore;* Hostiensis, *Summa Aurea, de electione et electi potestate* (I, 6), § *Quis possit eligere*, 29, a. v.

[70] "Aliud importat, si dicitur quem esse in 18 anno et aliud dicitur quem esse, seu debere esse 18 annorum, nam primo casu satis est ad illorum verborum verificationem quod quis 18 annum inchoaverit, in secundo vero casu debet esse completus. . . . Item secus esse, si diceretur, cum pervenerit in 18 anno, vel ad 18 annos, . . . quia quando dictio, in, iungitur ablativo, significat intrinsice; ideo sufficit quod sit in illo anno constitutus: sed quando iungitur cum accusativo, tunc significat extrinsice; unde debet esse extra illum annum."—*In Clem.*, ad c. 2, *de aetate et qualitate*, in Clem. 404 a. r.-b. v., nn. 6 & 7.

Article VI. Persons Lacking the Required Orders

Before the time of Pope Clement V (1305-1314) there was no general law demanding the subdiaconate as a qualification for electors. At the time of Pope Boniface VIII (1294-1303) all professed clerical monks, whether in major orders or not, were admitted to the elections in their religious churches and monasteries.[71] Sometimes, however, the particular law of a province or of a diocese excluded those who had not yet been ordained to the subdiaconate from participation in elections. Hostiensis related that a legate of the Holy Father had made such a law for the province of Provence in France.[72] Many bishops had such a law for their respective dioceses.[73]

In the Council of Vienne in France (1311-1312) Pope Clement V made the law that in elections in cathedral and collegiate churches, whether of seculars or of regulars, those who had not yet received the subdeaconship could not be admitted as voters.[74] This law of the Council, inasmuch as it mentioned only churches, and not monasteries, did indeed not seem to include elections which were concerned only with monastic affairs. This, however, was not the case. The rule applied to elections in monasteries just as well as to those in churches. Thus, the *glossa ordinaria* stated that, although all professed clerical monks had been admitted to elections in religious churches *and monasteries* at the time of Pope Boniface VIII, this was no longer the case at the time of Pope Clement V, because c. 2, *de aetate et qualitate et ordine praeficiendorum*, I, 6, in Clem. (which contains

[71] *Glossa ordinaria* ad c. 32, *de electione et electi potestate*, I, 6, in VI°, s. v. *conversi laici*.

[72] *Summa Aurea, de electione et electi potestate* (I, 6), § *Et qui nullo*, 28 a. r.; cf. *casus* ad c. 2, *de aetate et qualitate et ordine praeficiendorum*, I, 6, in Clem.

[73] *Casus* ad c. 2, *de aetate et qualitate et ordine praeficiendorum*, I, 6, in Clem.

[74] C. 2, *de aetate et qualitate et ordine praeficiendorum*, I, 6, in Clem.

the legislation of the Council of Vienne mentioned above), required that voters be at least subdeacons.[75]

The principle of law, as formulated in the *notandum* to c. 2, *de aetate et qualitate et ordine praeficiendorum,* I, 6, in Clem., read: "*. . . illicitum esse eum qui non sit in ordine ecclesiasticis misceri tractatibus.*"

The disqualification for lack of major orders did not apply, of course, in communities of nuns, or in communities made up solely of lay brothers.[76]

Article VII. The Non-Professed and Lay Brothers

Section 1. The Non-Professed

C. 32, *de electione et electi potestate,* I, 6, in VI°, excluded from elections all religious who had not been professed either explicitly or at least tacitly. C. 34, *de electione et electi potestate,* I, 6, in VI°, repeated the substance of this law but applied it specifically to nuns. By express profession was meant a profession made by word of mouth, or in writing, or both, or by a nod or other sign clearly expressing the person's intention to bind himself to the vows of religion. Tacit profession was that profession which was not made expressly, but which was implicitly contained in certain other acts.[77] An example of tacit profession is contained in c. 22, X, *de Regularibus et transeuntibus ad Religionem,* III, 31. This canon stated that a person was considered to be tacitly professed if he or she had worn the habit of the community for a year.[78] Since tacit profession occurred so

[75] *Glossa ordinaria* ad c. 32, *de electione et electi potestate,* I, 6, in VI°, s. v. *conversi laici.*

[76] C. 43, *de electione et electi potestate,* I, 6, in VI°; *glossa ordinaria* ad c. 32, *de electione et electi potestate,* I, 6, in VI°, s. v. *cum clericis;* Panormitanus, *In Clem.,* ad c. 1, *de aetate et qualitate praeficiendorum,* I, 6, in Clem., 403 a. r., n. 2.

[77] Reiffenstuel, lib. III, tit. 31, n. 158; Schmalzgrueber, *Ius Ecclesiasticum Universum* (5 vols. in 12, Romae, 1843-1845), lib. III, tit. 21, n. 155 (hereafter cited Schmalzgrueber).

[78] Cf. also *glossa* ad c. 22, X, *de Regularibus et transeuntibus ad Religionem,* III, 31, s. v. *per annum.*

easily, about the only ones excluded from voting by this law were novices and the young oblati.[79]

SECTION 2. LAY BROTHERS

The second half of c. 32, *de electione et electi potestate,* I, 6, in VI°, forbade *"conversi laici"* to participate in elections conducted by the clerics of the religious community. The term *"conversi laici"* had various meanings at different times in the history of monasticism. From the eighth till the tenth century, the term referred to lay servants attached to a monastery and living a semi-religious life. They were not religious in the canonical sense. At a later date the *"conversi laici"* were taken into the community to do manual labor and other work which would take a monk away from his monastery and his choir office. They were destined from the outset to remain lay brothers *("conversi laici")* for life. They took a vow of obedience and were religious in the strict sense.[80] This law of Pope Boniface VIII which excluded lay brothers from elections applied only to communities composed of both clerics and lay brothers. It did not apply to communities composed solely of lay brothers, nor to communities of nuns.[81] Before Pope Boniface's time (1294-1303), this rule existed as a particular law for the Cistercian Order. The *"conversi laici"* had been barred from the monk's chapter in the Cistercian Order as early as 1181.[82]

[79] *Glossa* ad c. 32, *de electione et electi potestate,* I, 6, in VI°, s. v. *tacite; Rosarium,* ad idem c., s. v. *cum professis,* 35 b. v.

[80] "... Loquitur de illis conversis qui sunt in monasteriis, qui quamvis sint expresse professi, non tamen sunt in clericos tonsurati." —*Rosarium,* ad c. 32, *de electione et electi potestate,* I, 6, in VI°, s. v. *cum professis,* 35 b. v., n. 3; *ibid.,* s. v. *conversi laici,* 35 b. v., n. 4; cf. Brockhaus, *Religious Who are Known as Conversi,* The Catholic University of America Canon Law Studies, n. 225 (Washington, D.C.: The Catholic University of America Press, 1946), pp. 7-27, and esp. p. 22.

[81] *Glossa* ad c. 32, *de electione et electi potestate,* I, 6, in VI°, s. v. *cum clericis;* c. 43, *de electione et electi potestate,* I, 6, in VI°.

[82] Brockhaus, *op. cit.,* p. 23.

ARTICLE VIII. MENDICANTS WHO TRANSFERRED TO A NON-MENDICANT ORDER

Pope Clement V, in the Council of Vienne, deprived of active and passive voting rights any religious who had transferred from a mendicant to a non-mendicant Order, even though he had made the transfer with the permission of the Holy See. The other members of the community were forbidden to accord such a transferee the right to vote.[83] The reason for this law, which is found in the law itself, was that all too often the religious who had transferred from a mendicant to a non-mendicant Order were restless and dissatisfied persons, and prone to stir up dissensions in the chapter.

ARTICLE IX. EXCOMMUNICATED PERSONS

In the early days of the Church there had been various kinds and degrees of excommunication. At the time of the *Decretum* of Gratian, however, there were only two kinds of excommunication, namely, minor excommunication and major excommunication. Pope Gregory IX defined the two types in c. 59, X, *de sententia excommunicationis,* V, 39. Minor excommunication was that excommunication which cut one off from the reception of the sacraments, whereas major excommunication was the excommunication which cut one off not only from the sacraments but even from communion with the faithful. A person suffering under minor excommunication did not lose his right to vote in ecclesiastical elections, though he did lose his right of becoming elected.[84] A person laboring under major excommunication, however, was deprived of both active and passive voting rights.[85] At a later date, Baldus (Baldo degli

[83] C. 1, *de Regularibus et transeuntibus ad Religionem,* III, 9, in Clem.

[84] C. 39, X, *de electione et electi potestate,* I, 6; c. 10, X, *de clerico excommunicato, deposito vel interdicto ministrante,* V, 27.

[85] Hostiensis, *Summa Aurea, de electione et electi potestate* (I, 6), § *Et qui nullo,* 28 b v.; Innocentius IV, *Commentaria,* ad c. 39, X, *de electione et electi potestate,* I, 6, s. v. *canonica,* p. 82, n. 1.

Ubaldi) (1319-1400) distinguished between those who had been *publicly* excommunicated (with major excommunication) and those who had *not* been *publicly* excommunicated. The former, he claimed, could be expelled from an election, whereas the latter could not.[86]

Article X. Clerics Under Suspension

Suspension was considered as a censure or as a vindictive penalty, by which a cleric was deprived of his use or exercise of ecclesiastical functions, relative to orders, offices or benefices.[87] The main species of suspension are suspension from office, suspension from orders, and suspension from benefice. Though all of these types of suspension are mentioned in medieval documents, a clear distinction was not always made between suspension from office and suspension from orders. Before the advent of "absolute" ordinations (ordination without canonical title), the order and the office for which a man was ordained, were so intimately associated with one another that suspension from either meant suspension from both.[88] Rainer says that after the twelfth century the distinction between suspension from office and suspension from orders was clearly made.[89] It seems, however, that Hostiensis did not make this distinction. He did not mention suspension from orders when summing up the various suspensions which disqualified a cleric as a voter.[90] If it had existed as a special suspension apart from suspension from office, he surely would have mentioned it, for it most certainly would have disqualified a cleric. Inasmuch as suspension from "conferring" the sac-

[86] Baldus (Baldo degli Ubaldi), *Super Decretalibus* (Lugdini, 1547), *de electione et electi potestate* (I, 6), c. *Illa Quotidiana,* s. v. *casus,* 66 b. r.

[87] Cf. Rainer, *Suspension of Clerics,* The Catholic University of America Canon Law Studies, n. 111 (Washington, D.C.: The Catholic University of America, 1937), p. 20.

[88] Cf. Rainer, *Suspension of Clerics,* pp. 11 & 16.

[89] *Ibid.,* p. 18.

[90] *Summa Aurea, de electione et electi potestate* (I, 6), § *Et qui nullo,* 28 b. v.

raments disqualified a voter,[91] one must conclude, *a fortiori*, that the more general suspension from orders (which indeed includes suspension from conferring the sacraments) would also have disqualified a cleric. Since, then, Hostiensis did not mention suspension from orders in his list, it must be concluded that, in his opinion at least, it did not exist as a suspension distinct from suspension from office.

Some commentators at the time of Hostiensis made a distinction between suspension from office and suspension from jurisdiction. Hostiensis and Bernard of Parma (d. 1266), the author of the *glossa ordinaria* to the Decretals of Pope Gregory IX, did not accept this distinction.[92] At any rate, the distinction was not of importance as far as elections were concerned, because the right to vote was not an exercise of true jurisdiction.[93]

Besides the general suspensions mentioned above, there were as many lesser suspensions as there were functions attached to orders, offices, and benefices. Thus, for example, there was suspension from the right to administer the minor order of tonsure, suspension from the right to grant a benefice, and suspension from the right to vote.[94]

With reference to their source, suspensions derived either *ab homine* or *a canone*.[95]

Suspension could be applied not only to physical persons, but also to moral personalities. When a moral personality was suspended, the corporate body was deprived of the exercise of the rights which it had as a unit. The rights which individual members of the group had as individuals were not affected, even though they acquired those rights through membership in the moral personality.[96] Since election was

[91] *Loc. cit.*

[92] *Loc. cit.; glossa* ad c. 8, X, *de consuetudine*, I, 4, s. v. *suspensis.*

[93] Hostiensis, *loc. cit.*

[94] C. 4, *de temporibus ordinationum et qualitate ordinandorum*, I, 9, in VI°; c. 3, 7, X, *de electione et electi potestate*, I, 6; c. 2, *de electione et electi potestate*, I, 6, in Clem.

[95] Hostiensis, *Summa Aurea, de electione et electi potestate* (I, 6), § *Et qui nullo*, 28 b. v.

[96] Cf. Rainer, *Suspension of Clerics*, pp. 22-23.

one of those rights which the moral personality exercised as a unit, it was one of the rights which the group could not exercise while under suspension.[97]

The principle of medieval ecclesiastical law was that suspended clerics could neither elect nor be elected.[98] This rule referred to general suspension *ab officio*. Hostiensis furnished a detailed account of the various suspensions which disqualified a cleric as a voter. He taught that any cleric suspended, whether *ab homine* or *a canone*, from office and benefice, or from office alone, was disqualified. Further, one suspended from "conferring" the sacraments was also disqualified.[99] It is strange that suspension from "conferring" the sacraments should have disqualified a cleric as a voter, since voting was not an exercise of the powers of orders. Hostiensis did not volunteer any explanation for this rule. It may be, perhaps, that the penalty was considered as a very severe punishment and was imposed only for very serious crimes, and that, consequently, such clerics were considered unworthy of participating in an ecclesiastical election.

Article XI. The Deposed and the Degraded

Deposition might be called a complete and perpetual suspension. Indeed, the penalty of suspension developed from the penalty of deposition and is a modified form of this punishment. Deposition included deprivation of all ecclesiastical offices, benefices, and dignities, and the suspension from all orders. Since deposition is a severer form of suspension, it is clear that it, like suspension, disqualified a cleric for voting.[100]

[97] Cf. *supra*, pp. 1-2; also, c. unic., *ne sede vacante aliquid innovetur*, III, 8, in VI°; c. 40, *de electione et electi potestate*, I, 6, in VI°; c. 1, *de electione*, I, 3, in Extravag. com.

[98] C. 16, X, *de electione et electi potestate*, I, 6; *glossa* ad c. 8, *de consuetudine*, I, 4, s. v. *suspensis; glossa* ad c. 23, X, *de appellationibus*, II, 28, s. v. *excommunicationis;* Hostiensis, *Summa Aurea, de electione et electi potestate* (I, 6), § *Et qui nullo*, 28 b. v.

[99] *Loc. cit.*

[100] C. 7, 10, D. L; c. 8, X, *de dolo et contumacia*, II, 14; c. 2, X,

Degradation always included deposition, and, consequently, always disqualified a cleric as a voter.[101]

Article XII. Individuals Under Personal Interdict

The penalty of personal interdict existed at the time of the Decretals,[102] but it seems to have been used very infrequently. The term *interdictus* was used quite loosely. When used in relation to clerics, it frequently meant *suspensus*.[103]

The canons which describe the effects of interdicts mention only the prohibition of the divine office, of the sacraments and the sacramentals, but nothing about elections. In c. 1, X, *de postulatione praelatorum,* I, 5, there is mention of the chapter of Sens, France, holding an election while the country was under interdict. This was, however, a *local* interdict, and one cannot conclude from this case that *personal* interdict did not disqualify a person. It must be admitted that one simply does not know whether or not personal interdict involved loss of voting rights.

Article XIII. Clerics of Irregular Status

There is only one instance, as found by the writer, in which an irregular cleric was disqualified. C. 18, *de sententia excommunicationis, suspensionis et interdicti,* V, 11, in VI°, declared that any priest who violated a local interdict by celebrating Mass in an interdicted place incurred irregularity reserved to the Roman Pontiff, and was therefore ineligible for admittance to elections.

de raptoribus, incendiariis et violatoribus ecclesiarum, V, 17.

101 "... degradamus, spoliamus et exuimus te omni ordine, beneficio, et privilegio clericali."—c. 2, *de poenis,* V, 9, in VI°; c. 7, X, *de crimine falsi,* V, 20; c. 27, X, *de verborum significatione,* V, 40.

102 C. 16, 24, *de sententia excommunicationis, suspensionis et interdicti,* V, 11, in VI°.

103 *Casus* ad c. 16, X, *de electione et electi potestate,* I, 6, uses *interdictis* and *suspensis* interchangeably; cf. c. 2, X, *de clerico excommunicato, deposito vel interdicto ministante,* V, 17; c. 16, *de sententia excommunicationis, suspensionis et interdicti,* V, 11, in VI°.

ARTICLE XIV. PERSONS BRANDED WITH INFAMY

Infamy, at the time of the *Corpus Iuris Canonici,* was of various kinds. There was an infamy of fact and an infamy of law. Infamy of law was either *secundum legem,* that is, of civil law, or *secundum canonem,* that is, of ecclesiastical law. There was also a peculiar *infamia canonica* (not to be confused with *infamia secundum canonem*), which was incurred through the commission of any mortal sin. Infamy could be contracted *per sententiam* or *ipso facto.*[104]

Infamy of fact did not usually suspend one from office, but if there was danger of scandal because the crime was exceptionally serious, the bishop could suspend the guilty cleric.[105] Infamy of fact, then, did not directly affect one's right to vote, but at times it could occasion the deprivation of one's voting rights inasmuch as it was the reason for suspension by the bishop.

Infamy of law, that is, of canon law, carried with it deposition from all offices and dignities, and rendered the culprit incapable of receiving any office or dignity in the future.[106] Infamy of law also excluded one from the exercise of all accredited ecclesiastical acts, among which acts was included voting in ecclesiastical elections.[107]

The peculiar severity of infamy of law consisted in the fact that it was perpetual, remaining after the delinquent had atoned for his crime.[108] Infamy of law could be removed only by the Supreme Pontiff, either through a *restitutio in integrum,* or by way of a dispensation.[109]

[104] *Glossa* ad c. 2, C. VI, q. 1

[105] *Glossa* ad c. 56, X, *de testibus et attestationibus,* II, 20; c. 10, X, *de purgatione canonica,* V, 34.

[106] C. 13, X, *de haereticis,* V, 7; c. unic., *de poenis,* XII, in Extravag. Ioan. XXII.

[107] *Locis citatis.*

[108] *Glossa* ad c. 2, C. VI, q. 1, s. v. *legis;* c. 5, *de poenis,* V, 9, in VI°; c. unic., *de poenis,* XII, in Extravag. Ioan. XXII.

[109] *Dictum* post c. 7, C. II, q. 3; *dictum* post c. 8, C. II, q. 3; c. 23, X, *de sententia et re iudicata,* II, 27; Hostiensis, *Commentaria,* ad c. 23, X, *de sententia et re iudicata,* II, 27, s. v. *restitutionis,* II, 169,

Article XV. The Simoniacal

Unlike the present law of the Code of Canon Law,[110] which perpetually deprives one guilty of simony of the right to vote, the law of the *Corpus Iuris Canonici* did not directly disqualify a simoniacal person. Indirectly, however, it did, inasmuch as it attached to this crime penalties which involved disqualification.

Simony was punished through the deposition of the guilty cleric from the office simoniacally obtained.[111] Deposition from the office was, of course, permanent.[112] Furthermore, one guilty of simony was to be deposed from all other offices and benefices which he held.[113]

All persons guilty of simony were anathematized, that is, excommunicated with major excommunication.[114] This excommunication was incurred automatically.[115] Pope Paul II (1464-1471), in a decree of November 23, 1464, used great detail to include in this punishment everyone, no matter of what dignity, who took part in any simoniacal transaction. He also reserved the remission of the excommunication to the Holy See.[116]

In addition to the punishments mentioned, persons guilty of simony were branded with perpetual infamy of law.[117]

a. v., n. 7; Panormitanus, *Commentaria,* ad c. 23, X, *de sententia et re iudicata,* II, 27, t. V, 119 b. r., nn. 12 & 13.

110 Can. 2392, n. 2.

111 C. 110, C. I, q. 1; c. 3, C. I, q. 3; c. 2. C. I., q. 7; c. 6, X, *de pactis,* I, 35; c. 2, X, *de simonia, et ne aliquid pro spiritualibus exigatur vel promittatur,* V, 3.

112 C. 11, X, *de simonia, et ne aliquid pro spiritualibus exigatur vel promittatur,* V, 3.

113 C. 2, X, *de confessis,* I, 28.

114 C. 6, 7, 110, C. I, q. 1; c. 1, 2, 9, C. I, q. 3; C. 23, X, *de iure patronatus,* III, 38; c. 8, 38, 39, X, *de simonia, et ne aliquid pro spiritualibus exigatur vel promittatur,* V, 3; c. 2, *de simonia,* V, 1, in Extravag. com.; c. 3, 5, *de poenis,* V, 9, in Extravag. com.

115 *Glossa* ad c. 7, C. I, q. 1, s. v. *anathematis;* c. 2, *de simonia,* V, 1, in Extravag. com.; c. 3, 5, *de poenis,* V, 9, in Extravag. com.

116 C. 2, *de simonia,* V, 1, in Extravag. com.

117 C. 15, C. I, q. 3; *glossa* ad idem c., s. v. *percellantur;* c. 4, C.

This infamy was not incurred automatically; it was to be imposed by way of a sentence, because the canons inflicting the penalty used such words as "*percellantur*" and "*damnari decernimus.*" The use of the passive voice and the imperative mode indicated that the penalty was to be imposed in the future.[118]

Since all three punishments attached to simony, namely, suspension, major excommunication and infamy of law, disqualified a person as a voter, it is evident that persons guilty of simony were never to be admitted to elections.

XV, q. 3; c. 13, X, *de simonia, et ne aliquid pro spiritualibus exigatur vel promittatur,* V, 3.

[118] Cf. *glossa* ad c. 42, X, *de electione et electi potestate,* I, 6, s. v. *priventur;* Hostiensis, *Commentaria,* ad idem c., s. v. *priventur,* I, 67 a. r., n. 51; Panormitanus, *Commentaria,* ad idem c., § *Nisi,* s. v. *priventur,* I, 440, n. 3.

CHAPTER III

DISQUALIFICATIONS IN CONSEQUENCE OF DELICTS

"*Delict*" in the title of this chapter is used in a very broad sense. It denotes any misdeed to which disqualification was attached.

A. *Delicts Committed by Individuals*

ARTICLE I. HERESY, SCHISM AND RELAPSE INTO JUDAISM

Heretics and schismatics, as a matter of principle, had no rights and no powers of governing in the Church. C. 31, C. XXIV, q. 1, states the principle in these words: "*Didicimus omnes omnino haereticos vel schismaticos nil habere potestatis, ac iuris.*"[1] From this general rule it can be concluded that heretics and schismatics had no right to vote in ecclesiastical elections.

Chapter three of the IV General Council of the Lateran (1215) excommunicated and anathematized all heretics.[2] This anathematization (major excommunication) was incurred automatically.[3] If the person who was guilty of heresy was a cleric, he was not only excommunicated, but was also degraded and handed over to the secular power for punishment.[4]

If, for a reasonable cause, a person was *suspected* of heresy, he had to purge himself. If he failed to do so, he was excommunicated. If he then made no effort to clear himself, and continued in the state of excommunication for a period of one year, he was to be condemned as a heretic.[5]

[1] Cf. c. 51, D. I, *de poenit.*

[2] Labbeus, XI, pars 1, 148; Mansi, XXII, 986; this decree of the Council was incorporated into the Decretals of Pope Gregory IX as c. 13, X, *de haereticis*, V, 7.

[3] Hostiensis, *Commentaria*, ad c. 49, X, *de sententia excommunicationis*, V, 39, s. v. *omnes haereticos*, IV, 121 a. v., n. 1.

[4] C. 13, X, *de haereticis*, V, 7.

[5] *Loc. cit.*

"Excommunication" in this case, and in all other cases where it was used without a modifier, signified major excommunication.[6]

Moreover, anyone who received, defended or supported heretics was also to be excommunicated. If such a person did not amend his life within a year's time, he was automatically infamous with infamy of law.[7]

Not only were heretics and their accomplices punished, but if they were not reconciled with the Church before their death, some of their descendants also were penalized. As a general rule, descendants were not punished for the sins of their forebears,[8] but this case was an exception. The descendants of heretics to the second generation were disqualified for all ecclesiastical benefices and public offices.[9] Actually, as c. 15, *de haereticis,* V, 2, in VI°, explained, this penalty was inherited to the *second* generation in the male line only; in the female line, it extended only to the *first* degree. Thus, a heretical father's sons, and his sons' sons, but not his daughters' sons, were disqualified. If the mother alone was heretical, her sons, but not her sons' sons, nor her daughters' sons, were disqualified.[10]

Schismatics, according to Helias Regnier (f. c. 1494), the author of the *Continuationes* of the *Liber Sextus,* were of two kinds. In the stricter sense of the word, a schismatic was one who denied the supreme authority of the papacy. In the wider sense, the notion of "schismatic" was referable also to those who, while not denying the theoretical supremacy of the papacy, refused obedience to the lawfully elected pope.[11] Juridically, schismatics were considered as heretics

[6] C. 59, X, *de sententia excommunicationis,* V, 39; Hostiensis, *Summa Aurea, de electione et electi potestate* (I, 6), § *Et qui nullo,* 28 b. r.

[7] C. 13, X, *de haereticis,* V, 7; c. 2, *de haereticis,* V, 2, in VI°.

[8] C. 10, C. I, q. 4; *glossa* ad c. 2, *de haereticis,* V, 2, in VI°, s. v. *filii.*

[9] C. 2, 15, *de haereticis,* V, 2, in VI°.

[10] *Glossa* ad c. 15, *de haereticis,* V, 2, in VI°, s. v. *inane.*

[11] *Continuatio* ad titulum *de schismaticis,* V, 3, in VI°.

and were punished with the same penalties.[12] In the case of schismatics who engaged in armed rebellion against the Supreme Pontiff, a somewhat more severe penalty was imposed. C. unic., *de schismaticis,* V, 3, in VI°, extended the disqualification of descendants to the fourth generation with reference to offices outside of Rome, and to all descendants with reference to offices in Rome.[13]

Those Christians who embraced Judaism, or who relapsed into Judaism after having been converted to the Faith, were to be numbered among the heretics, and were to be punished accordingly.[14]

Article II. Failure to Receive Orders

By statute law, by customary law, or also by ancient institution, certain offices postulated the previous reception of certain orders. Thus, at the time of the Decretalists, the offices of abbot, provost, dean, and archpriest postulated the order of the priesthood; the office of archdeacon presupposed the reception of the diaconate.[15] Whenever a person who lacked the required order was elected to such an office, he was under obligation to receive the required order within a period of a year, unless he became legitimately impeded. Failure to do so was punished with deprivation of the right to vote. This disqualification was only temporary; it lasted

[12] Cf. *glossa* ad c. 26, C. XXIV, q. 3, s. v. *et schisma; Continuatio* ad X, *de schismaticis,* V, 8 [the *Continuationes* of the Decretals of Gregory IX were written by Panormitanus (Abbas Siculus)]; *Continuatio* ad *de schismaticis,* V, 3, in VI°; c. unic., *de schismaticis,* V, 3, in VI°.

[13] This canon is a copy of the decree of Pope Boniface VIII, issued in 1279 against Cardinal Jacopo Colonna, Cardinal Pietro (Jacopo's nephew), and Cardinal Pietro's brothers, who had attacked the validity of Pope Boniface's election, and had rebelled against the Pope. The disqualification of descendants was applicable to the descendants of Cardinal Pietro's brothers. The Colonnas, however, were later reconciled to the Pope.

[14] C. 13, *de haereticis,* V, 2, in VI°.

[15] *Glossa* ad c. 2, *de aetate et qualitate et ordine praeficiendorum,* I, 6, in Clem., s. v. *annexi;* c. 1, X, *de aetate et qualitate et ordine praeficiendorum,* I, 14.

till the person had received the required order.[16] If a person became permanently impeded from receiving the necessary order through no fault of his own, Hostiensis contended that he could always be dispensed from the necessity of receiving the order, and could retain the office along with the right to vote. If, however, the impediment resulted through the person's own fault, he was to be deposed from his office.[17]

B. *Delicts Committed by a Group*

The delicts which will be treated now were usually perpetrated by the whole chapter or by a substantial part of it. Some of the delicts could be committed by an individual. Thus, for example, a lone individual could consent to interference on the part of lay persons in an election. For most of the delicts, however, a corporate action was necessary. Those delicts which postulated a corporate action did not, however, always presuppose co-operation of the majority of the voters. A minority of the voters could, for instance, "elect" an unworthy candidate.[18]

When part of the voting body, even the greater part of it, was guilty of a delict entailing the loss of voting rights, the right to elect was not taken from the body, but it devolved upon the innocent members.[19] The innocent members could, in certain instances, admit the guilty members to the election.[20] Thus, if some of the members of the chapter were deprived of their right to vote for having knowingly elected an unworthy candidate, the innocent members could admit

[16] C. 2, *de aetate et qualitate et ordine praeficiendorum,* I, 6, in Clem; *glossa* ad idem, s. v. *donec.*

[17] *Summa Aurea, de electione et electi potestate* (I, 6), § *Et qui nullo,* 28 a. r.; *Commentaria,* ad c. 1, X, *de aetate et qualitate et ordine praeficiendorum,* I, 14, s. v. *iusta causa,* I, 104 b. r., n. 3.

[18] Cf. *supra,* p. 2.

[19] C. 25, X, *de electione et electi potestate,* I, 6; *notandum* ad idem; Hostiensis, *Commentaria,* ad idem, s. v. *admittendos,* I, 53 b. r., nn. 6 & 7.

[20] C. 25, X, *de electione et electi potestate,* I, 6; *glossa* ad idem, s. v. *admiserant* et *admittendos;* Hostiensis, *Commentaria,* ad idem, s. v. *admittendos,* I, 43 b. r., nn. 6 & 7.

them to the new election.[21] It seems very surprising that the innocent members were allowed to admit the guilty persons, since the disqualification was established by the general law, and the members of the chapter had no power to dispense from the general law. The gloss attempts, rather unsatisfactorily, to explain the reason for this rule by saying that the guilty persons were disqualified, not in themselves, but in relation to the other members of the chapter.[22] Pope Innocent IV offered a different explanation. He stated that the right to elect devolved to the innocent members, and they could, if they wished, renounce their right to elect alone. Further, they could admit the others to the election, because the law, although it forbade the admission of laymen to an ecclesiastical election, did not forbid the admission of clerics. If the guilty members were admitted, they were present, not by right, but by favor.[23] The clearest and most satisfactory explanation was given by Panormitanus. Persons, he explained, could either be completely disqualified, or they could be deprived simply of the right to vote. Those who were completely disqualified lost not only their right to vote, but lost also their *capacity of receiving* the right to vote. If a person was not completely disqualified, but simply deprived of his right to vote, he was in the same relationship to the chapter as any non-member, and the chapter could admit him to the election just as they could admit any non-member (provided he was a cleric). For the admission of the guilty members, the unanimous consent of all the innocent members was required, for it was a matter which affected the right of each of the members, inasmuch as his vote was rendered less effective toward the choosing of a candidate.[24] Panormitanus did not detail which disqualifi-

[21] *Loc. cit.*

[22] *Glossa* ad c. 25, X, *de electione et electi potestate,* I, 6, s. v. *admiserant.*

[23] *Commentaria,* ad c. 25, X, *de electione et electi potestate,* I, 6, p. 69, n. 4.

[24] *Commentaria,* ad c. 25, X, *de electione et electi potestate,* I, 6, t. I, 378, nn. 3-5; *ibid.,* ad c. 40, X, *de electione et electi potestate,* I, 6, t. I, 426, n. 3; Reg. 29, R. J., in VI°.

cations were complete and which were simple deprivations. The various laws on disqualifications would have to be consulted for determining which of the disqualifications were complete and which were not. The right of the chapter to admit the guilty members (and non-members) to the election indicates how strongly the right to elect was regarded as a right of the chapter.

If the whole chapter was guilty of some delict, the right of election devolved to the next higher superior.[25] In the case of a cathedral chapter, the next higher superior was the bishop, or, when the see was vacant, the metropolitan.[26] This rule was modified in the *Liber Sextus*. The right to choose a bishop devolved to the metropolitan only when the delict consisted in the chapter's failure to elect within the time prescribed by the law; in all other cases the right devolved to the Holy See.[27]

Article I. Consenting to an Election Conducted with "Abuse by Secular Power"

As it was stated above, all lay persons were excluded from ecclesiastical elections.[28] If any member of the chapter freely consented to admit a lay prince or other person in power to an election *(electio per saecularis potestatis abusum)* he was automatically deprived of his right to vote for that time, and could be sentenced to suspension from all offices and benefices for three years.[29] This punishment was one of the reasons why members of the chapter, whenever they admitted an outsider who seemed to have the right to vote by reason of a custom or of a privilege, protested that his vote would be counted only if he could prove his right

[25] C. 7, X, *de electione et electi potestate,* I, 6.

[26] *Loc. cit.*

[27] C. 18, 37, *de electione et electi potestate,* I, 6, in VI°.

[28] Cf. *supra,* pp. 13-15; also p. 8.

[29] C. 25, IV General Council of the Lateran—Labbeus, XI, pars 1, 177; Mansi, XXII, 1014; c. 14, 42, X, *de electione et electi potestate,* I, 6; *glossa* ad c. 42, X, *de electione et electi potestate,* I, 6, s. v. *abusum, suspendatur, tunc, privati.*

to vote. If it was shown later that the layman who was admitted to the election under such a protest actually did not have the right to be present, the protest was taken as proof that the members did not knowingly and freely consent to his unlawful presence.[30]

ARTICLE II. ELECTING *"Contra Formas"*

Chapter twenty-four of the IV General Council of the Lateran (1215) enacted rather detailed instructions for conducting ecclesiastical elections. The decree reads as follows:

> Quia propter diversas electionum formas, quas quidam invenire conantur, et multa impedimenta proveniunt, et magna pericula imminent ecclesiis viduatis: Statuimus, ut, cum electio fuerit celebranda, praesentibus omnibus qui debent, et volunt, et possunt commode interesse, assumantur tres de collegio fide digni, qui secreto et singulatim voces cunctorum diligenter exquirant, et in scriptis redacta mox publicent in communi, nullo prorsus appellationis obstaculo interiecto: ut is collatione adhibita eligatur, in quem omnes, vel maior vel sanior pars capituli consentit. Vel saltem eligendi potestas aliquibus viris idoneis committatur, qui vice omnium ecclesiae viduatae provideant de pastore. Aliter electio facta non valet, nisi forte communiter esset ab omnibus, quasi per inspirationem Divinam, absque vitio celebrata. Qui vero contra praedictas formas eligere attentaverint, eligendi ea vice potestate priventur.[31]

The commentators analyzed this decree to determine what was substantial to the form and, consequently, necessary for the validity of the election. Hostiensis listed four-

[30] *Glossa* ad c. 43, X, *de electione et electi potestate,* I, 6, s. v. *abusum;* Hostiensis, *Commentaria,* ad. c. 50, X, *de electione et electi potestate,* I, 6, s. v. *sub huiusmodi protestatione,* I, 71 b. r., n. 1; Innocentius IV, *Commentaria,* ad idem, s. v. *protestatione,* p. 93, n. 1.

[31] Mansi, XXII, 1011; Labbeus, XI, pars 1, 176; c. 42, X, *de electione et electi potestate,* I, 6.

teen prescriptions as being of the substance, and Panormitanus listed eighteen.[32]

Because of these many requirements for its validity, the election by secret balloting *(per scrutinium)* was often abandoned for an election by duly appointed deputies *(per compromissarios)*, which was not subject to all these provisions. The election by deputies was either of a limited sort, in which the deputies had to inquire into the wishes of the members of the chapter and vote accordingly, or of a fuller type, in which the deputies elected according to their own good judgment.

Electors who elected *contra formas* were not automatically deprived of their right of suffrage, but they could be deprived by way of a sentence.[33] If the election was invalid because the mode of electing was defective in some way, it could be repeated as long as the voters had not yet been deprived of their vote through the imposing of a sentence.[34] In canon 50, X, *de electione et electi potestate*, I, 6, there is mention of a case wherein the members of a chapter were disqualified for failing to observe all the prescribed steps. It seems, however, that this penalty was inflicted only rarely.

The penalty for failing to observe the proper procedure was a rather mild one. It disqualified a voter for one turn only. This one turn included an attempted election which was, for some reason or other, invalid.[35]

[32] Hostiensis, *Commentaria*, ad c. 42, X, *de electione et electi potestate*, I, 6, s. v. *consentit*, I, 66 b. v., nn. 42-44; Panormitanus, *Commentaria*, ad idem, § *Quia propter*, I, 436-437, nn. 12-16.

[33] *Glossa* ad c. 42, X, *de electione et electi potestate*, I, 6, s. v. *priventur; ibid.* ad c. 50, X, *de electione et electi potestate*, I, 6, s. v. *privantes;* Hostiensis, *Commentaria*, ad c. 42, X, *de electione et electi potestate*, I, 6, s. v. *priventur*, I, 67 a. r., n. 51; Panormitanus, *Commentaria*, ad idem, § *Nisi*, s. v. priventur, I, 440, n. 3.

[34] C. 12, X, *de electione et electi potestate*, I, 6. The election could not be repeated if it was invalid because of defects on the part of the persons.

[35] Cf. c. 25, X, *de electione et electi potestate*, I, 6.

ARTICLE III. ELECTING AN UNWORTHY CANDIDATE

The canons of the Decretals of Pope Gregory IX repeatedly penalized those who knowingly elected unworthy candidates. The qualities postulated for a worthy candidate were listed in c. 7, X, *de electione et electi potestate,* I, 6. They were: maturity in his years *(aetatis maturitas),* sobriety in his morals *(gravitas morum),* proficiency in letters *(litterarum scientia),* and descent through lawful wedlock *(ortus ex legitimo matrimonio).*

The requisite age varied along with the office. For bishops the thirtieth year completed was required; for pastors, the twenty-fifth year begun.[36]

The requirement of sobriety of morals excluded criminals, the suspended, the excommunicated (including the persons under minor excommunication), etc.[37]

The knowledge required, Hostiensis related, differed with the order, the dignity, and the place.[38] A bishop had to be versed in the Old and New Testaments, in the canons of the councils, and also in secular knowledge.[39] For pastors it sufficed to know the penitential canons.[40] Archdeacons, since they were judges, were obliged to know the laws. Cantors had to know chant, and others had to have the particular knowledge needed in the exercise of their respective offices.[41] Abbots had to have a thorough knowledge of the

[36] C. 1, 2, 4, 5, D. LXXVIII; Hostiensis, *Commentaria,* ad c. 7, X, *de electione et electi potestate,* I, 6, s. v. *exegerit,* I, 40 a. r.-b. v., nn. 4 & 5.

[37] Hostiensis, *Commentaria,* ad c. 7, X, *de electione et electi potestate,* I, 6, s. v. *vita,* I, 40 b. v., n. 8; *Summa Aurea, de electione et electi potestate* (I, 6), § *Quis eligendus,* 29 a. r.

[38] *Commentaria,* ad. c. 7, X, *de electione et electi potestate,* I, 6, s. v. *et scientia,* I, 40 b. v., n. 8.

[39] C. 6, 7, D. XXXVIII; c. 1, D. XXXIX; c. 15, X, *de aetate et qualitate et ordine praeficiendorum,* I, 13; Hostiensis, *Commentaria,* ad c. 7, X, *de electione et electi potestate,* I, 6, s. v. *scientia,* I, 40 b. v., nn. 7-9.

[40] Hostiensis, *ibid.,* n. 10; Innocentius IV, *Commentaria,* ad c. 7, X, *de electione et electi potestate,* I, 6, s. v. *scientia,* p. 52, n. 1.

[41] Hostiensis, *ibid.,* nn. 11 & 12.

religious life.[42] The illiterate were excluded from all offices.[43]

Legitimacy was required for all candidates for dignities, higher offices *(personatus)*, and benefices to which the care of souls was attached.[44] The punishment for electing an unworthy candidate was disqualification for that turn, plus suspension from one's benefice for three years.[45] The suspension from one's benefice, however, did not include suspension from one's office, and did not, therefore, disqualify the elector during those three years.[46] The disqualification for one turn was incurred automatically. The canon stated "*privati sunt,*" not "*privandi sunt.*"[47] The penalty was not incurred for "nominating," that is, casting one's ballot for, an unworthy candidate if no common election followed.[48] Electors, though ordinarily they could not retract a vote once it was cast, could recall their vote any time before the capitular election took place if they had voted for an unworthy candidate.[49] In all cases, the penalty was not incurred unless the electors were aware of the candidate's unworthiness when they elected him.[50]

The penalty could be incurred by the members of the chapter even when the election was conducted by accredited

[42] C. 38, X, *de electione et electi potestate,* I, 6.

[43] Hostiensis, *ibid.*, n. 13.

[44] C. 7, 20, 25, X, *de electione et electi potestate,* I, 6; c. 18, X, *de filiis presbyterorum,* I, 18.

[45] C. 7, 25, 26, X, *de electione et electi potestate,* I, 6.

[46] *Glossa* ad c. 7, X, *de electione et electi potestate,* I, 6, s. v. *beneficiis.*

[47] *Ibid.*, s. v. *privatos;* Hostiensis, *Commentaria,* ad. c. 7, X, *de electione et electi potestate,* I, 6, s. v. *ordinetur,* I, 41 b. r., n. 46.

[48] "... non deprivati sint ... nisi adeo in eo perstiterint quod ex votis eorum communis electio subsequatur ..."—c. 7, *de electione et electi potestate,* I, 6, in VI°; "... consentiens scienter in indignum non est privatus potestate eligendi ipso iure, nisi ex illo consensu cum consensu aliorum fuerit secuta electio."— *glossa* ad idem, s. v. *perpetuo;* cf. *supra,* pp. 1-2.

[49] *Glossa* ad c. 7, *de electione et electi potestate,* I, 6, in VI°, s. v. *perstiterunt;* c. 58, X, *de electione et electi potestate,* I, 6.

[50] C. 7, 20, 25, 26, 40, X, *de electione et electi potestate,* I, 6.

deputies *(per compromissarios),* but only if the members of the chapter ratified the election performed by the deputies.[51]

Article IV. Postulating an Unworthy Candidate

The same punishment was imposed for postulating an unworthy person as was imposed for electing an unworthy person.[52] The question arises, however: "Who was unworthy with reference to postulation?" Those who were unworthy for becoming elected were not necessarily unworthy of postulation. Illegitimates, for instance, could not be elected to certain offices, but they could be postulated.[53] Indeed, the very reason for postulating a candidate instead of electing him was that he lacked some requisite qualification. Hostiensis and Pope Innocent IV taught that a person was unfit for postulation if he had committed some delict and then persevered in the crime.[54] Thus, a cleric who had violated a local interdict was declared unworthy of postulation by Pope Innocent III.[55] Those persons who lacked the required age, learning, or legitimacy, however, were not unfit for postulation.[56] At the time of Pope John XXII (1316-1334) the idea of unfitness for postulation was widened so that it included defects other than those envisioned by Hostiensis and Pope Innocent IV. Thus, a cleric under twenty-seven years of age could not be postulated for a prelacy in a cathedral church; a mendicant religious could not be postulated for a prelacy in a minor cathedral church belonging to a monastery of another religious order.[57] The idea of unworthiness in relation to postulation at the time of Pope John XXII had to be revised in such a manner that it in-

[51] C. 37, *de electione et electi potestate,* I, 6, in VI°.

[52] C. 40, X, *de electione et electi potestate,* I, 6.

[53] C. 20, X, *de electione et electi potestate,* I, 6.

[54] Hostiensis, *Commentaria,* ad c. 40, X, *de electione et electi potestate,* I, 6, s. v. *indignum,* I, 64 a. r., n. 13; Innocentius IV, *Commentaria,* ad idem c., s. v. *indignum,* p. 85, n. 7.

[55] C. 1, X, *de postulatione praelatorum,* I, 5.

[56] Hostiensis, *loc. cit.;* Innocentius IV, *loc. cit.*

[57] C. unic., *de postulatione praelatorum,* I, 2, in Extravag. com.

cluded also any lack of the required qualities for which a dispensation was normally not given.

Article V. Repostulating a Candidate Once Refused

If a chapter had postulated a person and the higher superior had refused to admit the postulation, the chapter could not again postulate that same person. If it did, the guilty persons were automatically deprived of their right to elect and to postulate.[58] The disqualification most probably applied to just that one turn, because the right to elect devolved upon the innocent members of the chapter, and it is highly unlikely that the legislator intended that the elections be conducted by a minority of the chapter for a longer period of time.[59] It is very probable that the delict of repostulating a rejected candidate was regarded as identical to the delict of postulating an unworthy candidate, for a person once refused certainly had to be considered as unfit for repostulation.

Article VI. Accepting a Postulated Candidate Before His Postulation Was Confirmed

If a cleric had been postulated for an office, for example, for the office of bishop, and the chapter admitted him to that office before the postulation was approved by the higher superior, the guilty members of the chapter were punished in the manner indicated in the preceding article.[60]

Article VII. Failing to Elect Within the Set Time Limit

"Lest the wolf be allowed to enter among the flock of the Lord because of the lack of a shepherd," the IV General Council of the Lateran (1215) prescribed that the election of prelates, in the churches of regulars as well as in the churches of seculars, be held within three months of the

[58] C. 2, X, *de postulatione praelatorum,* I, 5; Hostiensis, *Commentaria,* ad idem, I, 34 a. r., n. 2.

[59] Cf. c. 2, X, *de postulatione praelatorum,* I, 5.

[60] C. 23, X, *de electione et electi potestate,* I, 6.

occurrence of the vacancy. If the members of the chapter in the absence of any legitimate impediment or hindrance failed to hold the election within the set time limit, they were deprived of their right to vote for that instance.[61] For elections to *minor* dignities and benefices, a six months period of time was allowed.[62] The time was computed in the nature of a truly available time *(tempus utile)*, but its lapse continued if the persons were able to remove the obstacle which at the moment and in actual fact prevented them from making use of the time.[63] This penalty was incurred also when the deputies *(compromissarii)* chosen by the chapter failed to elect within the stated time.[64] The reason for this seemed close at hand. The chapter was considered in such a case to be at fault through its choosing negligent persons and through its failure to see to it that the deputies carried out their commission.[65]

[61] Mansi, XXII, 1011; Labbeus, XI, pars 1, 176; incorporated in c. 41, X, *de electione et electi potestate*, I, 6.

[62] C. 2, X, *de concessae praebendae, et ecclesiae non vacantis*, III, 8.

[63] C. 60, X, *de electione et electi potestate*, I, 6.

[64] C. 37, *de electione et electi potestate*, I, 6, in VI°.

[65] *Glossa* ad c. 37, *de electione et electi potestate*, I, 6, in VI°, s. v. *imputent.*

CHAPTER IV

REPETITION, DEVELOPMENT AND ADDITIONS TO THE DECRETAL LAW

In the thirteenth and fourteenth centuries there was a marked decline in the number of episcopal elections. Direct appointment by the Supreme Pontiff supplanted election as the principal means of selecting prelates. Decretal legislation had been concerned chiefly with episcopal and abbatial elections. With the eclipse of episcopal elections, the development of the electoral laws took place in the legislation for religious. This legislation came at times from the Holy See, at other times from the particular constitutions and rules of the various groups of religious. Sometimes one or the other law peculiar to a particular community exercised a strong influence on later general legislation. The development of the electoral laws, especially the laws of disqualification, was not very great or startling in the period between the Council of Trent and the publication of the Code of Canon Law. The laws of the Decretals on this matter were quite well developed and remained substantially the same down to, and even after the promulgation of the Code. The Council of Trent did not treat of elections at great length, for it was concerned with more fundamental matters, and indeed there was little to add to the laws already in force. There was no dearth of commentators on the subject of elections, but in their interpretations and explanations of the laws they followed the commentators of the preceding centuries quite closely.

Much of the legislation which follows concerns religious. It is not clear whether such legislation applied only to religious belonging to the Orders, or whether it applied also to the members of the institutes of simple vows. The difficulty arises from the fact that in pre-Code days the members of communities in which there was no profession of *solemn* vows were not, with the exception of the Jesuits, considered to be true religious.[1] Monsignor Nervegna (d. 1906), an advocate at the Roman Curia, said that the matter was disputed even in Rome.[2] Nervegna himself was of the opinion that the general laws for religious did apply to members of institutes of simple vows, unless the law exempted them in particular cases or unless the law, by its very nature, applied only to religious in solemn vows.[3] Nothing was decided officially before the publication of the Code of Canón Law. The constitutions of the different communities of simple vows, since they had to be approved by the Holy See, undoubtedly incorporated most of the general legislation for religious.

The particular laws of the various communities often added disqualifications which were not contained in the universal law. In the following articles these laws will be considered only occasionally, namely, when they illustrate a universal law or where they seem to be the forerunner of later universal legislation.

ARTICLE I. NON-MEMBERS

The universal law on this matter did not change. The particular law, in some instances, tightened the regulations. In the Order of Preachers, for instance, by a decree of Pope Clement VIII (1592-1605), registered in the acts of the General Chapter of Valladolid (1605), it was not only re-

[1] Benedictus XIV, const. *Quamvis iusto,* 30 aprilis 1749, § 13—*Codicis Iuris Canonici Fontes,* cura Emi Petri Card. Gasparri editi (9 vols., Romae [postea Civitate Vaticana]: Typis Polyglottis Vaticanis, 1923-1939; vols. VII-IX, ed. cura et studio Emi Iustiniani Card. Serédi), n. 298 (hereafter cited *Fontes*); S. C. Ep. et Reg., *Congregationis Presbyterorum Saecularium,* 16 sept. 1864—*Fontes,* n. 1993; Gregorius XIII, const. *Quanto fructuosis,* 1 febr. 1583, § 5—*Fontes,* n. 153.

[2] "Saepe disputatum fuit in S. Congregatione—utrum ordinationes generales, quae continentur in Bullis Summorum Pontificum pro *Regularibus votorum solemnium* editis, sint applicandae *Institutis votorum simplicium,* sive longe natis, sive nascituris, *exceptis excipiendis.*"—Nervegna, *De Institutis Votorum Simplicium Religiosorum et Monialium* (Romae: e Cooperativa Polygraphica Editrice, 1904), p. 22.

[3] *Ibid.,* p. 23.

quired that the member of the religious community be assigned to the house for which the election was taking place, but he had to be so assigned for at least two months prior to the election.[4]

Article II. The Absent

The Council of Trent (1545-1563) forbade superiors in religious Orders to appoint substitute voters to take the place of absent members of the chapter. It nullified any faculties in this regard which had been granted in the past.[5] Pope Innocent XII (1691-1700) repeated this prohibition in 1694.[6] In 1723 Pope Innocent XIII (1721-1724) refused a request of the Minister General of the Order of Friars Minor of the Observance for the faculties to supply the votes of absent missionaries who could not attend the general chapter because of the great distances.[7] The Pope considered the supplying of votes a threat to the liberty of the chapter, fearing, it seems, that such a power could be used to "pack the chapter." He reiterated the decree of his predecessor Pope Innocent XII, and strengthened it by prescribing that his own decree be mentioned in any future petition for dispensation from this law. Failure to do so was to be considered as subreption and obreption.

The Council of Trent issued no ruling forbidding absent voters to vote by proxy and, consequently, the pre-Tridentine practice of permitting proxies continued. It was held, however, that because of a prescription of the council which required that the election of superiors be undertaken by way of a secret ballot,[8] an absent voter could not give his proxy a mandate to vote for a particular designated person.[9]

[4] Castellini, *De Electione et Confirmatione Canonica Praelatorum* (Romae, 1625), p. 146, n. 77 (hereafter cited *De Electione*).

[5] Sess. XXV, *de regularibus*, c. 6.

[6] Const. *Christifidelium,* 16 febr. 1694, § 12—*Fontes*, n. 257.

[7] S. C. Ep. et Reg., *Ordinis Minorum Observatium,* 15 maii 1723—*Fontes*, n. 1840.

[8] Sess. XXV, *de regularibus*, c. 6.

[9] "Procuratores vero legitime constituti cum generali mandato ad eligendum non excluduntur, dummodo non habent mandatum de

The constitutions of the Order of Preachers forbade voting by proxy no matter how justifiable the voter's absence.[10] Voting by proxy was ruled out by the *Normae* of 1901, a set of rules which the Sacred Congregation of Bishops and Regulars followed in approving new religious congregations.[11] These *Normae* did not have the binding force of law, but they did serve as a master pattern for the constitutions of the many new congregations of simple vows which were established after such congregations were formally allowed by the Constitution *Conditae a Christo* of Pope Leo XIII.[12] The rules of the *Normae* were almost universally incorporated as particular laws into the constitutions of these new congregations.

Article III. Persons Lacking the Requisite Age

There was no direct legislation in the post-Decretalist period that increased the requisite age for voting in ecclesiastical elections. Indirectly, however, the age of electors in religious communities was raised, inasmuch as the age required for admission to religious profession was raised. The Council of Trent decreed: "In no religious Order, whether of men or of women, shall profession be made before the completion of the sixteenth year, and no one shall be admitted to profession who has been under probation less than a year after the reception of the habit."[13] A decree of the Sacred Congregation for Religious Affairs, issued on

certa persona eligenda, tunc enim votum non esset secretum"— *Sacrosanctum Oecumenicum Concilium Tridentinum, Additis Declarationibus Cardinalium,* ex ultima recognitione Ioannis Gallemart necnon remissionibus Augustini Barbosae et annotationibus practicis Cardinalis De Luca cum variis Rotae Romanae decisionibus (ed. novissima, Matriti, 1762), declarationes ad sess. XXV, *de regularibus,* c. 6, p. 342, col. 1.

10 Castellini, *De Electione,* p. 161, n. 96.

11 *Normae secundum quas Sacra Congregatio Episcoporum et Regularium in novis religionis congregationibus approbandis procedere solet* (Romae, 1901), n. 229 (hereafter cited *Normae*).

12 8 decembris 1900—*Fontes,* n. 644.

13 Sess. XXV, *de regularibus,* c. 15.

May 6, 1675, by special instruction of Pope Clement X (1670-1676), forbade anyone to be admitted to the clerical novitiate unless he had completed his fifteenth year, or to the novitiate for lay brothers unless he had completed his twentieth year.[14]

It is evident from the Council of Trent, sess. XXV, c. 17, that a dispensation could be granted for a girl to enter a convent at the age of twelve. If such a dispensation was granted, there was no law prohibiting her from voting immediately after her profession.

ARTICLE IV. PERSONS LACKING THE REQUIRED ORDERS

The fourth chapter of the twenty-second session, *de reformatione*, of the Council of Trent reiterated the legislation of Pope Clement V, which had required the order of subdeaconship as a prerequisite for voting in the elections of prelates in collegiate and cathedral churches. The wording of the law as well as a decision of the Sacred Congregation of the Council of May 22, 1577, as cited by Pignatelli (c. 1600-1675), seemed to indicate that this rule applied only to the elections held in cathedral and collegiate churches.[15] There are, however, indications that this law, in the absence of any contrary particular law in the Constitutions of the Order, was applicable also to the elections conducted by the chapters of religious Orders. Thus, a decision of the Sacred Congregation of the Council of February 1, 1653,

[14] *Etsi Decretis—Collectaneum in Usum Secretariae Sacrae Congregationis Episcoporum et Regularium* (A. Bizzarri, Romae: Typographia Polyglotta, 1885), pp. 274-275 (hereafer cited Bizzarri).

[15] The decision of the Sacred Congregation of the Council read as follows: "Si Constitutionibus Religionis caveatur etiam sacris non initiatum posse quemlibet professum habere vocem in Capitulo, non prohiberi a Concilio Tridentino, quin eam habeant etiam quod in sacris non sint; quoniam dictum decretum Concilii, sess. 22, cap. 4. comprehendit monasterium Regularium. Sed Ecclesiae Regulares, de quibus ibi est sermo, sunt Cathedrales, ut Pampilionensis, Caligurtana, etc., vel Collegiatae Regulares, ut sunt multae in Hispania." —Jacobus Pignatelli, *Consultationes Canonicae* (Coloniae Allobrogum: Gabrielis et Samuelis De Tournes, 1700), I, Consul. 226, n. 1.

also cited by Pignatelli, given in answer to a question proposed by certain priests and clerics of a Third Order of St. Francis, stated:

> Sacra Congregatio etc. censuit, c. 4, sess. 22. comprehendere etiam Regulares mendicantes; ita ut regulares, qui non sunt in ordine Subdiaconatus vocem non possint habere in Capitulis, et actibus capitularibus, si in Constitutionibus eiusdem Religionis aliter expresse non caveatur.[16]

The right of clerics who were not yet in major orders to vote in the elections of a clerical community, was considered as an *exception* to the decree of the Council of Trent. Samuelli (d. 1660) quoted the constitutions of the Capuchins, who enjoyed the privilege of allowing clerics who were not yet subdeacons (and even lay brothers) to vote as follows:

> I Clerici quantumque non siano Subdiaconi, et anco i Laici possino havere voce nell' electioni, per dicharatione e concessione di Pio Quinto di Santa Memoria, *non ostante il Decreto del Concilio Tridentino,* sess. 22. cap. 4. *de reform.*[17]

Article V. Persons Professed with Temporary Public Vows of Religion

The first instance of *temporary* public vows seems reflected in the vows prescribed by Pope Pius IX (1846-1878) for the military Order of the Knights Hospitalers of St. John of Jerusalem.[18] By his Apostolic authority the Pope changed the rule of this Order. Annual, temporary, simple vows for a ten year period were commanded for this body, which up till then had taken only perpetual solemn vows. On April 27, 1866, the Sacred Congregation of Bishops and Regulars decided that the members of the community who had not yet made their perpetual solemn vows did not have

[16] *Ibid.*, n. 4; cf. also nn 5 & 6, which contain a similar reply given to the Praemonstratentians in 1666.

[17] Samuelli, *Disputationum Controversiae de Canonica Electione* (Venetiis: apud Turrinum, 1644), p. 472, n. 4 (hereafter cited *De Electione*).

[18] Pius IX, *Militarem Ordinem,* 28 iulii 1854—Bizzarri, pp. 631-632.

the right to vote.[19] One of the reasons given by the Congregation for this decision was that, according to the common teaching of the authors, a person was not truly constituted in the religious state if his vows were not irrevocable on his part.

There were other instances of temporary vows before the twentieth century. The Vincentian Sisters of Szathmar, Hungary, for example, took vows using the formula, "For as long as I shall remain in the Community of the Sisters of Charity."[20] It is obvious that the lack of perpetual vows was not a disqualification in the example given, since all the Sisters took temporary vows.

Generally, however, temporary vows were rare till the formal approval was given to Institutes of simple vows by Pope Leo XIII in 1900.[21] It is true that Pope Pius IX had prescribed *simple* vows for a period of three years before the taking of solemn vows, but these vows were not *temporary*. They were perpetual and irrevocable on the part of the candidate.[22] The idea that irrevocability in the vows was an essential requirement of the religious life continued up to the publication of the Code of Canon Law.[23]

Temporary vows preceding perpetual vows became common with institutes of simple vows. The *Normae* of 1901,

[19] S. C. Ep. et Reg., *Ordinis Hierosolymitani,* 27 apr. 1866—*Fontes,* n. 1997.

[20] Cf. Archiv fuer katholisches Kirchenrecht (Innsbruck, 1857-1861; Mainz, 1862-), LXXII (1894), p. 518.

[21] Leo XIII, const. *Conditae a Christo,* 8 dec. 1900—*Fontes,* n. 644.

[22] S. C. super Statu Regularium, litt. encycl. *Neminem latet,* 19 mart. 1857—*Fontes,* n. 4381; S. C. Ep. et Reg., *Peculiaribus Adductus,* 19 mart. 1857—*Fontes,* n. 1976; S. C. super Statu Regularium, *Sanctissimus,* 12 iunii, 1858—*Fontes,* n. 4383; S. C. Ep. et Reg., *Perpensis,* 3 maii, 1902—*Fontes,* n. 2039.

[23] Cf. Larraona, *Commentarium pro Religiosis* (Romae, 1920-1934; ab anno 1935; *Commentarium pro Religiosis et Missionariis*), II (1921), 208 (hereafter cited *CpR* or *CpRM*); Wernz, *Ius Decretalium* (6 vols. in 10, Vol. I, 3. ed., Prati, 1913, Vol. II, 3. ed., Prati, 1915, Vol. III, 2. ed., Romae, 1908, Vol. IV, 2. ed., Romae, Pars I, 1911, Pars II, 1912, Vol. V, 3. ed., Prati, 1914, Vol. VI, 3. ed., Prati, 1913), III, n. 590, p. 249.

the master pattern for all new institutes of simple vows, set the rule requiring annual vows for a minimum of three years, and a maximum of six years, before perpetual profession.[24] Members with temporary vows enjoyed very few voting rights, due to the fact that in most instances the right to vote was resultant from the holding of certain offices for which members with temporary vows were ineligible. Nearly all the offices filled by way of an elective process were filled by candidates chosen by the superior general and his council[25] or by the general chapter.[26] But a member with temporary vows could not be superior general or a member of his council,[27] nor could he be a member of the general chapter, neither *ex officio* nor as an elected delegate.[28] One of the few elections in which the community as a whole had a share was the election of the delegates to the general chapter. In the election of the delegates members with temporary vows shared the right to vote along with the members with perpetual vows.[29]

In the election to decide whether a confessor should be retained for a second or third term, all Sisters, even those not otherwise qualified for voting, were entitled to vote. This applied both to religious Orders and also to institutes of simple vows.[30]

ARTICLE VI. PERSONS WITH SIMPLE VOWS IN ORDERS OF SOLEMN VOWS

The nature of the simple vows prescribed by Pope Pius IX was described in a declaration of the Congregation for Religious Affairs, issued the year after the taking of simple vows was first ordered. On June 12, 1858, the Congregation,

[24] *Normae*, nn. 103-105.
[25] Cf. *Normae*, n. 271, 5°.
[26] Cf. *Normae*, nn. 231 & 239.
[27] *Normae*, nn. 231 & 240.
[28] Cf. *Normae*, nn. 213-222, 231, 240, 311.
[29] *Normae*, n. 217.
[30] S. C. de Religiosis, decr. 3 febr. 1913, n. 2, b, & n. 16—*Fontes*, n. 4416.

answering a request of the Master General of the Dominicans, declared, among other things, that the religious in simple vows enjoyed the same privileges and favors as did those who were in solemn vows.[31] The period of years [six] in profession required in the Dominican Order for qualifying a member for active (and passive) voice was to be counted from the first profession. The religious in simple vows were to have the same right of suffrage in the acts of the chapters of their convents as those who were in solemn vows.[32]

This declaration did not clear up the matter completely. Several years later the Master General of the Dominicans proposed some questions concerning the answer given in 1858. Were members in simple vows, he asked, to have the right to vote in deciding whether a member of the community was to be admitted to solemn profession? As he pointed out, the members in simple vows in a house might outnumber those who were in solemn vows, and there was danger of collusion, since a member in simple vows might be afraid to vote against a confrère, lest the confrère, in turn, vote against him when the time came for his solemn vows. Pope Pius IX commanded the Secretary of the Congregation for Religious Affairs to answer in the negative.[33] This exception to the voting power of those who were in simple vows was repeated in 1902 by the Congregation of Bishops and Regulars.[34] Members in simple vows exercised the right of suffrage only on the local level. They could be elected only to minor offices, and not to any which would have entitled them to be present at a provincial or a general council.[35]

Article VII. A Third Sister Admitted to the Same Monastery

In June, 1701, the Congregation of Bishops and Regulars

[31] S. C. super Statu Reg., declar., 12 iunii, 1858, n. VI—*Fontes*, n. 4383.

[32] *Ibid.*, n. VIII.

[33] S. C. super Statu Reg., 7 febr. 1862—*Fontes*, n. 4387.

[34] S. C. Ep. et Reg., *Perpensis*, 3 maii 1902, n. 8—*Fontes*, n. 2039.

[35] S. C. super Statu Reg., 16 ian. 1891—*Fontes*, n. 4390; S. C. Ep. et Reg., decr. *Perpensis*, 3 maii 1902, n. 8—*Fontes*, n. 2039.

issued a decree declaring that, if a woman were admitted to a monastery to which two of her sisters already belonged, she would enjoy neither an active vote nor a passive voice in elections till one of the two sisters died.[36] This was perhaps the only entirely new disqualification, other than those inflicted for some crime, that was imposed in post-decretalist times.

Article VIII. Excommunicated Persons

In the year 1418 Pope Martin V (1417-1431) in the Council of Constance issued his famous Constitution *Ad Evitanda.*[37] This constitution relaxed the law on communication with excommunicated persons. Formerly all persons excommunicated with major excommunication were to be shunned *(vitandi);* but after this constitution was issued, excommunicated persons were to be considered as pertaining to the class of *vitandi* only if they had been expressly condemned by name by way of a judicial sentence, or if they had notoriously persecuted clerics. Since the faithful could now licitly associate with persons who had been excommunicated with a major excommunication as long as they were not of the class of the *vitandi,* the commentators concluded that such excommunicated persons could validly and licitly participate in ecclesiastical elections. The persons under major excommunication did not, however, according to the commentators, have a real *right* to vote and any of the other electors, if he so desired, could raise an exception of excommunication and have the excommunicated persons expelled from the election.[38] Only rarely was a dissenting voice

[36] Bizzarri, p. 336.

[37] *Fontes,* n. 45; Mansi, XXVII, 1192-1193.

[38] Schmalzgrueber, *Ius Ecclesiasticum Universum,* lib. I, tit. 6, n. 13; Santi, *Praelectiones Iuris Canonici* (5 vols. in 1, Ratisbonae: Pustet, 1886), lib. I, tit. 6, n. 7, p. 54; Ojetti, *Synopsis Rerum Moralium et Iuris Pontificis* (3. ed., emendata et aucta, 4 vols., Romae: ex Officina Polygraphica Editrice, 1909-1914), s. v. *electio,* n. 1943, col. 1720, and n. 1944, col. 1721; Wernz, *Ius Decretalium,* II, n. 357, esp. footnote 29, pp. 130-131.

raised against the admission of persons who were laboring under a major excommunication but who were not of the class of the *vitandi,* to elections. Hinschius (1835-1898) was one of the very few who held that the disqualification applied to all persons under major excommunication, whether they were or were not of the class of the *vitandi,* just as before the Constitution *Ad Evitanda.*[39]

Paralleling the case of the excommunicated, some authors thought that also the suspended and the personally interdicted should not be considered as disqualified unless they had been condemned by way of a judicial sentence.[40]

Article IX. The Simoniacal

The Council of Basle (1413-1449) was the first, it seems, to inflict the perpetual deprivation of the right to vote on those who had abused their right of suffrage to elect simoniacally. This council imposed the penalty of an automatically incurred deprivation of voting rights on those electors who were guilty of simony in the election of a bishop or of some other prelate.[41]

This penalty does not seem to have been specifically repeated before the publication of the Code of Canon Law. Popes Leo X (1513-1521) and St. Pius V (1566-1572) is-

[39] "Dass die *tolerati* ihr Stimmrecht behalten,... ist eine irrige Annahme, denn die Konstitution Martins V. hat die Wirkungen der Exkommunication nicht zu Gunsten des von Betroffenen beseitigt." Hinschius, *System des katholischen Kirchenrechts mit besonderer Ruecksicht auf Deutschland* (4 vols., Berlin: Verlag von I. Guttentag, 1869-1888), II, 660, footnote 5.

[40] Wernz, *Ius Decretalium,* II, n. 357, footnote 29, p. 131.

[41] "Et sic simoniace eligentes, praeter alias poenas, perpetuo sint ipso facto iure eligendi privati."—Mansi, XXIX, 62. The ecumenicity of this council is somewhat confused. Part of it was ecumenical; part of it was not. The best opinion seems to be that only the decrees of the first twenty-five sessions, and only such of these decrees as were not prejudicial to the authority of the Apostolic See, are to be considered as sharing an ecumenical character.—Cf. Schroeder, *Disciplinary Decrees of General Councils* (St. Louis, Mo.: Herder, 1937), p. 472. The law cited above is contained in the twenty-second session of the council.

sued decrees reaffirming all the penalties ever inflicted by their predecessors and by the general councils on persons guilty of simony, but they did not mention deprivation of active suffrage specifically.[42] On April 1, 1568, Pope St. Pius V decreed that anyone who committed the crime of confidential simony thereby lost whatever right he might have had in elections.[43]

Perpetual deprivation of the office to be incurred *ipso facto* was one of the punishments imposed on regular clerics who presumed to exercise an order to which they had been simoniacally promoted.[44]

ARTICLE X. HERETICS AND SCHISMATICS

With the rise of the protestant heresies, Pope Paul IV (1555-1559) found it necessary to renew the penalties attached to heresy and to schism. In his constitution of 1559 the Pope declared that all heretics and schismatics, and their abettors, no matter of what ecclesiastical or civil rank or dignity, incur all the penalties, viz., excommunication, suspension, interdict, and deprivation of dignities, privileges, etc., which had ever been inflicted by any of the Roman Pontiffs or any of the general councils.[45] Archbishops, patriarchs, primates, cardinals, and legates who were guilty of heresy or schism were *ipso facto* and perpetually disqualified as voters in the Church.[46] Those who abetted heretics or schismatics were rendered infamous with infamy of law, and were barred from all offices and from all elections.[47]

[42] Leo X (in Conc. Lateranen. V), const. *Supernae dispositionis*, 5 maii 1514, § 37—*Fontes*, n. 64; S. Pius V, const. *Hodie*, 14 nov. 1569, § 1—*Fontes*, n. 131.

[43] Const. *Quanta Ecclesiae*, §§ 5 & 6—*Fontes*, n. 125.

[44] Sixtus V, const. *Sanctum et salutare*, 5 ian. 1589, §§ 3 & 6—*Fontes*, n. 166.

[45] Paulus IV, const. *Cum ex Apostolatus*, 15 febr. 1559—*Fontes*, n. 94.

[46] *Ibid.*, § 3.

[47] *Ibid.*, § 5.

ARTICLE XI. PERSONS WHO PROCEEDED "*Contra Formas*" IN THE ELECTION

The Council of Trent prescribed that the election of superiors, temporary abbots, and other officials and generals, as well as abbesses and other superiors should be effected by means of a secret ballot.[48] This provision, which applied to all elections of major superiors of religious communities, was interpreted by the authors as excluding elections through deputies *(per compromissarios)* and elections by way of inspired agreement *(quasi per inspirationem)*, which had been formerly allowed.[49] According to the authors this interpretation was adhered to by the Sacred Congregation of the Council.[50] To elect through deputies or by way of inspired agreement now constituted a violation of the prescribed form, and the electors guilty of such a violation could be deprived by their higher superior of the right to vote for one turn.[51]

ARTICLE XII. PERSONS WHO FAILED TO GO TO CONFESSION, TO RECEIVE HOLY COMMUNION, AND TO TAKE THE OATH BEFORE THE ELECTIONS OF PRELATES

The Council of Basle (1431-1449) commanded that, in the election of bishops and of other prelates, the electors had to confess their sins, go to Mass, and receive the Holy Eucharist prior to the election. Further, before the balloting, they had to take an oath to elect him whom they considered best for the spiritual and temporal welfare of the Church. Failure to do any of these things resulted in an automatically incurred deprivation of the right of suffrage for one turn.[52]

[48] Sess. XXV, *de regularibus*, c. 6.

[49] Fagnanus, *Commentaria in Quinque Libros Decretalium* (5 vols. in 4, Venetiis: apud Paulum Balleonium, 1709), ad c. 42, X, I, 6, p. 288, nn. 20-30; Reiffenstuel, lib. 1, tit. VI, n. 347 ss.; Castellini, *De Electione*, Cap. CII, nn. 5 & 6, p. 173; Samuelli, *De Electione*, pp. 12-13.

[50] *Loc. cit.*

[51] Cf. Samuelli, *De Electione*, p. 16, Concl. V.

[52] Mansi, XXIX, 62.

Article XIII. Persons Who Failed to Elect Within the Set Time Limit

When the direct appointment of bishops by the Apostolic See supplanted the election of bishops by the cathedral chapter, it became necessary to have an *ad interim* designated administrator of the diocese to carry on the business of the diocese till the new bishop should be appointed. It would have been too cumbersome to have the whole chapter acting as administrator, and so the institution of the vicar capitular was begun. By prescription of the Council of Trent this vicar was to be elected by the cathedral chapter within eight days after the death of the ordinary. Upon failure to do so the members of the chapter lost their right to elect. The right to select a vicar capitular then devolved upon the metropolitan, or, if it was the metropolitan see that was vacant, the right devolved upon the oldest of the suffragan bishops. If the see was exempt, i. e., not part of a metropolitan organization, the right devolved upon the closest neighboring bishop.[53] This limit of eight days was an exception to the general rule which allowed three months for the filling of a vacant bishopric or abbacy, and six months for the filling of other prelacies. The very purpose in the choosing of a vicar capitular explains, of course, the shortness of the time limit set for his election.

[53] Conc. Trident., sess. XXIV, *de ref.*, c. 16.

CHAPTER V

INCREASED USE OF DEPRIVATION OF ACTIVE VOTING RIGHTS AS A PENALTY FOR OFFENSES NOT RELATED TO ELECTIONS

The use of deprivation of electoral rights as a penalty for crimes other than those committed in connection with an election was not entirely new with the post-decretalist period. The local Council of Trier (1277), for instance, deprived monks of their vote in the chapter if they presumed to leave the monastery without permission.[1] The Council of Ravenna (1314) applied the same penalty to *nuns* who left the cloister.[2] Generally, however, disqualification in elections, as a specific penalty, was imposed for offenses committed in connection with an election. This was in keeping with the principle that, as far as possible, punishment should be meted out in the same sphere in which the offense took place.[3] In post-decretalist times deprivation of electoral rights became a common penalty imposed for sundry offenses. It was not one of the more severe penalties, and was usually imposed along with much severer punishments. Religious were the usual subjects of this penalty. Since seculars very seldom had occasion to participate in an election, it would have been meaningless to impose this penalty on them.

The following articles will not be a complete account of all the offenses to which the penalty of disqualification in elections was attached. Some of the more common examples, and a few of the less common ones will be given. Such an enumeration may suffice to show the extent of the application of this form of penalty.

[1] Mansi, XXIV, 205-207.

[2] Mansi, XXV, 544-545.

[3] "... puniatur in eo in quo deliquit."—Hostiensis, *Commentaria,* ad c. 36, X, *de electione et electi potestate,* I, 6, s. v. *in poenam,* 62 b. r., n. 4.

ARTICLE I. VIOLATION OF THE CLOISTER

Failure to observe the cloister was one of the causes for the rise of the worldly spirit and the low ebb of the spiritual life in the monasteries of the Middle Ages. The Holy See was engaged in a constant struggle to keep the religious in their cloister and to keep the world out of it. Penalties were imposed for unauthorized entry into a cloister (passive violation of the cloister), and for unauthorized departure from it (active violation of the cloister). The usual penalty for violation of the cloister was excommunication.

SECTION 1. PASSIVE VIOLATION OF THE CLOISTER

Automatically sustained deprivation of active (and passive) electoral rights was one of the punishments incurred by a member of a community of regulars who violated the law of the cloister by visiting a convent of nuns without the proper permission, or by engaging in conversation with the nuns when he went to the convent for a legitimate purpose, such as saying Mass for the nuns. According to a decree issued by the Sacred Congregation of Bishops and Regulars in 1623, this penalty was imposed in 1590 by Pope Sixtus V (1585-1590). The decree of 1623 made it easier to obtain permission to visit a convent, but it did not relax the penalties imposed for any violation of the decree.[4]

SECTION 2. ACTIVE VIOLATION OF THE CLOISTER

The constitutions of the various religious communities usually deprived apostates and fugitives of their voting rights and privileges.[5] The universal law, however, though

[4] Bizzarri, pp. 22-24.

[5] Cf. *Constitutiones Fratrum Ordinis Praedicatorum,* dist. I, c. XX, const. IV—*Codex Regularium Monasticarum et Canonicarum* (6 vols., ed. L. Holtensius, ed. altera, cura M. Brockie, Augustae Vindelicorum, 1759), IV, 64-65; *Constitutiones Urbanae Fratrum Ordinum Minorum Conventualium S. Francisci,* c. III, tit. XXIV, n. 6 —*Codex Regularium Monasticarum et Canonicarum,* III, 339; *Constitutiones Monachorum Syrorum Maronitarum Ordinis S. Antonii Abbatis,* pars III, c. X—*Bullarium Pontificium Sacrae Congregationis*

it did impose other severe penalties, did not impose deprivation of voting rights except in a few cases. Thus, a religious who left his monastery to go to Rome without permission from the supreme moderator of the Order, or from the Cardinal Protector of the Order, incurred loss of active and passive electoral rights for two years.[6] A decree of 1601 granted the provincial superiors the power to give their subjects permission to go to Rome, but at the same time it reaffirmed the punishments contained in the earlier decree.[7]

SECTION 3. OFFENSES COMMITTED BY SUPERIORS IN REGARD TO FUGITIVE RELIGIOUS

Pope Sixtus V forbade local ordinaries to receive an unknown religious from outside their territories, unless the religious presented the written permission or command of his superior authorizing the journey. Ordinaries who violated this prohibition were perpetually deprived of active and passive electoral rights.[8] Those who gave hospitality to religious who had come to Rome without the proper permission incurred the same punishment as that meted out to the delinquent religious, namely, deprivation of active and passive voting rights for a period of two years.[9]

Pope Urban VIII (1623-1644) issued a lengthy decree on the subject of fugitives. Religious superiors were forbidden to allow any of their subjects to transfer to a stricter Order unless they had first received assurances from that Order that it would receive such transferees. Religious superiors were forbidden to give testimonial letters to expelled reli-

de Propaganda Fide (2. ed., 5 vols., Romae: Typis Collegii Urbani, 1839, cum Appendice ad *Bullarium,* 2 vols., Romae: 1858, Index Analyticus, Romae, 1868), II, 388.

[6] Clemens VIII, *Nullus omnino,* 25 iulii 1599, § 13—*Bullarium Diplomatum et Privilegiorum Sanctorum Romanorum Pontificum Taurinensis Editio* (24 vols. et appendix, Augustae Taurinorum, 1857-1872), X, 665 (hereafter cited *Bull. Rom. Tauri.*).

[7] Clemens VIII, decr. 20 mart. 1601—*Bull. Rom. Taur.,* X, 667.

[8] Sixtus V, *Cum de omnibus,* 26 nov. 1587, § 7—*Fontes,* n. 162.

[9] Clemens VIII, *Nullus omnino,* 25 iulii 1599, § 13—*Bull. Rom. Taur.,* X, 667.

gious. They were commanded to seek out fugitives and receive them back into the monastery. Local ordinaries were to force fugitive and apostate religious to return to their monasteries. Anyone who violated this decree, altered it, or undermined it in any way, was deprived of his right of suffrage.[10]

Article II. Violation of the Ecclesiastical Laws on Property

Any religious, whether man or woman, who was apprehended or convicted of exercising proprietorship in violation of the vow of poverty was deprived by the Tridentine legislation of voting rights and privileges for a period of two years.[11]

Perpetual disqualification in elections was incurred *ipso facto* by any superior of any Order, Congregation, Society, or Institute within the confines of Europe who alienated ecclesiastical property without the written permission of the Sacred Congregation of the Council. This penalty was enacted in a decree issued by the Sacred Congregation of the Council under special command from Pope Urban VIII on September 7, 1624.[12]

In an apostolic letter issued for religious missionaries in Japan and the East Indies, Pope Urban VIII strictly prohibited any missionary to engage in trade or any other worldly business. Loss of active electoral rights was among the penalties incurred by those who disobeyed this prohibition and by superiors who failed to punish those who were delinquent in this matter.[13] Pope Clement IX (1667-1669) extended this law to include missionaries in North and South America.[14]

[10] S. C. C., decr. 21 sept. 1624, §§ 3, 4, 5, 9, 10, 13—*Fontes*, n. 2454; *Bull. Rom. Taur.*, XIII, 202-205.

[11] Conc. Trident., sess. XXV, *de regularibus*, c. 2.

[12] *Fontes*, n. 2453.

[13] Urbanus VIII, litt. ap. *Ex debito*, 22 febr. 1633, § 8—*Fontes*, n. 211; *Bull. Rom. Taur.*, VI, 344-346.

[14] Clemens IX, const. *Solicitudo*, 17 iun. 1669—*Fontes*, n. 243; *Bull. Rom. Taur.*, VI, 344-346.

Article III. Offenses Committed by Superiors in Regard to the Admission of Novices

Pope Sixtus V, who had come from the ranks of the religious, knew the importance of excluding the unqualified from the monasteries. He, therefore, forbade those who were born of a sacrilegious or incestuous union, as also thieves, murderers, etc., debtors, and those who were subject to the rendering of an account regarding large sums of money to be admitted to the religious life. Superiors who received such unqualified persons into the novitiate were stripped of their voting rights.[15]

Pope Clement VIII (1592-1605) realized that the reformation of the religious Orders as prescribed by the Council of Trent could be obtained only through a proper and uniform training of novices. To insure such a training among the religious groups of Italy and the adjoining islands, he allowed candidates to be accepted only into such houses in the various provinces that were approved by the Holy See. Any superior who disobeyed the Pope's decree suffered the loss of all voting rights.[16] Pope Clement VIII repeated this decree in 1599, exempting from it, however, certain religious Orders that had retained their spiritual vigor.[17]

The age for the admission of postulants into the novitiate had been set at fifteen for clerical postulants, and at twenty for lay brother postulants. Many religious groups, desiring to retain young boys for singing in the choir and for waiting on the monks, evaded the law by accepting boys into the monastery not as novices but under the title of oblates, tertiaries, guests, or some other similar title. Pope Clement X (1670-1676) crushed this subterfuge with a decree of May 16 , 1675, issued through the Congregation for Religious Affairs. He forbade anyone to be admitted to the cloister before the age of fifteen as a clerical novice, and before the age of

[15] Sixtus V, const. *Cum de omnibus*, 26 nov. 1587, §§ 2, 4, 6—*Fontes*, n. 162.

[16] Clemens VIII, const. *Regularis disciplinae*, 12 mart. 1596—*Fontes*, n. 183.

[17] Clemens VIII, decr. *Sanctissimus*, 20 iun. 1599—*Fontes*, n. 186.

twenty as a brother novice. Within two months from the date of the issuance of the decree religious superiors were to send away from the monastery all those who were under the requisite age. Non-compliance with the decree resulted automatically in the deprivation of voting rights and in other assorted penalties.[18]

A hundred and seventy-three years later Pope Pius IX (1846-1878), through the Sacred Congregation for Religious Affairs, published a decree requiring that a candidate present testimonial letters from the ordinary of his place of origin as well as from the ordinary of any place where he had lived for more than a year after his fifteenth year, before he could be allowed to receive the habit in any religious community. These letters were to testify concerning the person's legitimacy, age, morals, life, reputation, station in life, education and learning, and whether or not he was laboring under any ecclesiastical censure, irregularity, or canonical impediment, and whether or not he was in debt or under any obligation of rendering an account for some office he had held. Any superior who admitted a candidate to investiture without these testimonial letters was deprived of his voting rights and privileges, and they could be restored only by the Holy See. Further, this decree was to be read in public at table on the first day of each January. Superiors who did not comply lost automatically their electoral rights.[19]

Article IV. Offenses Committed by Religious Superiors in Regard to the Presentation of Subjects for the Reception of Holy Orders

A superior of a community of regulars could send his subjects to a bishop other than the local ordinary to be ordained if the local ordinary was absent or if he was not ordaining at that particular time. To prevent all abuse of this privilege, the Sacred Congregation of the Council issued a decree in 1596 binding superiors who intended to send their sub-

[18] S. C. super Statu Reg., 16 maii 1675—Bizzarri, pp. 274-275.

[19] S. C. super Statu Reg., decr. *Romani Pontificis*, 25 ian. 1848—*Fontes*, n. 4375.

jects to other bishops to declare in the dimissorial letters the reason for the local bishop's absence or for his non-conducting of ordinations at that time. Disobedience of this decree by the religious superior entailed loss of voting rights.[20] In 1708, and again in 1733, the Sacred Congregation of the Council enforced this law in particular cases.[21] Pope Benedict XIV (1740-1758) incorporated the decree of 1596 into his constitution *Impositi Nobis* of 1747.[22]

ARTICLE V. FAILING TO ATTEND THE DIOCESAN SYNOD

The Sacred Congregation of the Council imposed an *ipso facto* incurred deprivation of the right to vote on "regular" religious who had the care of souls and who were not subject to a general chapter if they failed to attend the diocesan synod.[23]

ARTICLE VI. OFFENSES COMMITTED IN REGARD TO MASS STIPENDS

In 1697 Pope Innocent XII (1691-1700) published a lengthy decree in which he legislated on the matter of Mass Stipends. Religious who violated the decree were disqualified as electors and as candidates for election.[24]

ARTICLE VII. PRACTISING THE *"Artes Aromatoriae"*

A decree of the Congregation of Bishops and Regulars in August, 1707, forbade religious to engage in the manufacture or sale of aromatic spices, poisons, and drugs of any kind, except antidotes and chemicals. Violators of this prohibition suffered loss of their active and passive electoral rights and privileges besides the loss of offices and a suspension *a divinis*.[25]

[20] S. C. C., decr. 15 mart. 1596—*Fontes*, n. 2294.

[21] S. C. C., *Caputaquen.*, 28 ian., 11 febr. 1708, ad 2am—*Fontes*, n. 3060; *Brixen.*, 28 nov., 12 dec. 1733, ad IIIam and Vam—*Fontes*, n. 3411.

[22] Benedictus XIV, const. *Impositi Nobis*, 27 febr. 1747, § 5—*Fontes*, n. 376.

[23] S. C. C., 19 dec. 1604—*Fontes*, n. 2354.

[24] Innocentius XII, const. *Nuper*, 23 dec. 1697, §§ 7, 9, 24—*Fontes*, n. 260.

[25] S. C. Ep. et Reg., aug. 1707—Bizzarri, p. 338.

SUMMARY

The earliest legislation on disqualification in elections was developed in connection with the election of bishops and, to a lesser extent, the election of abbots. Because of the frequency and the importance of elections in the pre-fourteenth century times, deprivation of electoral rights was considered as a not unimportant penalty. The object of declaring and imposing electoral disqualifications at the time of the Decretals was to exclude incompetent voters and to prevent abuses in elections. Thus, those who were unfit by natural or canonical standards were disqualified. Furthermore, disqualification was imposed as a penalty for offenses committed in connection with elections. The obtaining of competent voters and the conducting of proper elections always remained the primary purpose of electoral disqualification, though such disqualification could serve also for other purposes. Thus in the post-decretalist period it came to be widely used as a general sort of penalty to be imposed for any kind of crime, even though the crime did not bear any relation to elections. After the fourteenth century this penalty lost much of its sting, for after that time the bishops were generally appointed by the Holy See, and no longer elected by the cathedral chapter. Thus, as this punishment became more common it also became less important. It was usually inflicted along with more severe penalties. As a punishment, disqualification in elections became more and more restricted to religious.

PART TWO

CANONICAL COMMENTARY

CHAPTER VI

INTRODUCTORY CHAPTER

ARTICLE I. DEFINITION OF SOME TERMS

SECTION 1. APPOINTMENT

Canonical appointment means the grant of an ecclesiastical office by the competent ecclesiastical authority, given in accordance with the rules of the sacred canons.[1] In canonical appointment three acts are discernible: the designation of a certain person *(vocatio)*, the grant of the title to the office together with all the rights and obligations connected therewith, and, finally, the formal taking of possession of the office *(missio in possessionem)*.[2] The three acts are not always separate and distinct. In the appointment of free conferral by a superior, for instance, the designation of the appointee and the grant of the title to the office occur in one single act. The third step, viz., the canonical entry into possession, is prescribed by law for some offices.[3] When it is required it is necessary for the licit exercise, and sometimes even for the valid exercise of official acts.[4] It is not, however, an absolute essential of canonical appointment. For some offices it is not demanded at all; in some other cases it can be dispensed with.[5] It is very rare in the case of religious offices.

SECTION 2. ELECTION

"Election" is sometimes used in a broad sense to mean the first step in canonical appointment, namely, the designation

[1] Can. 147, § 2.

[2] Cf. Maroto, *Institutiones Iuris Canonici* (2 vols., Vol. I, 3. ed., Romae: Apud Commentarium pro Religiosis, 1921, Vol. II, 1. ed., Matriti, 1919), I, 686 (hereafter cited Maroto).

[3] Cf., e.g., cans. 313, 334, 353, 1444, 1472.

[4] Cf. can. 1095, § 1, n. 1, where canonical entry into possession is required for the validity of a pastor's or a bishop's assistance at marriages in his territory.

[5] Can. 1444, § 1.

of the appointee, no matter how the designation is made.[6] In this general sense, election includes free appointment by the competent superior, presentation by a lay person enjoying the privilege of patronage, nomination by one enjoying the right to designate someone in virtue of some privilege other than the right of patronage, postulation of a candidate lacking some required quality, and, lastly, election in the specific sense.

Election in the specific and proper meaning of the word is a collegiate act by which the qualified members of a moral personality select by means of votes a qualified person to fill a vacant ecclesiastical office. Election does not confer upon a person the actual office, but it does give him a substantial right *(ius ad rem)* to acquire that office. The person acquires the title to the office *(ius in re)* upon confirmation by the proper superior or, when no confirmation is needed, by the acceptance on his part.[7] Election is a collegiate act of a corporate personality *(persona moralis)*, that is to say, it is an act of a group authorized to act in the name of the corporate personality. As such it is subject to the prescriptions of canon 101, which governs the acts of corporate personalities. The person designated in the election must have the qualifications demanded by law, otherwise he cannot be elected. A person without the required qualifications can be designated by way of postulation, but not by way of election. A person cannot be elected to an office unless that office is vacant.[8] In the definition of election given here the term

[6] Cf., e.g., cans. 232, § 1; 399, § 1; 446, § 1; 516, § 4; 560; 1359, § 1; 1360; 1393, § 3; 1520, § 1; 1580, § 2; 1589, § 1; 1598, § 3; 1607, § 1.

[7] Can. 176, § 2.

[8] Can. 150, § 1. This canon forbids canonical appointment (which includes election, cf. can. 148, § 1) to a non-vacant office. As it stands it is applicable to offices in the strict sense of the word (cf. can. 145, § 2), but by virtue of canon 20 it should be applied also to offices in the broad sense of the word. An office must be vacant before the elected person can acquire actual title to it; a situation wherein two persons simultaneously held title to the same office could result only in confusion and a breakdown of discipline. An additional reason for

"office" is to be taken in a broad sense. It is not to be restricted in such a manner that it would include only such functions as entail some participation in the power of orders or of jurisdiction, as defined in canon 145. Thus, such elections as those of religious superiors who enjoy only dominative power will also be included in this definition.

SECTION 3. FORMS OF ELECTIONS

Elections are of three different forms, namely, by ballot *(scrutinium),* by deputies *(per compromissum),* or by quasi-inspiration. Election by ballot occurs when the qualified voters cast their individual ballots for the candidate of their choice. Election by deputies is the form of election in

forbidding the holding of an election prior to the vacancy of the office would be that persons who would become qualified to vote shortly before the expiration of the current term of office could be unjustly deprived of their right to vote simply in view of the advanced date of the election. Abbo-Hannan [*The Sacred Canons* (2 vols., St. Louis: B. Herder Book Co., 1952), I, p. 225] say that in the case of an election concerning an office which is not retained by the incumbent for life but for a determined number of years, the election should ordinarily precede the vacancy. The present writer cannot accept this opinion since it is contrary to the clear wording of canon 150, § 1. Then too, the *Normae* of 1901 (and the Constitutions of the many religious communities which are modeled after the *Normae*) give no indication that an election can be held before the term of office has expired. On the contrary they indicate that the election takes place after the expiration of the term of office, for it provides that the superior whose office has expired shall act as vicar until the election of the new superior (cf. *Normae*, n. 225). It is true that in some religious Orders, e.g., the Capuchins, a superior can be elected even though the office is not yet vacant. This practice, however, is regarded as a special privilege [cf. Coronata, *Institutiones Iuris Canonici* (5 vols., Vols. I, II, III, & V, 2. ed., Vol. IV, 3. ed., Taurini: Marietti 1939-1948), I, p. 254, footnote n. 4, (hereafter cited *Institutiones*)].

Offices can become vacant by way of resignation, deprivation, removal, transfer, lapse of time (cf. can. 183, § 1), or by the death of the incumbent. In the case of offices which are filled recurrently, e.g., every three years, or every ten years, the term of office expires at the beginning of the same day of the month on which it began (can. 34, § 3, n. 5).

which one or several persons are authorized by the voters to choose an appointee in the name of all. Election by quasi-inspiration is had when all the electors, without previous discussion, unanimously and spontaneously agree upon one candidate without balloting. This third type of electing is not mentioned in the Code and is no longer permissible, except by way of a particular law.[9] Election by deputies, while still permissible, is very rare, since it requires the consent of each and every voter in the chapter.[10]

SECTION 4. ACTIVE AND PASSIVE VOTING RIGHTS

Voting rights and privileges are divided into two large subdivisions, namely, the right to vote *(vox activa)* and the right to be voted for *(vox passiva)*. Deprivation of passive voting rights will not be treated in this dissertation.

SECTION 5. DISQUALIFICATION

Disqualification is the incapacity of a person to perform certain acts validly. A person is disqualified by the natural law when he cannot perform those essentials which are required by the very nature of the act. Thus, an insane person cannot perform a human act *(actus humanus)* and therefore he is disqualified for voting, which is a human act. Natural disqualifications are sometimes incorporated in the positive law. Persons who are not disqualified by the natural law are sometimes deprived of their juridical capacity to act validly. This legal disability is the proper object of disqualifying laws properly so called.[11]

Disqualifying laws which *ipso facto* render contrary acts null and void are disqualifying in the fullest sense of the word. Those laws which do not render contrary acts automatically null and void, but only render them voidable by way of the sentence of a judge or of a superior are disquali-

[9] Cf. Schaefer, *De Religiosis* (4. ed., aucta et emendata, Romae: Editrice "Apostolato Cattolico," 1947), p. 232.

[10] Can. 172, § 1.

[11] Vermeersch-Creusen, *Epitome Iuris Canonici*, I, 103-104; Cicognani, *Canon Law*, p. 558; Beste, *Introductio in Codicem*, pp. 68-69.

fying in a lesser degree. Laws which prohibit an action, with or without threatening a penalty, but which do not render contrary actions either void or voidable are not disqualifying laws; such laws are purely prohibitory laws.[12]

A disqualifying law differs somewhat from an invalidating law. The former directly affects the performing person, whereas the latter affects the performed act. The result of both laws, however, is the same, viz., the performed act is null and void.

The main purpose of disqualifications in the Church is to protect the various institutes in the Church by excluding those who are unfit. Sometimes, however, a disqualification is imposed as a penalty. At still other times a disqualification may partake of the nature of both a safeguard for the institute and a punishment for the disqualified person. Thus, when those who are under the age of puberty are disqualified as voters, this disqualification is intended solely as a safeguard without any overtone of punishment. On the other hand, disqualification in elections is at times a vindictive penalty pure and simple.[13] An example of a disqualification imposed upon a person as both punishment for the person concerned and protection for the office is the disqualification of a person laboring under a sentence of censure or infamy of law.[14] Such a person is excluded from voting both because he is not fit to share in the choosing of persons to rule in the Church, and also because he is being punished for his delict.

Article II. The Source of the Right to Vote

Voting, as shown above, is part of the canonical act of choosing persons to fill vacant offices in the Church. Now, choosing persons for vacant offices is, quite obviously, part of the task of ruling the Church. Voting is, therefore, a participation, however limited, in the power of ruling the

[12] Cf. Beste, *op. cit.*, pp. 68-69; Vermeersch-Creusen, *op. cit.*, 104-105.

[13] Cf. can. 2291, § 11.

[14] Cf. can. 167, § 1, n. 3.

Church *(potestas regiminis vel iurisdictionis)*. The right to vote, then, must come from those who have been entrusted with the right and duty of ruling the Church.

The right to vote cannot come from civil authorities, for the State does not have the power to rule the Church. The Church, as is known from Fundamental Theology and Public Ecclesiastical Law, was established by Christ as a self-sufficient society *(societas perfecta)*, that is, as a society which has as its end the complete good of its order and which has *de iure* all the means necessary for attaining that end. A self-sufficient society in its own order is independent and fully autonomous.[15]

Likewise, the power to vote cannot come from the faithful within the Church. The Church was not established as a democracy, with the right to govern coming from the consent of the people. It was instituted by the will of Christ as an unequalized or hierarchical society, that is, as a society in which some members have more rights and powers than others.[16] There are in the Church those who rule and those who are ruled. This prevails not only as regards the administration of the sacraments *(hierarchica ordinis)* but also as regards teaching and ruling *(hierarchica iurisdictionis vel regiminis)*. The only ones in the Church having the right to rule by the divine law are the supreme pontiff and the body of bishops.[17] As a matter of fact, the Roman Pontiff and the bishops share the exercise of their ruling power by creating subordinate offices. This sharing is not required by the divine law, but it is a practical arrangement on the part of

[15] Cf. Ottaviani, *Institutiones Iuris Publici Ecclesiastici* (2 vols., Vol. I, 3. ed., Vol. II, 2. ed., Civitate Vaticana: Typis Polyglottis Vaticanis, 1947), I, 53; Hervé *Manuale Theologiae Dogmaticae* (4 vols., Vol I, 46. ed., Vols. II, III & IV, 42, ed., Pariis: Berche et Pagis, 1949-1952), I, 324.

[16] Hervé, *Manuale Theologiae Dogmaticae*, I, 282.

[17] Cf. The Council of the Vatican (1869-1870)—D. B., nn. 1823, 1827, 1828; Decretum *Lamentabili*—D. B., n. 2055; Oath against Modernism—D. B., n. 2145; Hervé, *Manuale Theologiae Dogmaticae*, I, 307, 337, & 464; cans. 218 & 219.

the Supreme Pontiff and the bishops.[18] If anyone, then, enjoys the right to vote in ecclesiastical elections he has this right, not by any claim of the natural law or of the positive divine law, but by a free grant of the Holy Father or of the local ordinary. The concession of this right is made not by way of a special grant to each individual, but in a general way, when the moral personality is given legal existence through a formal recognition by the proper authority.

The local ordinary can grant to certain of his subjects the right to elect to those offices which fall under his jurisdiction. Thus, he could establish a diocesan religious community and determine which members should vote. This right of the local ordinary can be restricted by the Roman Pontiff either through some special act or by way of the setting up of general rules and regulations, such as are contained in the Code. The Holy Father has this power to restrict the rights of the local ordinary by reason of the monarchical nature of the Church. The pope has full, supreme and immediate power of ruling the whole Church, and each and every member of the Church.[19] The power of the local ordinary over his subjects is full, immediate, and ordinary, but it is subordinate to the supreme power of the Roman Pontiff.[20] The right to vote, then, is always subject to and dependent upon the supreme power of the pope, who can take away the right completely or limit it in any way he sees fit.

Though the right to vote comes to a person ultimately from the Roman Pontiff or the local ordinary, it comes immediately from the constitutions of the moral personalities to which he belongs. Since it derives from the constitutions, it must be considered as a constitutional right *(ius constitutivum)*.

From this discussion of the nature and source of the right

[18] Cf. Coronata, *Institutiones Iuris Canonici, Inroductio, Ius Publicum Ecclesiasticum* (Romae: Marietti, 1948), pp. 71-73.

[19] Can. 218; The Council of the Vatican—D. B., n. 1827.

[20] Cf. Hervé, *Manuale Theologiae Dogmaticae,* I, 464-468; can. 329, § 1.

of suffrage it can be seen that the deprivation of that right is not a mere penance. Disqualification in elections is the deprivation of a constitutional right coming to one from the Roman Pontiff or the local ordinary. A superior who is subordinate to the one who granted the right cannot deprive a person of this right as he pleases;[21] he needs authorization from the higher superior. This authorization need not be given by means of a special act. It is to be found either in the universal law of the Code of Canon Law or in the particular law of the institute. The authorization may extend simply to the *imposition* of the penalty for violation of a specific law, or it may extend to the *institution* of the penalty. Thus, superiors who enjoy jurisdiction in the external forum of the Church and who can make laws and issue jurisdictional precepts are authorized by canon 2220, § 1, to attach penalties, among which are included the deprivation of voting rights,[22] to their laws and precepts. Superiors with only dominative power are not authorized by the Code of Canon Law to institute this penalty. They can be endowed with this power by the Constitutions of their institute, but, in fact, especially in institutes composed of women, they are often specifically denied this power.[23] Superiors with dominative power who are not empowered to establish this penalty can *apply* the penalty, but only in those cases which the Code of Canon Law and their Constitutions specify.

When a superior who enjoys jurisdiction in the external forum of the Church imposes the penalty of deprivation of voting rights upon one of his subjects, the deprivation includes all the voting rights which the culprit enjoys in the Church. When a superior who enjoys only dominative power, however, imposes the penalty on one of his subjects in the community, the deprivation includes only those voting rights which the culprit enjoys as a member of the community. Superiors with jurisdiction in the external forum when inflicting the penalty must proceed in a judicial way.

[21] Cf. Schaefer, *De Religiosis*, p. 241; *Normae*, n. 268.
[22] Cf. can. 2291, n. 11.
[23] Cf., e.g., *Normae*, n. 268.

Superiors with dominative power proceed not in a judicial way but in a paternal manner, i.e., as a father punishing a delinquent child.[24] Usually these latter superiors are ordered to act only in conjunction with their council.

Article III. Immediate Sources of Disqualifications

Section 1. Universal Law

The universal law on elections is contained in the Code of Canon Law in canons 160-182. Of these, canons 165 and 167 deal with disqualifications. As they stand, these canons do not deal with all elections; they deal only with elections to offices in the strict sense of the word. This is evident from the fact that Title IV of the Second Book of the Code is treating of offices in the strict sense[25] and of elections as a means of designating persons to fill such offices.[26] These canons are, however, applied to some other elections in virtue of the provisions of later canons. Thus, canon 507, § 1, prescribes that all elections performed by the chapters in religious communities, be conducted in accordance with canons 160-182. This rule holds also for communities of the common life, the members of which are not religious in the strict sense, since they do not take public vows.[27] Canon 697, § 2, directs that all the rules of canons 161-182 regarding elections are to be observed by associations of the faithful. By associations of the faithful are meant third Orders secular, confraternities, and pious unions.[28] Thus it is seen that the vast majority of ecclesiastical elections fall under the scope of canons 160-182 and of the disqualifications enacted in canons 165 and 167. The only elections not subject to the provisions of these canons are those few elections which take place outside of the electoral chapter.[29]

[24] Cf. Schaefer, *De Religiosis*, p. 205.

[25] Can. 145, § 1.

[26] Cf. can. 148, § 1.

[27] Can. 675.

[28] Can. 700.

[29] In many religious communities the election of the delegates to

Besides the general disqualifications mentioned in canons 165 and 167, there are more specific disqualifications, advertence to and mention of which are scattered throughout the Code of Canon Law. Most of these, though not all, receive mention in the penal section of the Code.[30] These disqualifications are not merely closer specifications of those which are mentioned in canon 167, § 1, nn. 3-5. If they were, they would be limited to the elections conducted by the electoral chapters. But these disqualifications are not to be limited in this manner, for there is no clause in these particular canons restricting their application to capitular elections. Thus, canon 2385 disqualifies an apostate from the religious life not only with reference to elections held in the chapter but in relation to all elections.

SECTION 2. PARTICULAR LAW

A person may be disqualified as a voter not only by the universal law but also by the particular law. Thus, the constitutions of a moral personality may impose disqualifications in addition to those which are enacted in the Code of Canon Law. The particular law may extend the import of the universal law to cases not covered by the Code. The constitutions of a religious community, for example, may apply the disqualifications of canon 167 to all elections, inclusive of such as are conducted outside the chapter. The constitutions may be stricter than the Code of Canon Law. They may, for instance, disqualify those who have been perpetually professed for a period of time of less than three years, whereas the Code simply disqualifies those who have not been perpetually professed.[31] The constitutions may also point to disqualifications not mentioned in the Code of Canon Law at all. They may, for example, disqualify a fugitive from the religious life for one or more turns. The

the general chapter takes place without the convocation of a local chapter.

[30] Cf., e.g., cans. 629, 2385, 2390-2403.

[31] Cf. can. 578, n. 3.

Code of Canon Law expressly permits the existence of particular laws in the matter of disqualification of electors.[32]

SECTION 3. PRE-CODE LEGISLATION AND THE LAW IN THE CODE

Some disqualifications no longer receive mention in the Code of Canon Law. All penal disqualifications of the universal law which no longer receive *explicit* mention in the Code, as also all non-penal disqualifications of the universal law which have not *at least implicitly* been retained in the Code, are abolished.[33]

The Code of Canon Law did not abrogate any of the disqualifications of the particular law. The Code did not abolish particular laws unless they were contrary to its canons.[34] No disqualification is contrary to the canons of the Code of Canon Law, for nowhere does the Code state that this or that reason may not or cannot serve as a ground for disqualifying an elector.

The pre-Code legislation on the disqualification of electors is of some importance even today, since most of the present laws on the matter come from pre-Code times. In accordance with canon 6, nn. 2, 3 and 4, the laws of the Code are to be interpreted in accordance with the pre-Code laws as far as that is possible.

[32] Cf. can. 167, § 1, n. 5.
[33] Can. 6, nn. 5 & 6.
[34] Can. 6, n. 1.

CHAPTER VII

DISQUALIFICATION OF NON-MEMBERS

Canon 165. *Nullus collegio extraneus admitti potest ad suffragium, salvis privilegiis legitime quaesitis; secus, electio est ipso facto nulla.*

In virtue of canon 165 all non-members are excluded from voting in ecclesiastical elections; any violation of this canon renders the whole election automatically invalid.

ARTICLE I. DISQUALIFICATION *"in Actu Primo"*

The disqualifications of electors in ecclesiastical elections are summarized in two canons, namely, canons 165 and 167. The disability of non-members is set off in a separate canon, canon 165; whereas all the other disqualifications are collected in canon 167. The reason for not having organized all the disqualifications in one canon was that there is a radical difference between the disqualification of canon 165 and the disqualifications contained in canon 167. Canon 165 deals with those who are disqualified as voters *in actu primo,* that is, those who lack some qualification prerequisite for admission to the voting body. Persons who are disqualified *in actu primo* have no title whatsoever upon which they could base the claim to the right to vote. Canon 167, on the other hand, treats of those persons who have the right to vote *in actu primo,* but who are forbidden to *exercise* their voting privileges *in actu secundo.* This latter group includes those who have all the qualifications required for membership in the voting body, but who may not validly exercise the voting rights acquired through membership in the voting body because of some additional determination, either good or bad. Thus, to demonstrate the difference, a person who has never joined a religious Order has no claim to vote in the Order's chapter and is included under canon 165, while an apostate from the Order has lost his right to use his voting rights and is included under canon 167, § 1, n. 5.[1]

It may be pointed out that a particular disqualification may in one instance bar a person from acquiring membership in a voting body, while in another instance it only suspends the person's use of his right. Thus, insanity prevents a person from being admitted to any voting body, but if a person should become insane after he has been admitted to the voting body, his right would be only suspended.

The distinction between disqualification *in actu primo* and disqualification *in actu secundo* is not without historical basis. Hostiensis (d. 1271), one of the most outstanding commentators on the decretals, stated that to be able to vote one needed to have the right to vote and needed also not to be impeded by any law. He divided his matter into two parts, the first treating of those who belong to the voting body, and the second part treating of those who were impeded from voting by some law.[2] His division corresponds accurately to the division between disqualifications *in actu primo* and disqualifications *in actu secundo*. Ioannes Andreae (d. 1348) in the *glossa ordinaria* mentioned that some commentators distinguished between those who lacked only the vote and those who lacked both vote and "*numerus*," that is, position or listing as a member of the voting body.[3] This distinction would parallel closely the distinction between disqualifications *in actu primo* and disqualifications *in actu secundo*.

[1] Cf. can. 2384.

[2] *Summa Aurea, de electione et electi potestate* (I, 6), § *Quis possit eligere*, 27 b. r.-29 a. v.

[3] "... excommunicatae, suspensae, et interdictae et similes personae & eligentes scienter indignam admittentur et computabuntur in numero; sed quae non sunt professae, vel minores, non: quia non faciunt numerum. Quidam vero dicunt exceptionem excommunicationis bene admitti contra eligentes, quia excommunicatio privat voce et numero.... Sed scienter eligens indignam, licet privetur voce, non numero ..."—*glossa ordinaria* ad c. 43, *de electione et electi potestate*, I, 6, in VI°, s. v. *non obstante*.

Article II. The Meaning of "*Extraneus Collegio*"

In spite of the seeming clarity of canon 165, some difficulty arises in determining the exact meaning of the term "*extraneus collegio,*" as used in this canon. When the voting *collegium* (collegiate moral personality) is not part of a larger *collegium* there is no problem. Thus, when this canon is applied to a cathedral chapter, anyone who is not a member of the chapter is an *extraneus collegio.* In religious communities and associations, however, the voting body is usually a special *collegium* within the community. The voting chapter, whether local, provincial, or general, forms a distinct juridical entity which is not coextensive with the respective local house, province, or society. The chapter is a *collegium* within a *collegium.* Does the term "*extraneus collegio*" as used in canon 165 refer to those who are not members of the religious community, or to all, including members of the religious community, who are not members of the electoral chapter? Would the admission of a fellow religious who is not a member of the chapter render the whole election invalid?

Some authors, in trying to determine the meaning of "*extraneus collegio,*" have sought a clear-cut definition of the word *extraneus.*[4] They have found such a definition in Passerini's classical work on elections, *De Electione Canonica.* Passerini (d. 1677) stated:

> Extraneus in proposito ille dici debet, qui non est membrum Collegii eligentium, et hic est ille, qui licet sit membrum Conventus aut Ecclesiae, pro qua est eligendus Praelatus, tamen non habet qualitatem aliquam necessarium ex lege, vel consuetudine ad hoc ut sit elector.... Et sic universaliter omnis ille, cui deficit aliqua qualitas seu conditio ex illis quae sunt necessariae ad eligendum, est extraneus a Collegio eligentium.[5]

[4] Cf., e.g., Parsons, *Canonical Elections,* Catholic University of America Canon Law Studies, n. 118 (Washington, D.C.: The Catholic University of America Press, 1939), p. 118; Maroto, I, 778.

[5] *Tractatus de Electione Canonica,* (Romae, 1693), III, 17 (hereafter cited *De Electione Canonica*).

Parsons (1911-1945) felt that the legislator had this definition in mind when drawing up canon 165.[6] This does not, however, seem to have been the case. Passerini's definition, as it stands, would include all who are disqualified, whether *in actu primo* or only *in actu secundo.* In fact, it seems that Passerini actually intended to include in his definition of *extranei* also those who were deprived only of the right to exercise their voting privileges. In the definition just quoted, Passerini stated that an *extraneus* is anyone who lacks *any* condition or quality required by law or custom. In a later chapter, where he treated of the conditions required for electors, he included among the conditions a free use of reason (which excluded the insane and those below the age of puberty), freedom from excommunication, from suspension, from interdict, from infamy, and freedom from any sentence depriving the elector of his right to vote.[7] In other words, the *extranei* of Passerini's definition included not only the *extranei* of canon 165 but also the disqualified voters of canon 167. A comparison of canons 165 and 167, however, shows that the disqualified voters of canon 167 are not included in the *extranei* of canon 165, because the effect of the admission of the disqualified voters of canon 167 is radically different from, and milder than, the effect of the admission of an *extraneus.*[8] The fact that pre-Code authors did not quote Passerini's definition seems also to argue against the contention that this was the generally accepted definition of *extraneus collegio.*

A better approach to the problem looks to the meaning and use of the term *collegium* among the pre-Code authors. A *collegium* meant a collegiate moral personality.[9] This

[6] *Canonical Election,* p. 118.

[7] *De Electione Canonica,* X, 10-141.

[8] Compare can. 165 with can. 167, § 2.

[9] Cf. Donatur [Hyacinthus Donatus Laynensis], *Rerum Regularium Quadrapartita Praxis Resolutioria* (2 vols., Neapoli, 1652), Pars III, tract. II, q. 4 (hereafter cited Donatus); Pirhing, *Ius Canonicum in Quinque Libros Decretalium Distributum* (5 vols. in 4, Dilingae, 1722), Lib. I, tit. 6, sec. I, § II, n. 9 (hereafter cited Pirhing); Passerini, *De Electione Canonica,* X, 7; Fagnanus, *Commentarium in*

definition alone would not be of much help in determining the meaning of *collegium* as used in canon 165, since both the chapter and the religious house were collegiate moral personalities. A survey of the commentaries written on elections, however, shows that *collegium,* when used in reference to elections, denoted the voting chapter of the community rather than the community itself. Pre-Code authors identified *collegium* with *capitulum,* using the terms synonymously and interchangeably.[10] The clearest statement on the matter is found in the work of Donatus. He wrote:

> Sed adverte, quod non omnes Religiosi faciunt Collegium et constituunt Capitulum, quamvis subsunt Praelato et iussu eiusdem diversis officiis reperiantur destinati.... Sed illi tantum, qui secundum Sacros Canones et propria statuta habent requisita ad capitulariter interessendum actibus et negotiis Capituli.[11]

Since, then, *collegium* was used in pre-Code commentaries on elections to mean the voting chapter and not the religious community, one should, in keeping with the principles of canonical interpretation, preserve that meaning in the interpretation of canon 165.

The text of the Code also supports the view that *collegium* refers to the voting chapter rather than to the community

Quinque Libros Decretalium, ad c. 1, X, I, 6, nn. 32 & 44; Hostiensis, *Summa Aurea,* 104 a. v., n. 2; Innocentius IV, *Commentaria,* p. 627-628.

[10] "... Capitulum seu Conventum, quae duo in iure sumuntur promiscue,... quamvis in praxi Capitulum vocari soleat Congregatio seu Collegium Clericorum saecularium, et conventus Congregatio Religiosorum."—Pichler, *Ius Canonicum,* Pars I, tit. VI, n. 19; "...qui non habent vocem, non sunt de Capitulo, seu Collegio..."—Pirhing, Lib. I, tit. 6, sec. 1, § 3, n. 14; Reiffenstuel, Lib. I, tit. 6, n. 159; *glossa* ad c. 47, X, *de electione et electi potestate,* I, 6, s. v. *vocem in capitulo;* c. 46, 50, *de electione et electi potestate,* I, 6, in VI°; Donatus, Pars III, Tr. II, qq. 3 & 6.

[11] Pars III, Tr. IV, q. 1; cp. Pars III, Tr. II, q. 7, where he stated: "Non omnes qui sunt in monasterio veniunt appellatione Capituli, sed illi tantum Patres, ad quos de iure aut de privilegio, vel consuetudine spectat interesse rebus capitulariter agendis...."

as a whole. Since canon 165 is speaking about elections, it is altogether logical to interpret *collegium* as referring to that *collegium* which is electoral, rather than to the *collegium* which is not electoral. Further, canon 507 applies canon 165 directly to the elections conducted by the voting chapter, and the *collegium* mentioned in canon 165 must be the *collegium* for which the law is specifically made, namely, the voting chapter. Also, to be consistent and logical the term *collegium* of canon 165 should retain the same meaning, whether the canon be applied to elections in religious communities and associations or to elections outside of such communities. Since *collegium* means the voting body when applied to elections outside of religious communities and associations, it would be inconsistent to say that it does not mean the voting body but the whole community when applied to elections within religious communities and associations.

The writer's interpretation of *collegium* is supported by the weight of the authority of the commentators. This interpretation is held by Larraona, Maroto, Goyeneche, Crnica, and others.[12] It seems that Gasparri (1852-1934), however, did not espouse this opinion. In his footnotes to canon 165 he cited only such pre-Code laws as dealt with persons who did not belong to the institute, and in his footnote to canon 167, § 1, n. 5, he cited a decretal law which dealt with the disqualification of the non-professed and of lay brothers (c. 32, *de electione et electi potestate,* I, 6, in VI°). It seems, therefore, that he did not consider the non-professed and lay brothers as *extranei,* as they would be considered according to the interpretation here offered by the writer.

[12] Larraona, "De Electionibus Religiosorum" *CpR,* IX, 335-336; Maroto, *Institutiones,* I, 778-779; Goyeneche, "Consultationes," *CpR,* VII, 390-391; Crnica, *Commentarium Theoretico-Practicum Codicis Iuris Canonici* (2 vols., Sibenik: Kačić, 1940), I, 174; Jone, *Commentarium in Codicem Iuris Canonici* (3 vols., Vol. I, Paderborn: Schöningh, 1950, I, 169; Parsons, *Canonical Elections,* p. 115-120; Haring, *Grundzüge des katholischen Kirchenrechts* (3. ed., 2 vols., Graz: Ulrich Mosers Buchhandlung, 1924), I, 203, note 5.

ARTICLE III. PERSONS INCLUDED AMONG THE "*Extranei*"

With the term *extraneus collegio* properly defined the task remains to list those who are included under the term. Collegiate moral personalities and individuals who enjoy the right to vote in ecclesiastical elections in virtue of some Apostolic privilege become *extranei* upon the cessation of the privilege. The cessation of privileges is governed by canons 60, 61, 65, and 70-78. In the case of a collegiate moral personality which enjoys voting rights by reason of an Apostolic concession, the individual members of the collegiate body become *extranei* not only upon cessation of the privilege but also upon lapse of membership in the body. The different groups which could receive voting privileges by a special grant of the Holy See are numberless, and so it is impossible to consider them all individually. The Holy Father, by way of example, could grant a parish the right to elect its pastor. In this case membership and non-membership in the parish would be determined in line with the rulings of canons 91-95. In this dissertation it is possible to consider those who are outsiders only in relation to those groups which commonly enjoy the right and privilege of voting in ecclesiastical elections. These groups are 1) the cathedral chapter and the body of diocesan consultors; 2) the voting body in religious communities and societies of the common life; and 3) the voting group in associations of the faithful. As a preamble to the discussion, all non-baptized persons are *extranei* in relation to ecclesiastical elections, for it is plain from the law of the Code that only the baptized have rights and privileges in the Church.[13] The Supreme Pontiff could, of course, grant a non-baptized person the right to vote in an ecclesiastical election, but this would be an exception to the common law or rule.

SECTION 1. THE CATHEDRAL CHAPTER AND THE BODY OF DIOCESAN CONSULTORS

The chief electoral function of the cathedral chapter is to

[13] Cf. can. 87.

elect a vicar capitular who rules the diocese during the vacancy between the death of the ordinary and the appointment of a successor.[14] In relation to the cathedral chapter, included among the outsiders are all those who have not been validly appointed as canons in accordance with canons 396, 403 and 1435, and all those who have lost their canonry. The position of canon can be lost through resignation, deprivation, removal, or transfer.[15] Suspension does not render one a non-member of the chapter.[16] Honorary canons cannot properly be said to belong to the cathedral chapter. Their title gives them the right to wear the insignia of a canon and the right to a stall in the choir, but it gives them no right to vote or to participate in any of the other administrative acts of the chapter.[17] They must be considered as *extranei* in relation to the chapter. Also excluded as non-members are those who hold inferior benefices in the cathedral church.[18] Canons who, after forty years of continuous and laudable service, have received a rescript from the Holy See declaring them *emeriti* remain members of the chapter. Such canons are freed from choir service but retain the right to receive the daily distributions, even the *distributiones inter praesentes* (meant for the ones in attendance at supererogatory functions), unless custom, the statutes of the chapter, or the intention of the founders and donors deprive them of this latter right. They retain all their rights except the right of option.[19]

In places such as the United States, where the institute of the cathedral chapter is not yet established, diocesan consultors are appointed to assist the bishop as his senate. As the cathedral chapter elects the vicar capitular to administer the diocese during its vacancy, so the diocesan consultors

[14] Can. 432, § 1.

[15] Can. 183, § 1; cans. 183-195; 584; 1438; 2266; 2298, n. 6; 2299, § 1; 2303; 2304; 2305.

[16] Cans. 2283 & 2265.

[17] Cf. cans. 407, § 2; 411, § 3.

[18] Can. 392, § 2.

[19] Can. 422; cf. Abbo-Hannan, *The Sacred Canons*, I, 247.

elect the administrator for the same task. The diocesan consultors are appointed by the bishop or, during the vacancy of the diocese, by the administrator with the consent of the other consultors.[20] The office of diocesan consultor is lost through resignation, deprivation, removal, transfer, and the lapse of the three-year term of office.[21] Since the office is not a benefice, it is lost immediately upon profession in a religious community, unlike the benefice of a cathedral canon, which is not lost till three years after religious profession.[22]

SECTION 2. RELIGIOUS COMMUNITIES AND SOCIETIES OF THE COMMON LIFE

In reference to a religious society all those who have not been validly professed in that society according to the norms of canon 572 are non-members. Novices, though they enjoy the spiritual privileges granted to the institute, are not formally incorporated in the society until they make their religious profession.[23] As regards elections, therefore, they must be regarded as non-members. To admit novices to participation in capitular elections would require special permission from the Holy See. Those who are in temporary vows are also barred from membership in the voting chapters, unless the constitutions of the society specifically permit their admission.[24] If a professed religious transfers to another religious society, he does not immediately become an *extraneus* in regard to his former community. His rights in the first community are not taken away; they are simply suspended until he has finished his novitiate and made his profession in the second community.[25] Religious in temporary vows who are dismissed from a community in accord-

[20] Cans. 424; 426, § 5.

[21] Cans. 183, § 1; 426, § 1.

[22] Can. 188, n. 1; can. 584.

[23] Cf. can. 567, § 1; Creusen, *Religious Men and Women in the Code* (4. English ed., Milwaukee: Bruce, 1940), p. 170.

[24] Can. 578, n. 3.

[25] Can. 633, § 1.

ance with canon 647 are freed from their vows and thereby become non-members of the community.[26] Those who are in perpetual vows when they are dismissed, whether automatically according to canon 646 or in consequence of the process outlined in canons 654-668, are not *ipso facto* freed from their vows, and hence do not by the fact of their dismissal become *extranei* in the sense of canon 165.[27] The vows create the formal link between the individual and the community. Religious who receive an indult of secularization are freed from their vows and are separated completely from the community.[28] They are non-members from the date the indult becomes effective. Religious who receive an indult of exclaustration from the Holy See remain bound by the vows as far as that is compatible with their state.[29] Their right to vote is suspended for the time of the exclaustration, but they do not become non-members in the meaning of canon 165. Membership in the general and provincial chapters respectively is usually dependent upon the holding of some office or upon having been duly elected as a delegate to the chapter.[30] Membership in the chapter is forfeited through loss of the office unless the constitutions of the society provide otherwise. The particular law of the institute usually provides that those who are capitulars by reason of some office should continue to be capitulars for that current chapter, even though they have not been re-elected to their former office by the chapter.[31] The constitutions of the many religious communities provide that the supreme moderator shall remain a member of the general chapter for life even after his office has expired.[32] Membership in the provincial chapter as also in the local chapter requires assignment to

[26] Can. 648.

[27] Cf. cans. 669; 672.

[28] Can. 640, nn. 1 & 2.

[29] Can. 639.

[30] The election of delegates to the chapter is generally not a capitular election and, therefore, is not governed by the Code, since canon 507, § 1, applies only to elections within the chapter.

[31] Cf. *Normae*, n. 213; *Constitutions of the Congregation of the Missionaries of Mariannhill* (Mariannhill: Mariannhill Mission Press, 1950), n. 228.

[32] *Ibid.*, n. 189; *Normae*, n. 214.

that particular province and house respectively. If a person is transferred from one house or monastery to another, or from one province to another, he becomes a non-member of the first house, monastery, or province from the day of his transfer.[33]

What has been said about religious communities applies, with the proper modifications, to communities of the common life also. In these latter societies the bond of union between the individual and the community arises not through vows, but through a promise or oath.

As a postscript it may be mentioned that in societies composed of clerics and lay brothers, the lay brothers are not disqualified from membership in the chapter unless the community has a particular law to that effect.[34] The Code did not repeat the disqualification listed in the decretals. Cappello says lay brothers are disqualified (except in non-clerical religious communities) by virtue of canon 166, which excludes laymen from participation in ecclesiastical elections.[35] Canon 166, however, is a repetition of pre-Code law[36] and should be interpreted as the pre-Code law was interpreted.[37] Now, the pre-Code legislation which excluded laymen *under threat of nullity of the entire election* was interpreted as not referring to lay brothers.[38] Canon 166, therefore, must be interpreted as not referring to lay brothers but only to lay persons who are neither clerics nor religious.[39] Though the Code of Canon Law does not disqualify lay brothers, the constitutions of the various religious communities usually do exclude them.

[33] Cf. can. 635, n. 1.

[34] Cf. Schaefer, *De Religiosis*, p. 238; *contra*, Cappello, *Summa Iuris Canonici* (Romae: Apud Aedes Pontificiae Universitatis Gregorianae, Vols. I & II, 4. ed., 1945, Vol. III, 3. ed., 1948), I, p. 253 (hereafter cited *Summa*).

[35] *Summa*, I, p. 253.

[36] Cf. c. 56, X, *de electione et electi potestate*, I, 6.

[37] Can. 6, n. 2.

[38] Pirhing, Lib. I, Tit. VI, sec. 1, § III, n. 18.

[39] Cf. Parsons, *Canonical Elections*, p. 121.

SECTION 3. ASSOCIATIONS OF THE FAITHFUL

In relation to associations of the faithful, they are non-members who have not been validly admitted to the association or who have been legitimately dismissed from it.[40] A person could, presumably, also resign from such an association. In that event he would cease to be a member when the association received official notification of his resignation. Membership in a third Order, but not in other associations, is lost when a person takes vows in a religious community.[41] Even though enrollment in the third Order revives if a religious is freed from his vows, yet the wording of the Code *(nequit pertinere)* shows clearly that a religious does not belong to the third Order after religious profession. Women cannot be admitted to associations known as confraternities except for receiving the indulgences and spiritual benefits granted to the members.[42] Since they assume none of the duties and obligations of members, they must be regarded as non-members as far as elections and other official business are concerned

Persons below the age of puberty can be admitted to membership in associations of the faithful. If the association has a special voting body those below the age of puberty would have to be excluded from that body[43] and, hence, would be *extranei.* If, however, there is no special voting body within the association but all the members participate in conducting the affairs of the association, then those below the age of puberty, though they would have to be excluded from voting, would not be *extranei.*

ARTICLE IV. CONDITIONS UNDER WHICH THE ELECTION IS NULL IN VIEW OF CANON 165

Before an election is rendered invalid by reason of canon 165 the following conditions must be verified: 1) The per-

[40] Cf. cans. 694 and 696.
[41] Can. 704, § 1.
[42] Can. 709, § 2.
[43] Cf. can. 167, § 1, n. 2.

son who is admitted must be a non-member of the voting body, not just a person who has had his voting rights suspended according to canon 167. 2) He must be *admitted.* This means that he must be admitted by the majority of the voters in accordance with canon 101, which regulates the acts of collegiate moral personalities. If he forces his way into the election over the protests of the majority, his action does not result in the invalidity of the whole election. Further, the admission must be formal (in contradistinction to material), that is to say, the voting body must be aware of the fact that he is not a member when they admit him to vote. If the voting body admitted a non-member under the false impression that he was a member, the election would not thereby be invalidated. 3) He must be admitted to vote. If he is present but does not cast a ballot, the election is not rendered invalid. 4) There must be no legitimately acquired privilege allowing the person to be present and to vote. Not only may the individual non-member acquire a privilege allowing him to vote in an election, but the voting body may acquire the privilege of admitting certain non-members to the election.

The admission of *one* non-member suffices to nullify the election. When canon 165 states, "*electio est ipso facto nulla,*" the term "election" should be understood as pointing to the ballotings in which the non-member took part. If there are several ballotings in an election and the non-member is expelled or leaves after the earlier ballotings, the subsequent ballotings and the resultant election would not be invalid.

CHAPTER VIII

DISQUALIFICATION OF MEMBERS OF THE VOTING BODY

ARTICLE I. DISQUALIFICATION OF PERSONS INCAPABLE OF HUMAN ACTS

Canon 167, § 1. *Nequeunt suffragium ferre:*

1°. *Incapaces actus humani.*

Election is, by its very nature, an exercise of intellect and will. The intellect considers the qualities of the various candidates, and the will makes a choice. In other words, electing is a human act. It is obvious, then, that those who are incapable of human acts in general are incapable of the particular human act of voting. The rule of canon 167, § 1, n. 1, is no more than a reiteration of the natural law. It should be noted that in reference to canon 167, § 1, n. 1, a person is not considered to be capable of human acts unless he is capable of acts which are perfectly voluntary *(voluntarium perfectum)*. By this is meant that a person must have that degree of knowledge and freedom of the will which are postulated for the committing of mortal sin. If a person's intellect is so clouded that he no longer is capable of committing mortal sin, but is still capable of committing venial sin, he would be disqualified for voting even though strictly he is capable of human acts.

Those who are incapable of human acts may be divided into two general classes, namely, the normal and the abnormal. Among the normal we have, first of all, infants. In Canon Law it is presumed that a person does not attain the use of reason till the completion of his seventh year.[1] At the other extreme of life we have the very old who are in their dotage. There is no definite age at which a person is considered so senile as to be incapable of human acts. It varies considerably in individual cases, both in time and in degree. In some

[1] Can. 88, § 3.

cases a person retains all his faculties unimpaired till his death at an advanced age. Aside from these habitual states there are temporary states in which a person is incapable of human acts. Besides the case of sleep, which is of no importance here, a person can lose his capacity to perform human acts by becoming intoxicated. It is not required that the intoxication be perfect, that is, an intoxication which deprives a person completely of his use of reason. Imperfect drunkenness suffices if it impairs the functioning of the reason to the extent that the person is incapable, here and now, of mortal sin. It is likewise of no consequence, in regard to the present matter, whether the intoxication be morally culpable or morally inculpable, since this disqualification is not intended as a punishment. What has been said about intoxication applies also to the condition induced through the use of drugs. Sickness sometimes causes a person to become delirious, and as a consequence renders him incapable of human acts. Passion, such as anger, may temporarily deprive a person of his power of thinking clearly. Thus a person in a blind rage should be expelled from the election because he has temporarily lost his right to vote.

Abnormal people may be classified either as mentally weak or as mentally unbalanced. The mentally weak include idiots, imbeciles, morons, and the sub-normal. Idiots have a mental age of two or three years and an I. Q. of up to 25. They lack judgment and are unable to foresee the consequences of their acts. In many instances they lead an almost purely vegetative existence. Imbeciles have a mental age of three to seven years and an I. Q. of 25 to 50. Morons have a mental age of six to twelve years and an I. Q. of 50 to 70. The sub-normal have an I. Q. of 80 to 90.[2] Idiots and imbeciles are obviously disqualified. In deciding whether or not a moronic person is capable of voting, one must consider not only his I. Q. but also his ability to keep his mind from wandering. Inadvertence is a chronic condition among the

[2] Cf. VanderVeldt-Odenwald, *Psychiatry and Catholicism* (New-York: McGraw-Hill, 1952), pp. 318-320.

feeble-minded. A moron with a mental age of eight years does not have as much thoughtfulness or advertence as an ordinary eight-year-old child. The whole life of the lower grade moron consists of a continuous succession of moments of inadvertence.[3] The higher grade moron and the subnormal person usually are not disqualified as electors.[4] It is impossible to draw a definite line of demarcation between those who are too absent-minded to vote and those who are not. Between the lower type moron and the highest type there is a considerable area of uncertainty. Cases of doubt, which will be discussed in a later article,[5] must be resolved in favor of the individual. The question of the voting rights of the mentally defective will seldom, if ever, arise as a practical problem in religious communities, societies of the common life, cathedral chapters, or bodies of diocesan consultors. The problem may arise, however, in some associations of the faithful.

The mentally unbalanced may be grouped as the psychotic, the psychoneurotic, and the psychopathic. It is not to the present purpose to go into a long discussion of these various groups. It suffices to point out that the psychotic live in a world of fantasy separated from reality, the psychoneurotic are only partially disabled and maintain contact with reality, the psychopathic, who evince a mixture of the traits of the psychotic and of the psychoneurotic, live most of the time in a state of unreality like that of the psychotic.[6] The psychotics are always disqualified. The psychopathic are disqualified except during their lucid moments. The psychoneurotic are usually not disqualified, but sometimes, depending upon the type of their neurosis, they are disqualified. Some types of neurosis, such as hysteria, seriously affect a

[3] *Ibid.*, pp. 323-324.

[4] These persons are generally capable of marriage. Cf. VanderVeldt-Odenwald, *op. cit.*, p. 325. Capacity to marry was one of the norms used by pre-Code authors to determine whether a person was mentally capable of voting. Cf. Castellini, *De Electione Canonica*, p. 141.

[5] *Infra*, pp. 159-160.

[6] Cf. VanderVeldt-Odenwald, *op. cit.*, p. 241.

person's ability to make an intelligent appraisal of the candidate's qualifications; other types of neurosis, such as hypochondria, do not. Persons who enjoy lucid intervals are capable of voting during those intervals.[7] Lucid moments, however, are not to be lightly presumed.[8] Once a person has been insane, it is presumed that he continues to be insane until it is proved that he has recovered his sanity.[9] This holds for permanent cures as well as for lucid intervals.

The commentators on the Decretals very often considered demoniacs along with the "*furiosi*" and the "*amentes.*" In a case of possession the devil takes over the inward control of the human limbs and organs. The devil cannot take over control of the intellect or will, so that, theoretically at least, it would be possible for a possessed person to perform internal human acts. They cannot, however, externalize their acts. Inasmuch as voting is not a purely interior act, it is evident that such unfortunate persons are disqualified as voters.

Article II. Exclusion of Persons Under the Age of Puberty

Canon 167, § 1. *Nequeunt suffragium ferre:*

2°. *Impuberes.*

To elect good superiors requires a certain amount of insight into human nature and an appreciation of the qualities required for carrying out a particular office successfully. Children usually lack the perspicacity necessary for choosing qualified superiors. They are easily deceived by a pleasing personality. It is easy to see, then, why children below the age of puberty are disqualified. The pre-Code commentators on the Decretals considered this disqualification one of the natural law, since children lack the discretion neces-

[7] Cf. Samuelli, *De Canonica Electione,* Tr. II, Contr. XXXII, Concl. VII; cf. can. 2201, § 2.

[8] Cf. VanderVeldt-Odenwald, *op. cit.,* p. 257-258.

[9] Samuelli, *op. cit.,* Tr. II, Contr. XXXII, Concl. V; *glossa* ad c. 3, X, *de successionibus ab intestato,* III, 27, s. v. *compotem.*

sary for deciding whether or not a person is fit for office.[10] It is not quite true to say that this is a disqualification deriving from the natural law. It is possible that a youth below the age of puberty would have sufficient maturity of judgment to elect wisely. The natural law does not set puberty as the dividing line between the age of wisdom and the age of foolishness. It is more exact to say that this disqualification is one of the positive ecclesiastical law with a solid foundation in fact.

The age of puberty, according to canon 88, § 2, is fourteen for boys, and twelve for girls.[11] The fourteenth and twelfth year, respectively, must be complete. Thus, a boy is disqualified in virtue of this canon till midnight of the day of his fourteenth anniversary of birth, and a girl is disqualified until midnight of the day of her twelfth anniversary of birth.[12] Augustine (1872-1943) required the age of fourteen for both boys and girls.[13] But this opinion seems contrary to the Code and contrary also to the pre-Code legislation and jurisprudence.[14]

The lack of the age of puberty will usually bar a person from acquiring membership in a voting body. This is especially true where the voting body forms a special body within a larger body. In this case the under-aged person would be disqualified *in actu primo,* i.e., he would be a non-member and, hence, excluded in virtue of canon 165. Where, however, the electing is done not by a special body but by the whole group, the members of that group under the age of puberty would be disqualified in virtue of canon 167, § 1, n. 2, and an election in which they took part would not be

[10] Cf., e.g., c. 32, *de electione et electi potestate,* I, 6, in VI°; Hostiensis, *Summa Aurea, de electione et electi potestate* (I, 6), § *Et qui nullo,* 28 a. r.; Castellini, *De Electione Canonica,* p. 137.

[11] Cf. c. 3, X, *de aetate et qualitate et ordine praeficiendorum,* I, 14; c. 32, 43, *de electione et electi potestate,* I, 6, in VI°.

[12] Cf. can. 34, § 3, n. 3.

[13] *A Commentary on the New Code of Canon Law* (8 vols., St. Louis: B. Herder Book Co., 1918-1922), II, 130.

[14] Cf. can. 88, § 2; *supra,* pp. 16-17.

subject to the automatically incurred invalidity imposed by canon 165.

Article III. Disqualification of Persons Laboring Under a Sentence of Censure or Infamy of Law

Canon 167, § 1. *Nequeunt suffragium ferre:*

3°. *Censura vel infamia iuris affecti, post sententiam tamen declaratoriam vel condemnatoriam.*

Section 1. Censures

A censure is defined in canon 2241 as a penalty by which a baptized person, guilty of some delict and remaining contumacious, is deprived of certain spiritual goods or of goods annexed to spiritual ones until, desisting from his contumacy, he is absolved. From this definition it is seen that a censure is a medicinal penalty, that is, a penalty which has as its primary object the correction of the delinquent. Censures can be imposed only upon one who is guilty of a delict.[15] A delict in Canon Law is a serious, external, and morally imputable violation of a law to which a canonical sanction, at least indeterminate, has been attached.[16] A delict always presupposes grave sin. Unless the law determines that an attempted delict itself constitutes a delictual misdeed, attempted delicts are not punished with censures.[17] The person who actually perpetrates the delict is not the only one who is punished. Those who are necessary cooperators as outlined in canon 2209, §§ 1-3, incur the same penalty as the main perpetrator of the crime, unless the law makes an express exception.[18] Censures may be incurred either automatically upon commission of the crime (*latae sententiae* penalties), or they may be incurred through the mandatory or facultative infliction of a penalty by way of a judicial sentence (*ferendae sententiae* penal-

[15] Can. 2241, § 1.
[16] Can. 2195, § 1.
[17] Cans. 2242, § 1; 2212, § 4.
[18] Can. 2231.

ties).[19] The *latae sententiae* penalties may be confirmed by means of a declaratory sentence. Penalties are presumed to be *ferendae sententiae* penalties unless the law clearly indicates that they are *latae sententiae.*[20] There are three kinds of censures, namely, excommunication, interdict, and suspension. Excommunication can be only a censure; interdict and suspension can be either censures or vindictive penalties. In doubt it is presumed that suspension and interdict are censures.[21]

I. *Excommunication.* Excommunication is a censure consisting of exclusion of a person from the communion of the faithful, to which exclusion are attached certain inseparable effects mentioned in the Code.[22] Excommunication can be inflicted only on physical persons, not on collegiate moral personalities.[23] Excommunicated persons can be either *tolerati* or *vitandi.* No one is a *vitandus* unless he has been expressly declared such by the Holy See, with this one exception that those who lay violent hands on the Holy Father are *ipso facto vitandi.*[24] If a *vitandus* casts a ballot in an election, his vote is always invalid.[25] The vote of a *toleratus,* however, is invalid only if there has intervened a condemnatory or a declaratory sentence.[26] The various crimes to which the penalty of excommunication is attached receive scattered mention throughout the fifth book of the Code.[27] Particular laws may sometimes have the penalty of excommunication attached.[28]

[19] Can. 2217, § 1, n. 2.

[20] Can. 2217, § 2.

[21] Can. 2255.

[22] Can. 2257.

[23] Can. 2255, § 2.

[24] Cans. 2258 & 2343, § 1, n. 1.

[25] Can. 2265, § 2.

[26] Cans. 2265, §§ 1 & 2; 167, § 1, n. 3.

[27] For *LATAE SENTENTIAE* excommunications cf. cans. 2314, §1; 2318, §§ 1 & 2; 2319, §§ 1-4; 2320; 2322, n. 1; 2326; 2327; 2332; 2333; 2334; 2335; 2338, §§ 1 & 2; 2339; 2341; 2342; 2343, §§ 1-4; 2345; 2346; 2347; 2350; 2351, § 1; 2352; 2360, § 1; 2363; 2367; 2368, § 2; 2369, § 1; 2385; 2388, §§ 1 & 2; 2392; 2405. For *FERENDAE SENTENTIAE* excommunications cf. cans. 2324; 2331; 2348; 2356; 2369, § 2.

[28] Cf., e.g., III Plenary Council of Baltimore (1884), n. 124.

II. *Interdict.* Interdict is a censure by which the faithful, while remaining in the communion of the Church, are forbidden certain spiritual goods or rights enumerated in the Code.[29] Interdict may be personal or local. Local interdict is that which directly affects a place, and only indirectly the people in the place. Personal interdict directly affects individuals.[30] A personal interdict is either general, as affecting a community or a collegiate moral personality, or particular, as affecting individual physical persons.[31] Local interdict, which can be general or particular, can be a censure,[32] but since a place as such can never vote, and since local interdicts do not forbid elections,[33] no consideration need be given to local interdicts in this work. A particular personal interdict, when total,[34] is always a censure and never a vindictive penalty.[35] General personal interdict can

[29] Can. 2268, § 1. [30] Can. 2268, § 2. [31] Cf. cans. 2269 & 2270, § 1

[32] Cf. Roberti, *De Delictis et Poenis* (Vol. I, Pars, I, 1930, et Pars II, 1938, Romae: Appolinaris), Vol. I, Pars II, p. 424.

[33] Cf. can. 2271.

[34] A particular personal interdict can be either total or partial. Interdict forbidding entrance into church is an example of a *partial* particular personal interdict. Such a partial interdict does not entail the incurring of the penalties enumerated in canon 2275. Cf. Vermeersch-Creusen, *Epitome,* III, p. 288; Beste, *Introductio in Codicem,* p. 945.

[35] Cf. Roberti, *op. cit.,* Vol. I, Pars II, p. 424. A hint of the fact that total particular personal interdict is always a censure is to be found in canon 2291, nn. 1 & 2, which, though it mentions all the other types of interdict (local interdict, general personal interdict, and interdict forbidding entrance into church), pointedly omits all mention of total particular personal interdict. It is true that the list of vindictive penalties contained in canon 2291 is not exhaustive, but, nevertheless, in view of the inclusion of all other types of interdict, the failure to mention total particular personal interdict is very strange if it is one of the vindictive penalties. The strongest argument, however, for the exclusively censural nature of total particular personal interdict is to be found in the consideration of the nature of the penalty itself. A person subject to this penalty is barred from reception of the sacraments (can. 2275, n. 2. It will be noted that none of the vindictive penalties mentioned in canon 2291 and canon 2298 excludes one from reception of the sacraments). This would mean that a person subject to a total particular personal interdict which

be either a censure or a vindictive penalty.[36]

A person subject to a total particular personal interdict is disqualified for elections in the same way as an excommunicated person is disqualified.[37] After sentence, whether de-

is to last for definite period of time, let us say three months, could not, even though sincerely repentant (cf. can. 2286), receive absolution from his sin till the period of time had expired. It is simply inconceivable to this writer that the Spouse of Christ, the good shepherd, would punish a person by forcing him, even though genuinely repentant, to remain in the state of sin. This is certainly contrary to the Church's attitude toward repentant sinners, and contrary also to the spirit of the Church's penal legislation (cf. can. 2214). If the legislator of the Code envisioned any vindictive penalty as barring a person from absolution from sin, he certainly would have made provision, similar to that made in relation to censures (cf. can. 2252 and 2254), for the easy dispensation from such vindictive penalties in cases of danger of death and in cases where it would be a hardship for the penitent to remain in the state of mortal sin for the length of time needed for obtaining dispensation from the competent superior. Another indication that the legislator did not envision any vindictive penalty as precluding the reception of absolution from sin is the fact that the prescriptions of canon 2250, §§ 2 & 3, and canon 2251 are nowhere in the Code applied to vindictive penalties.

Someone may allege that canon 1743, § 3, imposes total particular personal interdict as a vindictive penalty, basing his claim on the contention that the canon prescribes the imposition of the penalty for a determinate period of time (any penalty imposed for a determinate period of time must be a vindictive penalty, since censures cannot be imposed to last beyond the delinquent's recession from contumacy; cf. can. 2248, § 2). This argument, however, would not be based on proven fact, since canon 1743, § 3, by no means unequivocably states that the interdict is to be imposed for a determinate period of time. There is no rule of grammar or of canonical interpretation which demands that the phrase "*ad tempus a iudice pro rerum adiunctis definiendum*" found in the first independent clause of the canon, be applied also to the second independent clause of the canon. Though the punishment mentioned in the first clause is a vindictive penalty, there is no reason why the punishments mentioned in the second clause must also be vindictive penalties. It is not at all illogical to consider the two punishments contained in the second clause as censures.

[36] Cf. cans. 2244, § 2; 2291, n. 1. Cf. also Roberti, *op. cit.*, Vol. I, Pars II, p. 439.

[37] Can. 2275, n. 3.

claratory or condemnatory, his vote is invalid; before sentence, it is only illicit.[38]

Canon 2274, § 3, states that a community or a collegiate moral personality laboring under a general personal interdict is prohibited from exercising any of the spiritual rights which it has. Among the spiritual rights which a moral personality possesses is the right to elect.[39] The prohibition of canon 2274, § 3, affects those rights which the collegiate body has as a body; it does not affect, at least not directly, those rights which the members have as individuals, even if the members have acquired those rights by reason of membership in that collegiate body. The collegiate body, however, can exercise its rights only through its members,[40] and, therefore, whenever the collegiate body has a right to act, there is a corresponding right on the part of certain of its members to represent the collegiate moral personality in that action. Should the collegiate body lose its right to act, the individual members' right to represent the body in that particular action, of course, becomes meaningless. That election is considered as an act and right of the moral personality as such can be deduced from canon 2391. According to this canon a collegiate moral personality which elects an unworthy candidate is deprived of its right to elect for that instance. Since the collegiate body *as such* is punished, it is evident that the collegiate body *as such* is regarded as having conducted the election.[41]

Since canon 2274, § 3, does not state that the interdicted collegiate moral personality would act invalidly if it exercised any of its spiritual rights, it must be admitted that the

[38] Cans. 2275, n. 3; 2265.

[39] Cf. *glossa* ad c. 56, X, *de electione et electi potestate,* I, 6, s. v. *per laicos;* Roberti, *op. cit.,* Vol. I, Pars II, p. 440; Coronata, *Institutiones,* IV, p. 238.

[40] A collegiate moral personality sometimes acts through the agency of another moral personality, e.g., when a religious community elects through the agency of an electoral chapter. But even in this case the collegiate moral personality acts, in the final instance, through its individual members.

[41] Cf. *supra,* pp. 1-2.

moral personality is not disqualified in regard to elections *in consequence of this canon;*[42] by this canon it is only *forbidden* to elect. But when canon 2274, § 3, is considered in connection with canon 167, § 1, n. 3, it must be concluded that a moral personality is *disqualified* if there has been a sentence of interdict and if the interdict has been imposed as a censure. From the wording of canon 167, § 1, n. 3, no other conclusion seems possible. The canon does not distinguish between particular personal interdict and general personal interdict, and if the Code does not distinguish then one should likewise not distinguish. The moral personality is laboring under sentence of a censure and therefore must be considered disqualified.

What has been said about general personal interdict must be applied to persons laboring under sentence of the censure of interdict forbidding entrance into church.[43] It is altogether consonant with the wording of canon 167, § 1, n. 3, that persons laboring under this censure after sentence has been passed should be disqualified.[44] There do not seem to be any legal grounds for exempting them from disqualification.

The penalty of interdict is not of common occurrence. It is inflicted for only a few crimes, and these crimes themselves are rather unusual and infrequent.[45]

III. *Suspension.* Suspension as a censure is a penalty through which a cleric is forbidden the use of his office, his benefice, or both.[46] The effects of suspension are separable,

[42] Cf. can. 11.

[43] Cf. can. 2277. Interdict forbidding entrance into church can be a censure; cf. can. 2255, § 2; Roberti, *op. cit.*, Vol. I, Pars II, p. 449.

[44] Cf. *infra*, pp. 102-103; the reasoning there applied in relation to particular suspensions can be validly applied here also.

[45] For *LATAE SENTENTIAE* interdicts cf. can. 2338, § 4 (*interdictum personale particulare*); 2338, § 3; 2339 (*interdicta ab ingressu ecclesiae*); 2332 (*interdictum personale generale*). For *FERENDAE SENTENTIAE* interdicts cf. can. 1743, § 3; 2328; 2356 (*interdicta personalia particularia*); can. 2329 (*interdictum ab ingressu ecclesiae*).

[46] Can. 2278, § 1.

that is to say, there can be imposed a limited form of suspension which forbids the use of only one or of only some of the rights connected with an office or a benefice.[47] Suspension is a penalty limited exclusively to clerics.

Canon 2283 applies the same rules to those who are under suspension that prevail in regard to those who are excommunicated and their participation in ecclesiastical elections. A suspended cleric cannot, therefore, validly vote after sentence has been passed. Canon 2283 is treating only of general suspension, that is, suspension from office and benefice.[48] Although, then, only those who are under sentence of a *general* suspension are disqualified by canon 2283, still in virtue of canon 167, § 1, n. 3, those who are under sentence of a *particular* suspension inflicted as a censure are also disqualified. There is no indication in canon 167, § 1, n. 3, that only the severest forms of censure are meant, and, therefore, there is no justification for excluding the limited forms of suspension from its scope. At first it may seem strange that such censures as suspension from conferring a definite order, and suspension from the exercise of pontifical acts, should disqualify a person as a voter. It must be remembered, however, that this disqualification is incurred only when the penalty is a censure. This means that the person has committed a serious crime, a delict;[49] that he was contumacious even after being warned to recede from his contumacy, and even to such an extent that he allowed himself to be sentenced;[50] and, lastly, that he continues to be contumacious at the present time, not bothering to seek abso-

[47] Cans. 2278, § 2; 2279.

[48] Wernz-Vidal, *Ius Canonicum ad Codicis Normam Exactum* (7 vols. in 8, Vol. I, 2. ed., 1952, Vol. II, 3. ed. [a Aguirre recognita], 1943, Vol. III, 1. ed., 1933, Vol. IV, 1. ed., Tom. I, 1934, Tom. II, 1935, Vol. V, 3. ed., [a Aguirre recognita], 1946, Vol. VI, 2. ed. [a Capello recognita], 1951, Vol. VII, 2. ed., 1951, Romae: Apud Aedes Universitatis Gregorianae), VII, 336-337 (hereafter cited Wernz-Vidal); Roberti, *De Delictis et Poenis*, Vol. I, Pars II, pp. 475-477.

[49] Cf. cans. 2241, § 1; 2242, § 1.

[50] Cf. cans. 2233, § 2; 2242, §§ 1 & 2.

lution.[51] In the light of what has been said it is not surprising that persons under sentence of any kind of censure should be excluded. They are certainly undeserving of the right to vote. What has been said about a particular suspension incurred by an individual holds true also for a particular suspension incurred by a community or a collegiate moral personality. A community or a collegiate moral personality under a particular suspension is disqualified for elections, provided that there has been a sentence and provided that the suspension is incurred as a censure. This disqualification results not from canon 2285, § 3, which contains only a prohibition not a disqualification, but from canon 167, § 1, n. 3.[52]

A listing of the various suspensions inflicted by the Code is made in the footnote below.[53]

SECTION 2. INFAMY OF LAW

Infamy of law is not defined in the Code, but it can be described as a vindictive penalty which brands persons who are guilty of certain serious crimes as unworthy of the good esteem of their fellowmen, and denies them the normal exercise of the juridical personality which they possess in the society of the Church.[54] Infamy of law is a vindictive

[51] Cf. can. 2248, § 2, which plainly indicates that a person cannot be denied absolution as soon as he has receded from his contumacy.

[52] What has been said above (pp. 100-101) about an *interdict* incurred by a community or collegiate moral personality can be applied in this place to a *suspension* incurred by a community or collegiate moral person.

[53] *LATAE SENTENTIAE*: Cans. 671, n. 1; 2371; 2386 (*suspensio generalis*); can. 2366 (*ab audiendis confessionibus*); can. 2402 (*a iurisdictione*); can. 2374 (*ab officio recepto*); can. 2341 (*ab officio*); cans. 2366; 2400; 2372 (*a divinis*). *FERENDAE SENTENTIAE*: Cans. 2324; 2359, § 2; 2365; 2378; 2392, n. 3; 2394, n. 2 (*suspensio generalis*); cans. 2315; 2359, § 1; 2401 (*a divinis*); can. 2384 (*a beneficio*); can. 2379 (*ab ordinibus receptis*); can. 2377 (*ab audiendis confessionibus saecularium*).

[54] Cf. Tatarczuk, *Infamy of Law*, The Catholic University of America Canon Law Studies, n. 357 (The Catholic University of America Press, 1954), p. XI.

penalty, that is, it aims primarily at the restoration of the social order which has been disturbed in consequence of the commission of a crime, and only secondarily aims at the correction of the delinquent. Unlike censure, the vindictive penalty does not need to be dispensed from when the delinquent recedes from contumacy. It ceases only when there has elapsed the duration of time for which it was imposed, or when the competent superior dispenses from it. Vindictive penalties are not always imposed for a defined period of time; they may be imposed *ad beneplacitum superioris.*

Infamy of law is never a censure. It can be incurred automatically or in consequence of a sentence. If it has been incurred automatically it can receive confirmation through a declaratory sentence. Only the Holy See can attach the penalty of infamy of law to the violation of a law.[55] Authorities subordinate to the Holy See who hold jurisdiction in the Church can inflict this penalty only in accordance with the norms of the Code of Canon Law. Infamy of law cannot be imposed by way of a particular precept.[56]

Persons affected with a declaratory or a condemnatory sentence of infamy of law are disqualified as electors in ecclesiastical elections.[57] Canon 2294, § 1, states that those who are branded with infamy of law are incapable of performing authorized or accredited ecclesiastical acts. Some say that inasmuch as voting is included among the authorized ecclesiastical acts,[58] and inasmuch as canon 2294, § 1, does not postulate the previous passing of sentence, all persons branded with infamy of law, whether or not there has been a sentence, are disqualified.[59] In keeping with the

[55] Cf. can. 2293, § 2, which indicates that infamy of law is that infamy which is imposed in the cases expressly determined by the universally binding law.

[56] Cf. can. 1933, § 4; Coronata, *Institutiones,* III, pp. 378-379.

[57] Can. 167, § 1, n. 3; can. 2294, § 1. Infamy of law is incurred automatically for the crimes described in cans. 2320; 2328; 2343, § 1, n. 2; 2351, § 2; 2356; 2357, § 1. It is to be inflicted by way of sentence for the crimes described in cans. 2314, § 1, n. 2; 2359.

[58] Cf. can. 2256, n. 2.

[59] Cf., e.g., Wernz-Vidal, VII, 313-314, note 17.

general principle, "*generi per speciem derogatur,*"[60] however, it must be concluded that the more specific ruling of canon 167, § 1, n. 3, provides an exception to the more generic rule of canon 2294, § 1. It is submitted that a person suffering under the penalty of infamy of law is not disqualified unless sentence has been passed. This is the more benign interpretation, and in penal matters the more benign interpretation is to be followed.[61]

SECTION 3. THE SENTENCE

The disqualifications listed in canon 167, § 1, n. 3, are not incurred unless a condemnatory or a declaratory sentence has preceded. The reason for this seems to be that thus it is rendered easier to determine which voters are disqualified. In this number of the canon and throughout the whole canon the Code has limited itself to those disqualifications which are, at least in general, easily ascertained. The Code thereby forestalls endless quibbling and doubts.

The penalties mentioned in canon 167, § 1, n. 3, can be inflicted only by those who have jurisdiction in the external forum of the Church and by their delegates.[62] The following have jurisdiction in the external forum of the Church: 1) The Holy Father and Ecumenical Councils have jurisdiction over the entire Church; papal legates and delegates, the Sacred Congregations and Tribunals have jurisdiction within their sphere of competence. Cardinals have no jurisdiction in view of their cardinalatial dignity.[63] 2) Plenary councils, provincial councils, Metropolitans, residential bishops, abbots and prelates *nullius,* vicars and prefects Apostolic, pro-vicars and pro-prefects Apostolic, cathedral chapters and boards of diocesan consultors during the vacancy of the diocese, vicars capitulars and "diocesan administrators," and Apostolic administrators have jurisdiction with-

60 Reg. 34, R. J., in VI°.

61 Cf. can. 2219, § 1.

62 Cf. Beste, *Introductio in Codicem,* p. 913; Schaefer, *De Religiosis,* pp. 202-206.

63 Cf. can. 240, § 2.

in their respective territories.[64] Judges have jurisdiction in the juridical forum and can impose penalties in accord with the norms of the Code of Canon Law.[65] Vicars general have jurisdiction in the external forum but they may not impose penalties without a special mandate from the bishop.[66] 3) General and provincial chapters and major superiors in communities of exempt clerical religious have jurisdiction over their subjects.[67] Since their jurisdiction is purely personal, religious chapters and superiors cannot inflict the penalty of a *local* interdict.[68] Pastors, religious superiors in non-exempt religious communities, women religious, and laymen have no jurisdiction in the external forum of the Church. If a person is delegated to inflict a penalty, he must follow the rules of delegation as set down in canons 199-209.

Penalties can be imposed either by way of a judicial sentence or by way of an extrajudicial particular precept.[69] The word *"sententiam"* in the expression *"post sententiam"* in canon 167, § 1, n. 3, is not to be taken in the restricted sense of a judicial sentence enacted with all the solemnities of the court; it is to be taken in the same sense as *"sententia"* in the expression *"ferendae sententiae,"* namely, as any sentence whatsoever, whether imposed in a judicial trial or through an extrajudicial particular precept.[70] Authors generally hold that the expression *"post sententiam"* leaves room for the notion of penalties inflicted by way of particular precept.[71]

[64] Cf. cans. 281; 283; 291; 198; 329, § 1; 273; 323, § 1; 294, § 1; 309, §§ 2-4; 435, § 1; 427; 315, §§ 1 & 2.

[65] Can. 2220, § 1.

[66] Cans. 366, § 1; 2220, § 2.

[67] Cans. 501, § 1; 488, n. 8.

[68] Roberti (*De Delictis et Poenis*, Vol. I, Pars II, p. 426) states that religious superiors likewise cannot impose personal interdicts. He cites Wernz, *Ius Decretalium*, VI, n. 220, as his authority. But Wernz in fact stated the opposite, viz.: "Quae potestas Praelatorum regularium saltem ex consuetudine recepta restricta est ad ius infligendi interdictum personale, non vero locale."—*Ibid.*, note 497.

[69] Cf. cans. 1933, § 4; 2225.

[70] Cf. can. 2217, § 1, n. 2.

[71] Cf., e.g., Roberti, *De Delictis et Poenis*, Vol. I, Pars II, p. 387,

Not all penalties can be inflicted by way of particular precept, but only such as are enumerated in canon 1933, § 4, namely, penances, remedial penalties, excommunication, suspension, and interdict.[72] Of the penalties mentioned in canon 167, § 1, n. 3, therefore, the censures could be imposed by way of particular precept, the penalty of infamy of law could not be. The censures, however, can be inflicted by way of a particular precept only if the penalty has been threatened by way of a particular precept.[73] If a penalty is imposed through a judicial sentence, the delict must be public; if imposed by way of particular precept, the delict need not be public, but it must be certain.[74] Censures can be inflicted on unknown delinquents as long as the fact of the delict is certain.[75]

If the penalty is imposed through a judicial sentence, the formalities of canons 1868-1877 are to be observed; if it is imposed by way of a particular precept, it should ordinarily be administered in writing or before two witnesses.[76] If witnesses are used, they must be qualified to act as witnesses

commenting on excommunication *post sententiam;* Coronata, *Institutiones,* IV, p. 215.

[72] Authors dispute whether or not the listing of canon 1933, § 4, is all-inclusive. The majority of the authors thinks that it is, since in penal matters the restrictive interpretation is to be followed, and since the clear enumeration of these particular penalties would be meaningless if the list were not meant to be a complete one. Cf. Noval, *Commentarium Iuris Canonici,* Liber IV, *De Processibus,* Pars I, *De Iudiciis* (Romae: Marietti, 1920), pp. 495-496; Beste, *Introductio in Codicem,* pp. 843-844; Esswein, *Extrajudicial Coercive Powers of Ecclesiastical Superiors,* The Catholic University of America Canon Law Studies, n. 127, (Washington, D.C.: Catholic University of America Press, 1941), pp. 110-114; Coronata, *Institutiones,* III, pp. 378-379. *Contra,* Roberti, *De Delictis et Poenis,* Vol. I, Pars II, pp. 293-299.

[73] This is the interpretation given to the expression *"inflicta sit"* in canon 2225 by Beste (*op. cit.,* pp. 843-844, & 915). Cf. also Esswein, *loc. cit.;* and Noval, *loc. cit.* Roberti (*loc. cit.*) opposes this opinion also.

[74] Can. 1933, §§ 1 & 4.

[75] Cf. can. 2242, § 1.

[76] Can. 2225.

in court, since the purpose of having witnesses is to be able to prove *in court* that the precept was given.[77] If the precept were not imposed in writing or before witnesses, it would not necessarily be invalid, but it could not be enforced judicially.[78] A judicial sentence must always be in writing.[79] Both the judicial sentence and the particular precept must contain the basis in fact and in law for the penalty.[80] There are two exceptions to this rule. Canon 1605, § 1, indicates that the Tribunal of the Apostolic Tribunal does not have to advert to the basis in fact or in law for its decisions. Nor does the ordinary have to give the reasons in fact when with full and certified knowledge *(ex informata conscientia)* he suspends a cleric, unless he imposes the suspension as a censure.[81] The latter exception, however, is not pertinent in the present instance, since canon 167, § 1, n. 3, which is here under consideration, treats of suspension only as a censure. Before a penalty can be inflicted there must precede a warning that holds the threat of punishment, and before a censure can be imposed there must precede a warning that the person recede from his contumacy.[82] If serious scandal was given, or if the nature of the delict was of a special gravity, no threat of punishment need precede the imposing of the penalty.[83] Nor need the warning that the person recede from his contumacy be given when a suspension *ex informata conscientia* is imposed.[84] If the sentence or the particular precept is invalid for any reason, the penalty is not incurred, for an invalid sentence or precept is without force in the Church.

Canon 2232, § 2, points out that a declaratory sentence is retroactive to the time of the commission of the crime. An

[77] Cf. can. 1757; Cicognani, *Canon Law*, p. 637.

[78] Can. 24.

[79] Cf. cans. 1894, nn. 3 & 4; 1585.

[80] Cf. cans. 1873, § 1, n. 3; 1894, n. 2; 2225.

[81] Can. 2188, nn. 1 & 2.

[82] Cf. cans. 2222, § 1; 2233, § 2.

[83] Cf. can. 2222, § 1.

[84] Can. 2187.

occasional author has applied this canon to canon 167, § 1, n. 3, by saying that a vote when cast by a person under censure or infamy incurred *ipso facto* is rendered null by a later declaratory sentence.[85] This interpretation is contrary to the explicit words of canon 167, § 1, n. 3, which postulates a previously rendered sentence. It is also based on an erroneous conception of the meaning of the retroactivity of laws or sentences. A retroactive law can never alter facts, so that an act which once was valid will later become invalid. What happens is this: legal recognition is no longer accorded to a past valid act, so that the past act no longer presents a legitimate title for possession or operation. Retroactivity affects only the *presently enduring* effects of the past act.[86] The present declaration of the censure or the infamy of law does not, therefore, render a person disqualified in the past, nor does it make his past vote invalid.

Article IV. Disqualification of Persons Who Have Enrolled in or Publicly Adhered to a Heretical or a Schismatical Sect

Canon 167, § 1. *Nequeunt suffragium ferre:*

4°. *Qui sectae haereticae vel schismaticae nomen dederunt vel publice adhaeserunt.*

Canon 167, § 1, n. 4, disqualifies those who have enrolled in or publicly adhered to a heretical or a schismatical sect. This disqualification is not surprising, since defection from the faith and rebellion against the Vicar of Christ are among the most serious of all delicts. Even though a person repents of his treasonous act, yet his crime indicates a weakness of character. This disqualification has the nature of an irregularity that arises from some delictual misdeed *(irregularitas ex delicto)* rather than the nature of a punishment.

[85] Cf., e.g., Augustine, *A Commentary on the New Code of Canon Law*, II, 130.

[86] Cf. Roelker, "Acquired Rights and the Retroactivity of Laws," *The Jurist* (Washington, D.C.: 1941—), IV (1944), 495; Cicognani, *Canon Law*, p. 555.

The Code of Canon Law defines a heretic as one who, after baptism, while still remaining a Christian, pertinaciously denies or doubts about any of the truths which must be believed with a Catholic and divine faith.[87] If one were to follow this definition in interpreting the expression *"sectae haereticae"* as it occurs in canon 167, § 1, n. 4, then one could include only Protestant sects, since of the non-Catholic sects they alone retain the name Christian. Atheistic sects, pagan cults, Mohammedanism, and the Jewish religion would not be included. This interpretation does not prove acceptable to the writer of this dissertation. It is true that the restrictive interpretation is to be followed in the interpreting of disqualifying laws, but the meaning of the law should never be restricted unreasonably.[88] It is unreasonable to think that the legislator intended to disqualify those who defect from the Church and join a Protestant sect, but not those who defect and join, for instance, a Mohammedan sect. The sin is of the same species in both cases. There is no reason for thinking that the legislator was using "heretical" in such a narrow meaning. "Heretical" can also mean "opposed to the Catholic Faith," and it is in this wide sense that it should be understood in the present instance. Heretical sects are all those that teach anything contrary to the Catholic Faith, whether they are Protestant, Jewish, Mohammedan, or pagan. Also included are atheistic sects.[89] Societies, such as the Masons, which do not have a religious (or atheistic) end as their *primary* purpose are not consid-

[87] Can. 1325, § 2.

[88] Pope Pius XII has only recently rebuked those canonists who restrict the meaning of penal laws unreasonably. In a Motu Proprio, issued on December 25, 1953, he stated: "Ecclesiae bonum postulat ut, quantum fieri potest, caveamus ne, incertis privatorum hominum de germano canonum sensu opinionibus et coniecturis, Iuris canonici stabilitas in discrimen vocetur, neve, subtilitatibus et cavillationibus immorando, contra apertam legislatoris voluntatem, legum violatoribus indulgeatur iniuste, quod nervum ecclesiasticae disciplinae disrumpit."—*AAS*, XLVI (1954), 88.

[89] Pont. Com. ad Cod. auth. Interp., 30 iulii 1934—*AAS*, XXVI (1934), 494.

ered as heretical sects.[90]

The notion of "sect" involves the idea of a society, of an association, or of some collegiate moral personality, formally organized in some stable form, though no hierarchical set-up is required.[91]

A sect is schismatical if it refuses obedience to the Supreme Pontiff or if it rejects communion with the members of the Church subject to the Supreme Pontiff.[92] A group may refuse obedience to the Holy Father either because it denies the primacy of the Pope, or because it denies the right of the incumbent to the office.[93] If the sect denies the primacy, it is not only schismatical but also heretical, since primacy is an article of faith. Heretical sects are all schismatic, but the term "schismatic" is commonly applied only to those sects which deny simply the dogma of the primacy of the Pope. Schismatic sects would include the dissident oriental sects, and also any organized group which formed around an antipope or which attempted to depose the legitimately elected Pontiff. A group is not schismatic if it refuses to obey a single precept but does not deny the right of the Holy Father to command.[94]

To incur the disqualification listed in canon 167, § 1, n. 4, it does not suffice to hold heretical or schismatical opinions privately; enrollment in or public adherence to a sect is required. "*Nomen dederunt*" as used in this canon and elsewhere in the Code is a technical expression; it means "to enroll in." One enrolls in a sect by offering one's name to be

[90] Compare canon 2314 with can. 2335. Cf. Schaefer, *De Religiosis*, p. 424. The Communist party as such would not be an atheistic sect, since its primary purpose is social and political rather than religious. The atheistic leagues of the Communist movement are, of course, atheistic sects. Persons who join the Communist party are apostates, and as such incur excommunication reserved to the Holy See (cf. *AAS*, XLI [1949], 334), but they are not permanently disqualified as they would be for joining an atheistic sect.

[91] Cf. Larraona, "Commentarium Codicis," *CpRM*, XVI (1935), 429.

[92] Cf. can. 1325. [93] Cf. *supra*, pp. 31-32. [94] Cf. can. 2331.

inscribed on the roster of the sect, or by undergoing the initiation ceremony of the sect,[95] by taking the official oath of allegiance to the sect, and the like. Enrollment, unlike adherence, does not have to be public; even occult enrollment entails the disability here in question. Public adherence to a sect would be established by such acts as publicly defending the errors and proclaiming oneself a member of the sect, by renting a pew in a sectarian church, or by repeatedly attending at sectarian services and meetings. It does not include such acts as contributing to a sectarian collection or occasionally attending sectarian services out of curiosity. Acts which normally are performed only by a member of the sect would constitute adherence to the sect because such acts indicate that the person considers himself as a member of that group. An act constitutes *public* adherence if the act is commonly known or if it is an act which will readily become known.[96]

The disqualification of canon 167, § 1, n. 4, is not incurred by those who are born in heresy or schism, but who in later life are converted to the true faith. This is the interpretation given by the Pontifical Commission for the Authentic Interpretation of the Code in regard to canon 542, which disbars from the religious life those who have adhered to a non-Catholic sect.[97] This interpretation can be safely applied to canon 167, § 1, n. 4, since the nature of the disability is the same in both cases. Those who were baptized Catholics but were reared from infancy as heretics or schismatics and who later returned to the Church can also be said not to incur this disqualification. The just cited reply of the Pontifical Commission for the Authentic Interpretation of the Code stated that the disability in canon 542 is to be applied to those who *defected* from the faith and adhered to a non-Catholic sect. One can hardly point to an infant as having *defected;* one would rather regard him as having been torn away from the Church. Therefore such persons, when

[95] E.g., submitting to sectarian baptism.
[96] Cf. can. 2197, n. 1.
[97] Oct. 16, 1919—*AAS*, XI (1919), 477.

they later return to the Church, are not to be included under the listing in canon 542 nor, *a pari,* under the listing of canon 167, §1, n. 4. The defection must be a fully personal act which cannot be excused.[98]

The disqualification contained in canon 167, § 1, n. 4, applies not only to those who have defected and still belong to a non-Catholic sect, but also to those Catholics who indeed defected from the Church but later returned to it.[99] This can be seen from the verbs *dederunt* and *adhaeserunt* which are in the perfect tense, indicating, therefore, past acts. Especially as regards *adhaeserunt,* the wording in the Code would not have employed the past tense if reference were to be made to a present adherence only. When a reference is intended for those who at present adhere to or are enrolled in a non-Catholic sect, the Code clearly indicates this by using the present tense or the passive participle.[100]

Those who defect from the faith and enroll in or publicly adhere to a non-Catholic sect automatically incur the censure of excommunication and automatically become infamous with infamy of law,[101] and so could be disqualified not only in virtue of number 4 of canon 167, § 1, but also in virtue of number 3 of the same canon. There are some notable differences, however, between these two numbers. The penalty is incurred in virtue of number 3 only if there has been a previously imposed sentence; in virtue of number 4, however, the penalty is incurred even if there has been no sentence. Also, the disqualification arising from number 3 ceases upon an absolution from the censure or dispensation from the infamy of law; the disqualification arising from number 4 is perpetual.[102]

[98] Cf. Larraona, "Commentarium Codicis," *CpRM,* XVI (1935), 431-432.

[99] Oesterle, *Praelectiones Iuris Canonici* (Vol. I, Romae: Collegio S. Anselmi, 1931), I, 96; Jone, *Commentarium in Codicem Iuris Canonici,* I, 171; cf. Schaefer, *De Religiosis,* pp. 237 & 424; Larraona, "Commentarium Codicis," *CpRM,* XVI (1935), 431.

[100] Cf., e.g., cans. 693; 765, n. 2; 795, n. 2.

[101] Can. 2314, § 1, nn. 1 & 3.

[102] Cf. Larraona, *loc. cit.* Larraona is commenting on canon 542

Schaefer (d. 1948) was of the opinion that a tacit dispensation from the disqualification imposed by canon 167, § 1, n. 4, is implied in a dispensation from the disability imposed by canon 542 (which bars from the religious life those who have enrolled in or publicly adhered to a non-Catholic sect).[103] If the competent superior, Schaefer said, grants the right to enter the religious life to a person who has lapsed from the faith and later has returned, this permission should be understood to include the right to acquire all the rights which members of the religious community have. This opinion is sound, but it seems more feasible in practice to ask specifically for a dispensation from the law contained in canon 167, § 1, n. 4, in the petition for the dispensation from the law contained in canon 542.

Article V. Persons Disqualified in Consequence of the Legitimate Sentence of an Ecclesiastical Judge, or Through Some Prescript of the Law, Universal or Particular

Canon 167, § 1. *Nequeunt suffragium ferre:*

5°. *Carentes voce activa sive ob legitimam iudicis sententiam sive ex iure communi aut particulari.*

Number 5 of canon 167, § 1, provides a general all-inclusive rule which encompasses all the disqualified persons who have not been dealt with in the foregoing numbers of this canon or in canon 165. Only vindictive penalties are treated here, since censures have been treated above, in number 3 of this canon.

For the sake of clarification one would do well to point out which are the vindictive penalties that disqualify persons as electors. Clarification is needed especially in regard to those penalties which are described in the Code as censures. Some of these penalties cannot be imposed as vindictive penalties, and of those which can be imposed as vindic-

but his commentary can be applied to canon 167, § 1, n. 4, in view of the similarity of the two canons.

[103] *De Religiosis*, p. 237.

tive penalties most do not have a disqualifying effect when imposed as vindictive penalties.

First of all, excommunication can never be imposed as a vindictive penalty; it is always a censure.[104] A total particular personal interdict cannot be imposed as a vindictive penalty.[105] A general personal interdict and an interdict forbidding entrance into church can be inflicted as vindictive penalties, but they do not disqualify an elector.[106] Suspension can be imposed as a vindictive penalty.[107] General suspension, i.e., suspension from office and benefice, inflicted by way of sentence upon an individual disqualifies that individual as an elector.[108] Suspensions imposed upon a com-

[104] Can. 2255, § 2.

[105] Cf. *supra,* pp. 98-99, esp. footnote n. 35.

[106] A general personal interdict and an interdict forbidding entrance into church are personal interdicts, but they do not entail the disqualification applied to the personally interdicted by canon 2275, n. 3, since canon 2275 is understood as applying only to those who are under a total *particular* personal interdict; cf. Coronata, *Institutiones,* IV, 239. Canon 2275 certainly does not apply to a community under general interdict. Penalties imposed upon a community as such should affect the community as such, and not the members of the community as individuals. But almost all of the penal effects mentioned in canon 2275 can affect only individuals, indicating that the legislator did not envision these penalties as applicable to communities. Canon 2275 likewise does not apply to persons under an interdict forbidding entrance into church. The penalties listed in canon 2277 have already been mentioned in canon 2275. It would be meaningless for the Code to repeat these effects if those under interdict forbidding entrance into church were already included in canon 2275. It would be more meaningless to repeat only part of the prohibitions of canon 2275. The effects of a general personal interdict and of an interdict forbidding entrance into church are limited to those effects mentioned in canon 2274 (which contains a prohibition but no disqualification) and canon 2277 respectively, unless some other canon (as canon 167, § 1, n. 3) attaches some additional effect.

[107] Can. 2255, § 2.

[108] Can. 2283. The canons of the Code which treat of suspension (can. 2278-2285) deal with it as a censure. Nowhere in the Code are the effects of suspension as a vindictive penalty described. It must be concluded, therefore, that the effects of suspension as a vindictive penalty are the same as the effects of suspension imposed

munity as also particular suspensions do not disqualify persons from voting.[109] Besides general suspension there are other vindictive penalties which involve electoral disqualification. Deposition, which goes one step further than general suspension in severity, disqualifies a cleric as a voter.[110]

as a censure. Cf. Roberti, *De Delictis et Poenis,* Vol. I, Pars II, pp. 476-477. For delicts which are punished with general suspension inflicted as a vindictive penalty cf. cans. 2342, n. 1; 2347, n. 2; 2350, § 2; 2370; 2387.

[109] A community of clerics under suspension is not disqualified by canon 2285, § 3, since the penalty imposed upon a community by that canon is only a prohibition not a disqualification. Nor is the community disqualified by canon 2283, since, as is commonly held, canon 2283 applies only to general suspension from office and benefice inflicted upon an individual cleric; cf. Roberti, *De Delictis et Poenis,* Vol. I, Pars II, pp. 475-478; Wernz-Vidal, VII, 336-337; Vermeersch-Creusen, *Epitome,* III, 292; Coronata, *Institutiones,* IV, 256, note 3. The effects of suspension inflicted upon a community should be limited to the effects mentioned in canon 2285, just as the effects of *interdict* imposed upon a community are limited to the effects listed in canon 2274. The penalties imposed by canon 2285 are the penalties imposed upon the excommunicated by canon 2265. The penalties listed in canon 2265 are directly intended for imposition on individual persons (excommunication can be imposed only on individuals), and most of them are penalties not suited for imposition on a community as a moral personality. Particular (partial) suspensions should not be included in canon 2283 either. Since vindictive penalties do not presuppose contumacy, it would be strange if a person punished with a mild partial suspension incurred simultaneously the severe penalties listed in canon 2265.

[110] The disqualifications imposed by canon 2283 are applicable in cases of deposition. It was stated above (p. 116, footnote n. 109) that canon 2283 applied only to cases of general suspension, i.e., suspension from office *and* from benefice, and the suspension implied in every deposition is suspension from office (cf. can. 2303, § 1). But inasmuch as the *deprivation* of all benefices is implied in deposition (can. 2303, § 1), and inasmuch as *suspension* from benefice is thereby rendered impossible, the suspension from office is as general a suspension as is possible under the circumstances. Canon 2283 is to be applied, therefore, to this suspension from office. Since deposition is always imposed by way of a solemn judicial sentence (can. 1576, § 1, n. 2), the electoral disability imposed upon deposed clerics by canon 2283 is truly a disqualification, not merely a prohibition (cf. can. 2265, §2). For delicts which are punished with general

Degradation, inasmuch as it always implies deposition, also disqualifies a cleric.[111] Disqualification for all authorized or accredited ecclesiastical acts, when imposed as a real disqualification and not simply as a prohibition, disqualifies a person for electing, since electing is one of the authorized or accredited ecclesiastical acts.[112] The specific penalty of deprivation of active and passive voting rights may also be imposed.[113] This penalty may be inflicted for certain offenses as prescribed in the law, or it may be imposed in place of some more severe penalty when the case warrants it.[114]

It would not be feasible to treat in detail each and every crime that is punished with any of the above-mentioned penalties. Those crimes, however, which are punished with the specific penalty of deprivation of voting rights will be treated in detail later in this article.

SECTION 1. PERSONS DISQUALIFIED IN CONSEQUENCE OF THE LEGITIMATE SENTENCE OF AN ECCLESIASTICAL JUDGE

I. *The meaning of "Iudicis Sententiam"*

"*Iudicis sententiam*" in canon 167, § 1, n. 5, should not be restricted to include only those sentences which are imposed by the judge in formal trials, but should be extended to include also precepts imposed extrajudicially. It is true that

suspension inflicted as a vindictive penalty cf. cans. 2342, n. 1; 2347, n. 2; 2350, § 2; 2370; 2387.

[111] Cf. can. 2305, § 1. Cf. cans. 2314, § 1, n. 3; 2343, § 1, n. 3; 2354, § 2; 2368, § 1; 2388, § 1, for crimes which are punished with degradation.

[112] Cf. can. 2256, n. 2. There is only one case in the Code of the imposition of disbarrment from authorized ecclesiastical acts as a true disqualification, viz., can. 2294, § 2, which disqualifies those who are infamous with infamy of law. As stated above (pp. 104-105), however, election is not to be included in the authorized ecclesiastical acts mentioned in canon 2294, § 2. The disqualification for all authorized ecclesiastical acts could be imposed by particular law, and in that case election would be included among the authorized ecclesiastical acts.

[113] Can. 2291, n. 11.

[114] Cf. can. 2223, § 2 & § 3, n. 3.

iudex is commonly taken to mean the judge in a solemn trial, yet it must be admitted that an ecclesiastical superior is exercising true judicial power when inflicting penal precepts. He is a judge in the true sense of the word. Not all the formalities of a solemn trial are observed when penal precepts are imposed, but the substance of a trial—the accusation, the opportunity for defense, and the decision or sentence—are there. Even declarations of disqualification issued by religious superiors who enjoy only dominative power and not true jurisdiction should be included in the term *"iudicis sententiam."* This is a broad interpretation of the term but it is to be noted that it is not in conflict with canon 19, which declares that the restrictive interpretation is to be followed in interpreting laws which decree a penalty. Number 5, of canon 167, § 1, unlike the preceding numbers of that canon, does not in fact decree any penalties; it simply points in a general way to the disqualifications which arise from sources other than canon 167. Since declarations by religious superiors who enjoy only dominative power are a source of electoral disqualification, they should be included under the term *"iudicis sententiam."*[115]

Deprivation of voting rights imposed by a religious superior who enjoys only dominative power extends to only those voting rights which the delinquent enjoys as a member of the religious community. In practice, however, a religious will seldom, if ever, enjoy any voting rights outside his community. The penalty of deprivation of voting rights can be imposed for those crimes, often listed in the constitutions of the community, which seriously disturb the in-

[115] It is more logical to include them under the disqualifications arising from a judicial sentence than to include them under the disqualifications arising from the law, universal or particular. All disqualifications arise ultimately from the law, but the fact that "judicial sentence" and "law" are given as separate sources of disqualification indicates that number 5 of canon 167, § 1, is treating of the *immediate* source of the disqualifications. In canon 167, § 1, n. 5, "disqualifications arising from the law" includes only those disqualifications which the law imposes automatically, without the interposition of a sentence.

ternal order of the community. The constitutions will determine which superiors are authorized to impose the penalty. Usually the constitutions limit this authorization to the supreme moderator acting in conjunction with his council. In imposing the penalty the superior proceeds as a father does in punishing a delinquent child; no judicial trial is needed.[116]

The only vindictive penalty involving loss of voting rights which can be imposed by way of a jurisdictional precept is a general suspension. With the exception of a general suspension, the penalties which, according to canon 1933, § 4, can be imposed by way of a jurisdictional precept either do not disqualify at all or do so only when inflicted as censures.

Of the crimes which can be punished with penalties entailing loss of voting rights, some are described in the universal law, others are described in the particular law. In this work only the crimes listed in the universal law will be treated.

II. *Individual Offenses Punishable with a Sentence Depriving a Person of the Right to Vote*

a. Religious who are guilty of conspiring against the authority of the Roman Pontiff, of his legates, or of their own proper ordinary, or against the legitimate mandates of these superiors, as well as religious who are guilty of inciting subjects to disobedience against these superiors, are to be deprived of their active and passive voting rights and privileges.[117]

Members of communities of the common life do not incur this penalty, since strictly they are not religious.[118] Members of associations of the faithful likewise do not incur this penalty. To commit the crime described, a conspiracy must take place. A conspiracy must include at least two persons. The attempt to incite subjects to disobedience constitutes

[116] Cf. Schaefer, *De Religiosis*, p. 205.

[117] Cf. can. 2331, § 2.

[118] Cf. can. 673.

the delict whether the attempt is successful or not.[119] Under the term "legates" are included legates *a latere,* nuncios, internuncios, and Apostolic delegates.[120] Persons who conspire against a mandate that exceeds the power of the legate, or against any mandate contrary to the positive divine or the natural divine law do not incur this penalty, for such mandates are not legitimate.

Since canon 2331, § 2, used the jussive subjunctive, the penalty must be imposed upon those found guilty of the crime, unless the conditions described in canon 2223, § 3, n. 3, prevail.

b. Active and passive voting rights are to be taken from religious who issue laws, mandates, or decrees against the liberty and the rights of the Church.[121]

"Religious," as in the preceding case, means religious in the strict sense of the word. All laws, mandates, and decrees are included under the sanction of this canon, whether they be ecclesiastical laws or civil laws. A religious will seldom be in a position to pass civil legislation, but he may become a co-operator by voting for a civil law harmful to the legitimate interests of the Church. Any legislation which interferes with the rights and liberties of the *whole* Church or of any *part* of the Church constitutes the crime contemplated in this canon. Privileges granted to the Church by the civil power do not come under this canon. Thus, if bishops in certain Catholic countries are granted seats in the legislative councils of those countries, this is a privilege granted by the civil government and not a right of the Church. A law withdrawing this privilege would not be a violation of the rights of the Church.

c. Religious who directly or indirectly impede the exercise of ecclesiastical jurisdiction by having recourse to the lay authorities are to be deprived of their active and passive voting rights.[122]

[119] Cf. can. 2212, §§ 3 & 4; Beste, *Introductio in Codicem,* p. 965.

[120] Cf. cans. 265; 266; 267.

[121] Cf. cans. 2336, § 1; 2334, n. 1.

[122] Cf. cans. 2336, § 1; 2334, n. 2.

"Jurisdiction" may be ordinary or delegated, judicial or non-judicial, sacramental or non-sacramental, of the internal forum or of the external forum. The impeding of any sort of ecclesiastical jurisdiction falls within the scope of this canon. It must, however, be jurisdiction that is impeded. If the exercises of orders is impeded, the crime would not fall under this canon. Recourse to the lay authority is essential to this crime. If one were to impede the exercise of ecclesiastical jurisdiction by means of a personal interference, but without recourse to the lay authority, one would not incur the penalty enacted in this canon.

d. Religious who enroll in a Masonic sect or in some other association of the same kind which plots against the Church or the legitimate civil authority shall be deprived of active and passive voting rights and privileges.[123]

One is to be penalized by deprivation of his voting rights for *enrolling* in the forbidden society, even though subsequently he takes no part in the organization's activities. Even enrollment as an honorary member is included. A person can enroll by giving his name to the society, by submitting to the initiation ceremonies of the society, by taking an oath of loyalty to the society, or by any other act which the society uses as a sign of admittance to membership. Included among the societies dealt with in this canon are such societies as the Society of the Finians, the Society of the Carbonari, the Communist Party, the Ku Klux Klan, the Society of the Nihilists, the Society of the Anarchists, the Katipunan Society, the various branches of Freemasonry, and the Society of the Knights Templars. It is sometimes difficult to judge whether a specific government is or is not the legitimate government. A government which has usurped power can in the course of time become the legitimate government if it substantially attains the ends for which governments are established.

e. Religious who introduce or admit women, of whatever age they may be, into the cloister of men religious in solemn

[123] Cf. cans. 2336, § 1; 2335.

vows shall be deprived of their active and passive voting rights.[124]

This penalty is to be imposed only for the violation of the cloister of a community of *men* religious, and then only if the community is one whose members profess solemn vows. "Cloister" is to be taken in the strict sense of the papal cloister, set up in accordance with canon 597, § 3. It does not include parts of the house set aside as restricted by the local superior. If a woman religious were to enter the cloister of a community of men religious by *stealth,* she would not be subject to the penalty of this canon. But if she were to induce a man religious to admit her or to introduce her into the cloister she would be a co-operator in the crime forbidden by this canon and as such would be liable to the penalty described in this canon. If a man religious in simple vows were to introduce a woman into the papal cloister of a group of men religious, he would be guilty of the crime envisioned in this canon. The canon does not require that the religious who commits the crime be in solemn vows, or that he belong to the community whose cloister is violated.

The deprivation of voting rights is a preceptive penalty.

f. Religious who forge or falsify letters, decrees, or rescripts of the Holy See, or who knowingly use such letters, decrees, or rescripts shall be deprived of active and passive voting rights.[125]

Forgery consists in the fabrication of a complete document. Falsification is any addition, suppression, or substitution that changes the meaning of the document substantially. Documents of the Holy See include documents from the Holy Father and from the Congregations, Tribunals, and Offices which assist the Holy Father in ruling the universal Church.[126]

Two distinct delicts are treated in canon 2360. The one is the *forgery or falsification* of a document of the Holy See; the other is the use of such documents. The delict of

[124] Cf. can. 2342, n. 2.

[125] Cf. can. 2360, §§ 1 & 2.

[126] Cf. can. 7.

forgery is complete when the document is completed, i.e., drawn up, signed, and sealed. Falsification is completed when the substantial change is completed. The delict of forgery or falsification does not postulate any subsequent use of the spurious document. False documents can be used, for instance, in support of one's claim to certain rights or privileges, or in support of one's theological or canonical theories. Even if the false documents are used in support of orthodox and traditional teaching, the delict is committed. In using the document, however, the person must be aware of the forgery or falsification; otherwise he does not commit the delict.[127] Generally it will be presumed that the person using a document forged (or falsified) by someone else does not know of the forgery, since the fact of the forgery will seldom, if ever, be a notorious fact.[128]

This penalty is preceptive as far as religious are concerned. It could be imposed on clerics, but it is not preceptive in their regard.[129]

g. Priests who are guilty of the crime of solicitation as mentioned in canon 904 shall be deprived of active and passive voting rights and shall be declared disqualified for receiving them in the future.[130]

Solicitation is the act of provoking another to sin either formally or materially against the sixth commandment. The person solicited can be of either sex. The delict is commit-

[127] Though the canon uses the adverb *scienter*, perfect knowledge and freedom are not required, but only such as is necessary for committing serious sin. Canon 2229, § 2, applies only to *latae sententiae* penalties.

[128] Cf. can. 16, § 2. The statement in canon 16, § 2, namely that a person is presumed to be ignorant of the non-notorious deeds of another, is more fundamental than the statement in canon 2200, § 2, namely that malice (and therefore full knowledge and consent) is presumed in the external forum whenever an external violation of the law has been effected. Presumptions are based on what usually happens (cf. Reg. 45, R. J., in VI°). Persons generally do not know the non-notorious deeds of another, and this fact does not change when people are committing external violations of the law.

[129] Cf. can. 2360, § 2.

[130] Cf. can. 2368, § 1.

ted if the priest solicits the penitent to sin with him, with someone else, or even alone. It does not matter whether the sin to which the penitent is solicited is a sin in action, word, or thought.[131] The act of solicitation may consist in words or actions. Words or actions which are innocent in themselves will constitute solicitation if subsequent acts show that they contemplated the approach to a sin against purity. The attempt to incite to sin constitutes the delict; it matters not whether the penitent does or does not respond to the confessor's solicitation. To constitute the delict of solicitation mentioned in canon 904, the solicitation must occur in connection with confession, that is, in confession, immediately before or after confession, or in the place of confession under the pretense of confession.

The penalty imposed for solicitation is preceptive. It is to be imposed on all priests guilty of the crime whether they be religious or secular. They are not only to be deprived of the voting rights and privileges which they have, but they are to be declared incapable of ever receiving any such rights and privileges in the future.

h. A confessor who presumptuously violates the seal of confession indirectly shall be liable to the penalties listed in canon 2368, § 1.[132] The penalties listed in canon 2368, § 1, are the penalties which are to be imposed for the crime of solicitation. A confessor who is guilty of indirectly violating the seal of confession, therefore, is to be deprived of all his voting rights and privileges and is to be declared incapable of receiving any such rights and privileges in the future.

The seal of confession is directly violated when both the sin confessed and the identity of the penitent are clearly manifested. Indirect violation of the seal occurs when the sin confessed is mentioned and, although the identity of the penitent is not clearly revealed, there is danger that his

[131] Thus, if a confessor were to inform his penitent that the idle entertainment of impure thoughts is not sinful, he would be guilty of the crime of solicitation.

[132] Cf. can. 2369, § 1.

identity may become known; or, on the other hand, when the penitent is identified and, though the sin is not manifested, there is danger that the sin may become known, or that suspicions concerning the sin may be aroused. Some authors regard the use of sacramental knowledge which redounds to the harm of the penitent or of the sacrament as an indirect violation of the seal. If, however, there is no danger of revealing the penitent and his sin, then the use of the sacramental knowledge could be considered as an indirect violation of the seal only in a very broad sense and would not constitute the crime described in canon 2369, § 1.[133]

No special significance is to be attached to the use of the term *praesumpserit,* since this penalty is of a *ferendae sententiae* character and canon 2229, § 2, applies only to *latae sententiae* penalties.

i. Religious who seriously violate the law of community life as prescribed by their constitutions are to be gravely admonished and if they fail to make amends they are to be punished even with the deprivation of active and passive voting rights.[134]

Community life involves two elements, one, living together, and two, sharing with others in the ordinary needs of life such as food, clothing, and furniture.[135] Community life in the fullest sense embraces both of these elements. If community life is taken in this sense, it would be violated if a religious were to withdraw himself from community exer-

[133] The Code of Canon Law seems to imply a distinction between the violation of the seal (can. 889) and the unlawful use of sacramental knowledge (can. 890). An instruction of the Holy Office issued on June 9, 1915, strongly condemned the unlawful use of sacramental knowledge, "*even though it be done without substantial violation of the sacramental secret*..."—Bouscaren, *Canon Law Digest* (3 vols., Vol. I, 1934, Vol. II, 1943, Vol. III, 1954, [Annual Supplements 1953— , ed. by Bouscaren-O'Connor], Milwaukee: Bruce Publishing Company), I, 413-414. Cf. Vermeersch-Creusen, *Epitome,* III, 363.

[134] Cf. can. 2389.

[135] Cf. can. 673; 594, § 1.

cises (prayers, meals, work, and recreation), or if he were to violate the vow of poverty. In the development of the legislation on the matter, however, the expression "common life" took on the specific meaning of community of goods.[136] Since canon 2389 is a penal canon, authors limit the violations of the common life to violations in matters relating to the common goods or property.[137] The constitutions of each particular community will determine more exactly than canon 594, § 1, how the community of goods is to be observed. The constitutions may also determine what constitutes a serious violation. This penalty is applicable also in communities of the common life. The canon mentions only religious, but the Pontifical Commission for the Authentic Interpretation of the Code has revealed that it applies also to communities of the common life inasfar as the members live a common life.[138] Imposition of the penalty is mandatory.

SECTION 2. PERSONS AUTOMATICALLY DISQUALIFIED BY THE UNIVERSAL LAW

The disqualifications imposed by way of a sentence have been dealt with in the preceding section. In this section will be treated those qualifications which are incurred automatically. Most of these disqualifications are of a penal character.[139]

[136] Cf. Wernz-Vidal, III (*De Religiosis*), pp. 379-380.

[137] Cf., e.g., Vermeersch-Creusen, *Epitome*, III, 375; Schaefer, *De Religiosis*, pp. 672-675; Coronata, *Institutiones*, IV, 661, and I, 786; Beste, *Introductio in Codicem*, pp. 993 & 409.

[138] *AAS*, X (1918), 347.

[139] Parsons (*Canonical Elections*, pp. 124-127) identified the disqualifications listed in canon 167, § 1, n. 5, with penal disqualifications *exclusively*. "*Carentes*," he said, has a penal meaning in connection with "*sententiam iudicis*"; therefore it should have a penal meaning in connection with "*iure communi aut particulari*" also. This argument is far from convincing. It is not "*carentes*" that has the penal note, but "*iurdicis sententiam.*" "*Carentes*" means simply "lacking" in connection with "*iudicis sententiam*" and in connection with "*iure communi aut particulari.*" If this number of the canon embraced only penal disqualifications, non-penal disqualifica-

I. *Penal Disqualifications*

a. A religious who has apostatized from the religious life, even though he later returned to his religious house, shall forever lack active and passive voting rights.[140]

An apostate from the religious life has been defined in the Code as a religious having perpetual vows, either solemn or simple, who unlawfully leaves the religious house with the intention of not returning, or who, though he has left the house legitimately, does not return to it because he intends to withdraw himself from religious obedience.[141] From this definition it can be seen that the delict of apostasy presupposes 1) that the religious be perpetually professed; 2) that he leave or remain outside of his religious house unlawfully, and 3) that he have the intention of not returning. Religious in temporary vows and members of communities of the common life cannot commit this delict. Women religious in perpetual vows can commit this delict and are subject to the penalties enacted in canon 2385.[142] The intention of not returning to the religious house must be manifested through some external act. The intention of not returning is presumed if the unlawful absence extends over a period of more than one month.[143] The use of the word "*caret*" shows that the penalty is incurred automatically.

b. Electors who, contrary to the liberty of the Church, solicit or freely admit unlawful interference from a layman or from the secular power in an election conducted by a college of clerics or religious are automatically deprived of the right to vote for that time.[144]

tions, such as those which are listed in canons 639 and 629, § 2, would not be included at all under canon 167 or any other canon in this section of the Code. Parsons treated the disqualification listed in canon 639, namely, of exclaustrated religious, under this number of canon 167. It is not clear how he could have considered exclaustration as a penalty.

140 Cf. can. 2385.

141 Can. 644, § 1.

142 Cf. can. 490.

143 Can. 644, § 2.

144 Cf. can. 2390, § 2.

Allowing a layman to vote, or even to be present when his presence could intimidate any of the electors, would constitute unlawful interference. Such interference renders the election invalid.[145] It is only in connection with elections conducted by clerics or religious that the penalty of canon 2390, § 2, is incurred, for the canon mentions only these elections. This canon does not apply to elections conducted by associations of the faithful or by communities of the common life. "Layman" in this canon is to be taken in the strict sense; it does include a lay religious. This is the more benign interpretation, and it is also the interpretation followed in the pre-Code law.[146] To incur the penalty the electors must admit the layman freely. If they are forced to admit him, they are not subject to this penalty. The disqualification lasts for that one turn, that is, for that particular election.[147] If, as is usually the case, elections to various offices are conducted at the same chapter, the electors who invited or freely admitted lay interference are disqualified for all the elections to which they invited or freely admitted the lay person. The delict is not perpetrated when, though the lay interference has been invited, the lay person did not respond to the invitation.

c. Those who commit the crime of simony in connection with any ecclesiastical office, benefice, or dignity are automatically and perpetually deprived of any right to elect, present, or nominate that they may have.[148] Simony is defined in canon 727, §§ 1 & 2. Simony in contravention of the divine law is the deliberate will to buy or sell for a temporal price something intrinsically spiritual, or some temporal thing annexed to a spiritual thing in such a way

[145] Can. 166.

[146] Cf. *supra*, p. 88. If a lay religious who did not belong to the chapter were allowed to vote the election would be invalid (cf. can. 165) but the members who admitted the lay religious would not incur the disqualification prescribed by canon 2390, § 2.

[147] The election, of course, is invalid and must be repeated. Cf. can. 166.

[148] Cf. can. 2392.

that it could not exist without the spiritual thing, or some spiritual thing connected with a temporal thing in such a way that the spiritual thing is the partial object of the sale. Simony in contravention of the ecclesiastical law is the exchange of temporal things connected with spiritual things for other temporal things connected with spiritual things, or of spiritual things for spiritual things, or even of temporal things for temporal things, when this has been forbidden by the Church because of the danger of irreverence to spiritual things. "Buying," "selling," or "exchanging," when used in connection with simony, is to be taken in the broad sense to include any agreement, even if not carried out, or even if only tacit, in which the simoniacal intent is not indeed expressly manifested but may be deduced from the circumstances.[149] The element of agreement requires that a simoniacal offer be made, either tacitly or expressly, by one party, and accepted, either tacitly or expressly, by the second party. A simoniacal offer, if refused, would constitute only an attempted delict *(conatus delicti)* and would not induce the penalty of canon 2392.[150] The penalty listed in canon 2392 is incurred whether the perpetrated simony violates the divine law or the ecclesiastical law.[151] The penalty of disqualification is incurred only if the simony is committed in connection with an ecclesiastical office, benefice, or dignity. The delict is committed, however, if simony

[149] Can. 728.

[150] Cf. cans. 2212; 2228.

[151] Cf. Vermeersch-Creusen, *Epitome*, II, 9; *ibid.*, III, 377-378; Beste, *Introductio in Codicem*, pp. 993-994. Simony in contravention of the ecclesiastical law is truly simony and, therefore, should be punished as such. Further, it would be meaningless for the law to declare certain transactions simoniacal by reason of the ecclesiastical law if no penalty or if no nullifying effect were attached thereto. If, however, the simony which offends against the ecclesiastical law did not entail the same penalties, and if it did not have the same nullifying effects as those which derive through simony which offends against the divine law, then it would entail no penalty and it would have no nullifying effects, for nowhere in the Code is any penalization attached specifically and exclusively to simony which offends against the ecclesiastical law.

is committed in any connection with an office, benefice, or dignity, whether in the acquisition, bestowal, transfer, renunciation, suppression, or exercise thereof. "Ecclesiastical office" must be strictly interpreted according to the definition of canon 145. Although the deprivation of voting rights is perpetual, it applies to only those rights which the person has at the time of the commission of the crime; the canon does not disqualify the culprit from obtaining other voting rights in the future.[152]

d. All who legitimately enjoy the right of electing, and who show disregard for the authority of the one who has the right of confirmation by presuming to confer an office, benefice, or ecclesiastical dignity, are automatically deprived of their right to elect for that turn.[153]

Confirmation is not needed for all elections.[154] It is only when it is needed and it is nevertheless neglected that this penalty is incurred. The guilty members alone incur the penalty, for the canon does not make it applicable to the collegiate body as such. To make the canon applicable to the whole electoral body would be a violation of canon 19[155] and canon 2219, § 1.[156] The right to elect for that instance, therefore, will belong to the innocent members of the electoral body. If all the members should be guilty of the crime and, consequently, deprived of their right to vote, the right to fill the office for that time will devolve to the superior who would have had the right to confirm the election, or who next succeeds to the right of appointment.[157] Since canon 2393 contains the word "*praesumpserint,*" any diminution

[152] Cf. can. 2368, § 1, which not only deprives the culprit of the voting rights which he has but also renders him ineligible for receiving such rights in the future.

[153] Cf. can. 2393.

[154] Cf. can. 176, § 2.

[155] Canon 19 states that laws which restrict the free exercise of one's rights are to interpreted restrictively.

[156] Canon 2219, § 1, states that the more benign interpretation is to be followed in penal matters.

[157] Cf. can. 178.

of responsibility will excuse from the incurring of the penalty.[158]

e. If the electors have postulated a candidate and the postulation is not sent to the competent superior within the prescribed time, the postulation is automatically void and the electors are deprived, for that turn, of the right to elect or postulate, unless they can prove that they were legitimately impeded from sending the postulation.[159]

Canon 181, § 1, demands that the postulation be sent within eight days to the superior who has the right of confirming the election, if he has also the faculties to dispense from the candidate's impediment; otherwise the postulation is to be sent to the Roman Pontiff, or to someone else who has the faculty to dispense. It is clear from canon 181, § 2, that the eight-day period is to be reckoned as usable time. The obligation to send the postulation to the competent superior is incumbent upon the whole electoral body, and the penalty for failing to send the postulation is incurred by the whole chapter.[160]

If the postulation of a candidate who is fit for postulation is refused by the superior or by the person postulated, the electoral college must proceed to a new election within a month.[161]

f. A collegiate body of electors that knowingly elects a candidate who is unworthy is automatically deprived, for that time, of the right to proceed to a new election.[162]

There exists a great deal of confusion among modern commentators as to the meaning of "unworthy candidate." Some authors consider as an unworthy candidate anyone

158 Cf. can. 2229, § 2. The different ways in which liability can be diminished are described in cans. 2200-2206.

159 Cf. can. 181, § 2.

160 Cf. Coronata, *Institutiones,* I, 309, footnote n. 5.

161 Cf. can. 182, § 1; can. 176, § 1. Canon 176 does not treat of postulation specifically, but all the regulations of Article II, Title IV, Book II of the Code, which deals with elections, are applicable to postulation except in so far as Article III of that section of the Code specifies differences. Postulation is only a substitute for election.

162 Can. 2391, § 1.

who has some impediment or lack of quality which cannot be, or usually is not, dispensed from.[163] Others hold that unworthiness arises only from some delict or through some penalty; they hold that only moral deficiencies render a person unworthy. Defects in knowledge or age, they say, render a person unfit *(non-idoneus)*, but not unworthy *(indignus)*.[164] A survey of the pre-Code legislation on this matters shows both opinions to be erroneous. A study of the Decretals of Pope Gregory IX shows that a candidate was considered *indignus* if he lacked any of the qualities required by law. Thus, chapter 7, X, *de electione et electi potestate*, I, 6, the principal source of the present canon, deprived electors of their vote for one time if they elected anyone who was not qualified with reference to *age, morals, learning*, or *legitimacy of birth*. The rubric to paragraph four of this chapter of the Decretals calls an *unqualified* candidate *indignus*. Candidates who are designated as unworthy in the rubric to c. 22, X, *de electione et electi potestate*, I, 6, turn out in the body of the decretal to be persons lacking the required *orders, learning*, or *age*. The rubric to c. 25, X, *de electione et electi potestate*, I, 6, calls one who is illegitimate unworthy. Chapter 4, X, *de aetate et qualitate et ordine praeficiendorum*, I, 14, reads: "*Ad regimen ecclesiarum non debet institui indignus scientia, moribus, vel aetate . . .*"[165] The commentators on the Decretals also used the term *indignus* to denote a candidate disqualified in any way whatsoever. Thus Reiffenstuel (1642-1703) wrote: "*Indignus vero cui deest aliqua ex qualitatibus ad ministerium beneficiale de iure requisitis.*"[166] Pichler (1670-1736) stated: "*. . . eligendus sit dignus, nempe sit*

[163] Cf., e.g., Woywod, *A Practical Commentary on the Code of Canon Law* (2 vols. in 1, New York: John F. Wagner, 1952), II, 574; Beste, *Introductio in Codicem*, p. 933.

[164] Cf., e.g., Vermeersch-Creusen, *Epitome*, III, 376; Coronata, *Institutiones*, IV, 665 with footnote n. 7.

[165] Cf. also cc. 20, 40, 44, 53, X, *de electione et electi potestate*, I, 6; c. 18, *de electione et electi potestate*, I, 6, in VI°.

[166] Lib. I, tit. VI, n. 235; cf. *ibid.*, n. 21.

legitimo toro natus, debita aetate instructus, gravitate morum et literarum scientia commendabilis, etc. . . ."[167] Further, the pre-Code legislation made no distinction between *non-idoneus* and *indignus*. Thus cc. 7, 22, 40, 53, X, *de electione et electi potestate,* I, 6, and c. 29, X, *de praebendis et dignitatibus,* III, 5, use *indignus* and *idoneus* as contraries.[168] In accordance with canon 6 one must retain the historical meaning of the term *indignus* and interpret the present legislation in the light of the pre-Code legislation which it reiterates.[169] An unworthy candidate, therefore, is the same as an unfit candidate, that is, a candidate lacking any quality whatsoever that is required by law.

Some authors object to identifying an unworthy candidate with an unfit candidate. They say a distinction must be made, basing their contention on the difference between canon 1465, which allows a person who has presented an *unfit* candidate to make a new presentation, and canon 2391, § 3, which deprives of the right of presentation any person who has presented an *unworthy* candidate.[170] It must be noted, however, that canon 2391, § 3, is dealing with the case wherein a person *knowingly* presents an unworthy candidate, whereas canon 1465 is dealing with the case wherein the candidate is *found* to be unfit. The difference between canon 2391, § 3, and canon 1465 is that in the one case the unworthy candidate was known by the patron to be unworthy, whereas in the other case he was not known to be unworthy.[171]

[167] Lib. I, tit. VI, § IV, n. 21; cf. also Schmalzgrueber, Lib. I, tit. VI, nn. 19-21; Pirhing, Lib. I, tit. VI, nn. 42-43.

[168] The Decretals are quite consistent in using *idoneus* rather than *dignus,* and *indignus* rather than *non-idoneus.*

[169] Canon 2391, § 1, is only a partial repetition of the pre-Code law inasmuch as c. 7, X, *de electione et electi potestate,* I, 6, not only deprived guilty electors of their vote for that turn, but also suspended them from their benefice for three years.

[170] Cf., e.g., Coronata, *Institutiones,* IV, 665; Woywod, *A Practical Commentary on the Code of Canon Law,* II, 574.

[171] This interpretation of canons 1465, § 1, and 2391, § 3, is in accord with the pre-Code law on the matter, for in pre-Code law if a

It must be remembered that the unfitness of the candidate must bear a relationship to *election.* Those authors who say that an unworthy candidate for election is one who labors under an impediment that cannot or usually is not dispensed from, have made the error of taking unworthiness in relation to *postulation* and applying it to elections.[172] The Decretals clearly distinguished between unworthiness in relation to election and unworthiness in relation to postulation. Thus, an illegitimate candidate was unworthy of election but not of postulation.[173] A consideration of the difference in the nature of election and the nature of postulation will show the basis for making the distinction. In postulation the electors are petitioning for a favor, whereas in election they are exercising a right.[174]

The Code of Canon Law does not define precisely when a candidate must be worthy. It would not seem unjustified to adopt for election the norm set in relation to presentation.[175] Canon 1463 allows the candidate till the day of his acceptance of the presentation to become qualified. A candidate who has been elected, therefore, should also be allowed till the day of his acceptance of the election to become qualified.[176] Using canon 1463 as a pattern, one may fully define an unworthy or unfit candidate as one who, on the day of election or at least on the day of his acceptance, lacks any

person unknowingly presented an unworthy candidate he was allowed to present another candidate, but if he knowingly presented an unworthy candidate he was deprived of his right of presentation for that time. Cf. Pichler, lib. III, tit. XXXVIII, n. 10. In canon 1465 a person who presents two unworthy candidates in a row is deprived of his right of presentation, not for the reason that his manner of acting connotes malice, but simply because it points to incompetence or carelessness.

172 Cf. can. 182, § 1.

173 Cf. c. 20, X, *de electione et electi potestate,* I, 6.

174 Cp. can. 176, § 2, and can. 181, § 3.

175 Cf. can. 20.

176 A candidate has eight days of usable time dating from the notification of his election within which to accept the election (cf. can. 175).

of the qualities required by the universal or particular law, or by the law of the foundation.

The penalty established by canon 2391, § 1, is incurred whether the elected candidate lacks a quality required for validity of the election, or only one required for the licitness of the election.[177] The election itself, however, is automatically invalid only if the lacking quality is required for the validity of the election.[178] If the lacking quality is required for *licitness* and the election is one which requires confirmation, the proper superior can refuse to confirm the election.[179] If the lacking quality is required for licitness and the election is one that does *not* require confirmation, the election is valid but it can be nullified by the competent superior.[180] If the competent superior does invalidate the il-

[177] Cf. Schmalzgrueber, Lib. I., tit. VI, n. 19. For lack of qualities which render an election invalid cf. cans. 154; 504; 505; 2265; 2275; 2283; 2345; 2346; 2390, § 2; 2394, § 1; 2395; 2413; 2294, § 1. For lack of qualities which render an election illicit but not invalid cf. cans. 367, § 1; 2265, § 1, n. 2 & § 2; 2294, § 2.

[178] Cf. can. 11. Coronata, who maintains that an unworthy candidate is one who is morally unfit (cf. *Institutiones*, IV, 665) holds that the election is automatically invalid (cf. *ibid.*, 666). This opinion, however, is scarcely tenable. According to canon 2265, § 1, n. 2, and § 2, the election of an excommunicated person, who is certainly morally unfit, is valid, unless the excommunication has been inflicted or confirmed by way of a sentence. Other authors, though they do not explicitly say so, seem to imply that the election is automatically invalid (cf., e.g., Beste, *Introductio in Codicem*, p. 993; Vermeersch-Creusen, *Epitome*, III, 376). Even if one were to hold the opinion that a candidate unworthy of election is one who is under some impediment that cannot be or usually is not dispensed from, one could not say that the election of an unworthy candidate must always be automatically invalid. Excommunication is an impediment that is seldom, if ever, dispensed from, and yet, as already stated in this paragraph, the election of an excommunicated person is not always automatically invalid.

[179] Cf. can. 177, § 2.

[180] Cf. can. 153, § 3. Can. 153, § 3, is in that article of the Code which deals with free appointment (libera collatio), but it is applicable also to elections (and the other forms of canonical provision). There are authors (cf., e.g., Vermeersch-Creusen, *Epitome*, I, 247) who hold that some of the canons in the article entitled "*De Libera*

licit election, he obtains for that time the right to fill the vacant office by way of a free appointment.[181] If the superior should not choose to nullify the illicit election, the penalty of canon 2391, § 1, is not to be applied for the next future election, since the canon forbids the collegiate body to proceed to a new election only for the one particular time, i.e., the current election.

The deprivation is incurred by the whole collegiate body, and not by the guilty members alone. This is a change from the legislation of the Decretals.[182] The wording of canon 2391, § 1, especially when compared with paragraph two of this same canon, shows clearly that the whole collegiate body incurs the loss of its right. It cannot be validly objected that the legislator would not want to deprive the innocent members of their right. The Code in other instances does deprive innocent members of the rights which they have as members of a moral personality. Thus, canons 2274 and 2283 allow the whole community to be interdicted or suspended, and thereby allow all the members to be deprived of their rights, even though not all of the members were guilty of the delict for which the punishment is imposed.[183]

Collatione" are meant for all forms of canonical provision. This certainly seems true of canons 153; 154; and 156, §§ 1 & 2. But even if canon 153, § 3, is not directly applicable to elections it can still be applied in virtue of canon 20. If someone were to object that canon 20 does not allow the use of a supplementary source of legislation in the case of the infliction of penalties, one would have to point out that the nullification of the illicit election is not intended as a penalty. The purpose of the nullification is to safeguard the office and the common good.

[181] Cf. can. 178.

[182] Cf. cc. 25, 53, X, *de electione et electi potestate,* I, 6.

[183] Coronata (*Institutiones,* IV, 665-666) says that only the guilty members are to be punished, since the collegiate body consists in the "*sanior pars,*" and the part that elected the unworthy candidate cannot be said to be the "*sanior pars.*" This explanation is rather imaginative, but if followed out logically it would lead to the conclusion that the crime described in canon 2391, § 1, could never be committed. A collegiate body can never knowingly elect an unworthy candidate except through its guilty members; but if its guilty

The collegiate body must know of the candidate's unworthiness when electing him if it is to incur the penalty. The electors are obliged to investigate the qualifications of the candidates, and the burden of proof, therefore, will be upon the electors to show that they did not know of the defect in the candidate. The electors are presumed to know the qualifications required by law.[184] If, however, they could prove that they did not know the law or the lack of qualifications, they would be excused from incurring the penalty. Since canon 2391, § 1, contains the word *"scienter,"* and since the penalty is a *latae sententiae* penalty, any diminution of liability, either on the part of the intellect or on the part of the will, exempts from the penalty.[185]

g. If the competent superior rejects the postulation of a candidate, the right to elect returns to the collegiate body, unless the electors knowingly postulated one who labored under an impediment which cannot be or usually is not dispensed from; in this case the right of making provision belongs to the superior.[186]

The wording of this canon, "the right to elect returns to the collegiate body, unless . . . ," indicates clearly that this penalty is incurred automatically. This penalty is the same as the penalty imposed for *electing* an unworthy candidate. Canon 182, fortunately, contains its own definition of a candidate unworthy of postulation, and thereby precludes much argumentation. Impediments which cannot be dispensed from are those which derive from the positive or natural divine law. Those which usually are not dispensed from can be known only from past decisions of the Holy See and from sound common sense. The requirement of legitimacy is often dispensed from. Lack of the required

members do not help constitute the collegiate body, the collegiate body cannot elect through them. The Code clearly states: *"Collegium quod scienter indignum elegerit. . . ."*

[184] Can. 16, § 2.

[185] Can. 2229, § 2. Affected ignorance is regarded as not diminishing liability (cf. can. 2229, § 1).

[186] Cf. can. 182, § 1.

age is often dispensed from if the discrepancy between the candidate's age and the age required by law is not very notable. Moral requirements, such as freedom from the sentence of censure, will not be dispensed from. If the collegiate body can show that it did not know that the candidate's impediment is usually not dispensed from, it would not incur the penalty. Any diminution of liability will excuse the collegiate body from incurring the penalty since this is a *latae sententiae* and the canon contains the word "*scienter.*"[187]

II. *Non-Penal Disqualifications*

The non-penal disqualification of non-members of the electoral body is dealt with in canon 165. The disqualifications of the natural law are dealt with in canon 167, § 1, n. 1. There remain, accordingly, very few non-penal disqualifications to be treated in this present section.

a. Religious who enjoy the cardinalatial or episcopal dignity lack active and passive voting rights and privileges even after laying down their office and returning to their religious community.[188]

This disqualification applies only to religious in the strict sense; it does not apply to the members of communities of the common life.[189] The probable reason for the disqualification listed in canon 629, § 2, is that, on the one hand, it would be unbecoming for a cardinal or bishop to be put on an equal footing with the other electors, and, on the other hand, it would be unfair to the community to give him any more power than the other electors. An additional reason may be that, as a result of his long absence from the community, the returning cardinal or bishop would not be well informed on the qualifications of the various prospective candidates and on the affairs of the community in general.

[187] Cf. can. 2229, § 2.

[188] Cf. can. 629, § 2.

[189] Canon 629 is not among the canons on religious which the Code makes applicable also to communities of the common life. Cf. cans. 673-681.

If a cardinal or bishop who has returned to his community is postulated for an office which carries with it the right to vote, and the postulation is admitted, the admission of the postulation would be an implicit dispensation from the disqualification. This dispensation would last only for the duration of the office.[190]

b. Religious who receive an indult of exclaustration from the Apostolic See lack the right to vote or to be voted for during the time of the exclaustration.[191]

Though canon 639 mentions only indults received from the Apostolic See, the deprivation of voting rights results also from an indult of exclaustration received from the local ordinary.[192] The disqualification lasts for the period of time that the indult is actually used, not for the time that the indult is granted.[193]

c. If the election is not held within the prescribed time, the right of free appointment devolves upon the superior who has the right of confirming the election or who has the successive right of making provision for the office in question.[194]

According to canon 161 an election may not be deferred

[190] Cf. can. 66, § 3.

[191] Cf. can. 639.

[192] Pont. Com. ad Cod. auth. Interp., 12 novembris 1922—*AAS*, XIV (1922), p. 662.

[193] A religious could return before the indult expired, since the indult is a favor granted for his benefit, and he is not obliged to use a favor granted for his own benefit (cf. can. 69). The formula of the indult regularly acknowledges the religious superior's right to recall the exclaustrated religious to the cloister even before the indult expires; cf. Schaefer, *De Religiosis*, pp. 911-912.

[194] Cf. cans. 178 & 161. The loss of the right to elect because of failure to elect within the given time period is listed here among the *non-penal* disqualifications because the Code itself seems to consider it as a non-penal disqualification. Thus, canon 178 distinguishes between loss of the right to elect because of failure to elect within the set time-period and penal loss of the right to elect. The time limit, then, merely determines the extent of the electoral body's right of election, without imposing any grave obligation upon the group to use that right. Failure to elect within the time-limit would not be a delict but merely the failure to use one's right.

beyond three months (usable time), which three months are to be reckoned from the day on which notice of the vacancy is received. The three months' period of time is to be computed according to canon 34, § 3; the first day is not counted unless the notification of the vacancy was received at the very beginning of the day. Once the election has begun it cannot be said that it is still being deferred, and, therefore, it suffices to have begun the election within the three-month limit, even though the completion of the election should occur after that time period. Further, canon 161 states that the right to choose devolves upon the superior only if the time has lapsed without being used. If the election has begun, the time cannot be said to have lapsed without being used.[195] Since the three-month period is to be computed as usable time *(tempus utile)*, it does not run if the electoral body does not know of the vacancy or if, through no fault of its own, it is impeded from electing.[196] It seems indeed necessary but also sufficient that the president of the electoral college, who is to summon the electors, know of the vacancy for the time to commence to run. It does not seem necessary that all or even a majority of the electors know of the vacancy. In the opinion of this writer, only such ignorance as prevents the *collegium* from making use of its right should be considered as impeding the running of the time. But once the president knows of the vacancy, the *collegium* can begin to exercise its right, inasmuch as the president can convoke the electors. The election can be impeded by other factors besides ignorance of the vacancy. Thus, if the summons cannot be issued for some reason, one can duly regard the running of the time to be interrupted as long as the reason continues to exist.[197]

[195] The wording of canon 161 should be interpreted restrictively, since the canon is one which restricts the voters' right (cf. can. 19). Parsons (*Canonical Elections*, p. 97) stated that the election must be *completed* within three months, but he did not offer any basis for his view.

[196] Can. 35.

[197] Ordinary obstacles which prevent the use of one's rights are

Provided that they have been summoned to the election, how many electors must be impeded from attending before the college would be considered as impeded from electing? If the particular law of the college requires a quorum for the validity of the election, then there would have to be impeded only so many electors whose absence would suffice to neutralize the quorum.[198] The Code of Canon Law, however, sets no quorum requirement.[199] Therefore, if only one voter answers the summons, he has the right of electing.[200] It must be concluded, then, that, once the summons has been issued, all the electors must be impeded before the time available for holding the election *(tempus utile)* would be interrupted.[201]

Canon 176, § 1, orders that, should the chosen candidate refuse to accept the election, the electoral college must proceed to a new election within a month after receiving notice of the candidate's refusal. This time is usable time, and is to be computed in the same manner as the three-month period mentioned above. The canon allows only one month for the college to proceed to a new election regardless of how much of the three-month period originally allotted for the election had elapsed before the first election was held. Thus, if the first election was held toward the end of the three-month period the chapter has a full month for the new election. Likewise, if the first election was held toward

not considered as impeding the flow of the *tempus utile*. Thus, sleep or press of business are not impediments which interrupt the *tempus utile*.

198 The *Normae* of 1901 (n. 223) required a quorum of two-thirds of the voters. If one more than a third of the electors was prevented from attending, the collegiate body was impeded in the use of its right.

199 Canon 162, § 3, demands that at least two-thirds of the electors be summoned, but it does not demand that two-thirds answer the summons.

200 Cf. can. 163; Parsons, *Canonical Elections*, p. 110.

201 It is presupposed, of course, that there is no quorum requirement.

the beginning of the three-month period, the chapter still has only a month to proceed to the new election.

Canon 432 permits only eight days after the notification of the vacancy of the see within which to elect a vicar capitular. This time runs not as a *tempus utile* but as a *tempus continuum,* that is, it lapses without an interruption or break. The election must be completed within the eight-day period.

The particular capitular statutes may restrict or lengthen the time set by the Code of Canon Law for the holding of the election.

d. A collegiate body may have the right of presentation. In such a case the candidate for presentation would be chosen by the collegiate body by way of an election. If a collegiate body enjoys the right of presentation, it must, provided there be no legitimate impediment, make the presentation within four months after receiving notification of the vacancy of the office, unless the law of the foundation or entrenched custom prescribes a shorter time.[202] If the presentation is not made within the prescribed time, the church or the benefice is conferred for that turn by way of free appointment.[203] The time allotted for presentation is usable time, and is computed in the manner indicated in the foregoing sections. Custom or particular law can shorten, but it cannot lengthen, the four-month period. If a second presentation is to be made,[204] the patron, in this case the collegiate body, is not given a month's time within which to select a new candidate, as are the electors when a second election is needed. The patron has that portion of the four-month period which has not yet been used in making the first presentation. The time between the first presentation and the subsequent notification of the renunciation, rejec-

[202] Cf. can. 1457.

[203] Can. 1458, § 1.

[204] A second presentation would be called for if the candidate were to refuse the presentation, or if he were found to be unworthy, or if he were to die before he could be canonically instituted, cf. can. 1465, § 1; can. 1468.

tion, or death of the presented candidate is to be considered as neutralized *(tempus obstructum)*. Thus, for example, if a patron presented a candidate one month after notification of the vacancy of the office, and that candidate died two weeks after the presentation but before the canonical institution had taken place, the two weeks between the presentation and the death of the candidate is neutralized time, and the patron has the three months still remaining of the four-month period to make the second presentation.

SECTION 3. PERSONS DISQUALIFIED BY THE PARTICULAR LAW

The particular law of the various communities, associations, or chapters may list additional disqualifications. These disqualifications may be penal or non-penal. To learn these disqualifications it would be necessary to consult the constitutions of the various individual groups. These disqualifications can be found most often in the constitutions of the communities of religious. They are not, however, limited to these communities. Cathedral chapters, bodies of diocesan consultors, and societies of the faithful can also have special laws disqualifying certain persons as voters. Deprivation of voting rights is frequently imposed by the particular law as a penalty for violation of the secrecy of the chapter. Very often communities of the common life adopt penalties which the Code of Canon Law applies only to religious in the strict sense.

ARTICLE VI. EFFECTS OF THE ADMISSION OF DISQUALIFIED VOTERS UPON THE ELECTION

Canon 167, § 2. *Si quis ex praedictis admittatur, eius suffragium est nullum, sed electio valet, nisi constet, eo dempto, electum non retulisse requisitum suffragiorum numerum, aut nisi scienter admissus fuerit excommunicatus per sententiam declaratoriam vel condemnatoriam.*

The vote of a disqualified voter is invalid. This does not, however, have any effect upon the validity of the election except in two instances. The first instance, as is to be expected, is the case wherein it appears that an invalid vote has decided the election. The second case is one in which a person laboring under the sentence of excommunication has been knowingly admitted to the election.

Whenever there is the possibility that an invalid vote has decided the election, an investigation must be conducted for discovering whether or not such was actually the case. If there is no possibility that the invalid vote (or votes) decided the election, there is no need of any investigation. Thus, if only one invalid vote was cast and the person elected received one or more votes beyond the required majority, it is evident that the invalid vote did not decide the election, even if it was cast for the victor.

The Code of Canon Law does not prescribe any mode of procedure to be followed in the task of determining whether or not an invalid vote played a decisive part in the election. The electoral body may adopt whatever procedure it deems best, but the secrecy of the ballots of the qualified voters must not be violated.[205] It is possible that the unqualified voter was unaware of his disability and cast his vote in good faith. In such a case the simplest procedure to follow would be to ask the disqualified voter whether or not he voted for the victorious candidate. On the other hand, if the disqualified voter acted in bad faith, or is suspected of having so acted, it would not be advisable to question him, since he can hardly be considered trustworthy.[206] If the ballots have not yet been burned, and the vote of the disqualified elector can be identified, the ballot should be opened. Thus it could be seen whether or not he voted for the person elected.[207] If

[205] Cf. can. 169, § 1, n. 2. The secrecy of the invalid ballots need not be maintained, since invalid ballots are not, legally speaking, any ballots at all. Courtesy, however, may require that, as far as feasible, the secrecy of such ballots be preserved, especially when they were cast in good faith.

[206] Cf. Coronata, *Institutiones*, I, 276.

[207] It is not a violation of the secrecy of the ballot to mark the ballots with a sign or even one's name, even though the tellers should learn for whom the individual electors voted. The secrecy is not violated by the fact that the tellers know for whom the electors voted,

the voting was conducted *viva voce* to the tellers, the tellers may be requested to testify whether or not the disqualified voter cast his ballot for the person who has the majority of votes.[208] If, however, the ballots have been burned, or if the tellers do not remember for whom the disqualified voter cast his ballot, the best procedure would be to *reconstruct* the election. In this reconstruction each elector, excluding the disqualified one, would write the name of the candidate for whom he voted on a slip of paper similar to a ballot sheet. These slips could then be collected by the tellers and counted. The result will then be identical with the result the election would have had, had the disqualified voter not taken part, and it will be clear whether or not the leading candidate received a majority without the invalid vote. It should be pointed out to the electors that this procedure is only a poll, not a new election, and they are not free to write down any name they choose, but only the name of the candidate for whom they originally voted. This poll may also be conducted by way of the mails. In this case the superior, preferably with the aid of his council, could conduct the poll. To preserve the secrecy of the electors' votes, the electors should send their poll slips in a sealed envelop inside an outer envelope, and the poll slips should be collected in a common urn, to be counted when all the slips have been received. The poll slips should be identical and it would, therefore, be advisable for the superior to send out the slips from his office.

It may, however, be impossible to learn whether or not the election was decided by an invalid vote. Thus, for exam-

for it is permissible to vote *viva voce,* in which case the tellers know the vote of each elector; cf. Schaefer, *De Religiosis,* p. 242; Coronata, *Institutiones,* I, 281. It would be advisable to put the name or sign under a folded or pasted flap which would be opened only when an investigation were being conducted.

208 The tellers should not be asked to name the person for whom the disqualified elector voted, for this may prove embarrassing to the the candidate named. They should only be asked whether or not the disqualified elector voted for the candidate who received the majority of the votes.

ple, the poll may be inconclusive because some of the electors have died between the time of the election and the poll.[209] If the investigation should prove inconclusive, the election is to be allowed to stand. Coronata says that the election must be repeated if it is not clear that it was valid.[210] But this is contrary to the wording of canon 167, § 2, which clearly states that the election is valid unless the invalidity is evident. It is the invalidity of the election which must be proved, not the validity. If, *de facto,* the election was decided by an invalid vote, the Church supplies for the invalidity.[211] The Church will supply for the invalidity of acts performed during a full term, or during a partial term, of office. Thus, if a considerable time after the election has taken place it is learned that the election was decided by an invalid vote, all the official acts performed up to that time by the invalidly elected person should be considered valid.

The second instance wherein the admission of a disqualified voter to the election affects the validity of the election is that in which an elector laboring under a sentence of excommunication is knowingly admitted. Excommunication is the severest of all ecclesiastical penalties. The admission of an elector laboring under any penalty other than excommunication, does not automatically nullify the election. The invalidation of an election for knowingly admitting a person laboring under a sentence of excommunication is similar to the invalidation which occurs when a non-member is admitted to vote.[212] Only one elector under a sentence of excommunication need be admitted for the election to become null and void. The electoral body must admit the elector *knowingly;* it must know both that the elector is excommunicated and that there has been a sentence, either con-

[209] The poll should be taken even if one or the other of the electors had died. The deceased elector may not have voted for the leading candidate and in this case the poll could show that the candidate had a majority without the vote of the deceased elector and without the vote of the disqualified elector.

[210] *Institutiones,* I, 276.

[211] Cf. Parsons, *Canonical Elections,* p. 130.

[212] Cf. can. 165.

demnatory or declaratory. The excommunicated person must be knowingly admitted by the *majority*. Thus, if only a minority of the electoral college knew of the sentence of excommunication, the election would not be automatically invalid. The electors must admit the disqualified voter *freely*. If a minority forced the others to admit the excommunicated elector, the election would not be *ipso facto* null on this particular ground.[213]

The Code of Canon Law does not deprive the electoral body of its right of proceeding to a new election if the election was invalid because the deciding vote was cast by a disqualified elector, or because a person under a sentence of excommunication was knowingly admitted to the election. The college could, however, if seriously guilty, be deprived of its right by way of a judicial sentence.[214] If not deprived of its right, the college may proceed to a new election. The new election must be conducted within the three-month time limit set by canon 161, unless the competent superior grants an extension. In calculating the time period it is necessary to distinguish between the case in which the electoral body admitted a disqualified voter *knowingly* and the case in which it did so *unknowingly*. In the latter case the time between the first election and the discovery of the invalidity of that election would be considered as impeded time; in the former case it would not be so considered, inasmuch as it was in consequence of the college's own fault that the usable time was lost.

ARTICLE VII. ELECTORS WHO ARE FORBIDDEN TO EXERCISE THEIR RIGHT OF VOTING

Some electors are forbidden by the Code of Canon Law to *exercise* their right to vote. Their right is not taken from

[213] In the case described, it may very well be that the election would be invalid because many of the votes were invalid for lack of being given freely; cf. can. 169, § 1, n. 1. If it can be shown that any vote which was needed for establishing the majority was invalid in consequence of grave fear, the whole election would not be valid.

[214] Cf. can. 2291, n. 11.

them, but they may not licitly make use of their right.[215] The canons sometimes prohibit specifically the exercise of the right to vote; more often they forbid the exercise of all authorized ecclesiastical acts, which include the right to vote.[216] Canons which suspend a person from the positions *(munus)* which he holds in the church, automatically suspend him from the use of the voting rights, if any, which are connected with those positions.[217] Suspension of ecclesiastical favors *(gratiae)* involves suspension of those voting rights which one has acquired by way of a privilege.

a. Anyone under excommunication incurred automatically, and not confirmed by way of a declaratory sentence, is forbidden to act in the capacity of an elector.[218] If he voted, however, his act would not be invalid, unless he is a *vitandus*.[219]

b. An elector laboring under the censure of a particular personal interdict incurred automatically, is barred from voting.[220] If the censure is confirmed by way of a declaratory sentence, however, the person is no longer merely barred, but is truly disqualified.[221]

c. A cleric who is suffering under a general suspension inflicted as a *latae sententiae* penalty is barred from partici-

[215] A simple prohibition does not imply nullity in consequence of the violation of the act that is forbidden. A prohibition can, however, be changed into a disqualification by an additional provision in another canon. Thus, for example, the prohibition of canon 2256, n. 2, which forbids a person who is barred from the exercise of authorized ecclesiastical acts, to act as sponsor at baptism or confirmation, is changed into a disqualification by canons 765 and 795. Where there is no such additional provision, however, the prohibition affects only the licitness, and not the validity of an act.

[216] Can. 2256, n. 2.

[217] *Loss* of the position would make one a non-member of the electoral body.

[218] Can. 2265, § 1, n. 1; cf. also can. 2263.

[219] Can. 2265, § 2. A person becomes a *vitandus* (one to be shunned socially) *automatically* only in one instance, namely, if he lays violent hands on the Holy Father; cf. can. 2258, § 2.

[220] Can. 2275, n. 3.

[221] Cans. 167, § 1, n. 3; 2275, n. 3; 2265, § 2.

pating in ecclesiastical elections.[222] As long as there is no sentence, his right is not taken away, but the exercise of it is forbidden. The suspension could be incurred either as a censure or as a vindictive penalty.[223]

d. A community under a general personal interdict is prohibited from using the spiritual rights which it has.[224] The right of electing is a spiritual right,[225] and is, therefore, one of the rights which the community cannot licitly exercise while under the interdict. A general personal interdict deprives the community of those rights of voting which it has as a body or a unit.[226] A general personal interdict may be either a censure or a vindictive penalty.[227] When the interdict is a vindictive penalty it is only a prohibition, whether it has been incurred automatically or imposed by way of a sentence, because nowhere does the Code of Canon Law attribute a truly disqualifying effect to a general personal interdict when it is a vindictive penalty. When it is a censure, however, a sentence would render the penalty truly incapacitating by reason of canon 167, § 1, n. 3.

e. A community of clerics which has been suspended as a body may not exercise the spiritual rights which it has as a community.[228] This penalty differs from a general personal interdict only in this, that the latter can be inflicted on any group, whereas the former can be imposed only on a body of clerics.

f. Persons who are infamous by reason of infamy of fact may not vote, since they must be repelled from the exercise of all authorized ecclesiastical acts.[229] A person incurs in-

[222] Cans. 2283; 2265, §§ 1 & 2.

[223] As explained above (pp. 115-116, footnote 108), the canons on suspension (can. 2278-2285) apply to suspension both in the nature of a censure and also in the nature of a vindictive penalty.

[224] Can. 2274, § 3.

[225] Cf. *glossa ordinaria* ad c. 51, X, *de electione et electi potestate,* I, 6, s. v. *iuri contrarium.*

[226] Cf. can. 2274, § 3.

[227] Can. 2255, § 2; 2291, n. 1.

[228] Can. 2285, § 3.

[229] Can. 2294, § 2; 2256, n. 2.

famy of fact when, because of some delict committed, or because of some morally bad behavior, he has, in the opinion of the ordinary, lost his good repute among righteous and serious-minded Catholics.[230] Infamy of fact is not a penalty;[231] the restrictions placed upon persons suffering under infamy of fact are intended not as punishments, but as a protection for the dignity of the sacred orders and of the ecclesiastical offices and functions. Infamy of fact does, however, result in the restriction of one's rights and, therefore, must be strictly interpreted.[232] The ordinary, not necessarily the ordinary of the place, and he alone has the right to decide whether a person has lost his good repute. This decision must be expressed in some sort of declaration. Only if there has been such a declaration by the ordinary, can a person be considered as infamous by reason of infamy of fact. The ordinary must investigate to determine 1) whether or not the person has actually lost his good name, and this among serious-minded members of the faithful, and 2) whether or not this loss of his good name was due to the morally bad behavior or to some delict attributable to that person. If either of these cannot be verified, the ordinary is not justified in declaring a person infamous in fact. Thus, if the person has actually been guilty of morally bad conduct, but good Catholics do not know or do not believe the rumors regarding this conduct, a person is not infamous. On the other hand, if the person has actually lost his good reputation, even among good Catholics, and this is due, not to any bad action on his part, but to malicious slander, he is not, juridically, infamous.[233]

230 Can. 2293, § 2.

231 Cf. can. 2291, which mentions only infamy of law as a vindictive penalty. Infamy of fact could be considered as an *irregularitas ex delicto.*

232 Can. 19.

233 Coronata (*Institutiones,* IV, 268) says that infamy of fact can be declared by a diocesan law or statute. It is difficult to see how the declaration of the *existence of a fact* can be made matter for a law. A law certainly cannot decide whether or not a particular group of persons are serious-minded people. Nor can a law decide

It may be noted that those who suffer under infamy of *law* incurred *ipso facto* but not confirmed by way of a declaratory sentence, are not barred from voting. It is true that canon 2294, § 1, disqualifies all those who are infamous by reason of infamy of law from the exercise of authorized ecclesiastical acts; but, as pointed out above,[234] voting is not included among those authorized ecclesiastical acts from which a person laboring under automatically incurred infamy of law is barred, since canon 167, § 1, n. 3, specifically requires a sentence before infamy of law will disqualify. Nowhere in the Code of Canon Law is there any canon excluding a person who is infamous by reason of infamy of law, from voting if there has not been a sentence. They may not, therefore, be excluded from ecclesiastical elections. It may be pointed out that the admission of a person laboring under infamy of law will not cause scandal, unless, of course, the same crime has brought on infamy of fact.

g. Those who are suspect of heresy and do not remove the cause of the suspicion after being warned are to be excluded from the exercise of the authorized ecclesiastical acts.[235] Suspicion of heresy arises only from those crimes which are specifically designated in the Code of Canon Law.[236] The exclusion from the exercise of the authorized ecclesiastical acts is to be imposed by way of a sentence, after the warning has been given and no sign of repentence has been manifested.

h. Anyone who makes an unsuccessful attempt on his own life is to be barred from the exercise of the authorized ecclesiastical acts.[237] This is a case in which the attempt to commit a delict does in itself constitute a delict.[238] The penalty must be imposed by way of a sentence.

whether a person has actually committed the action which would render him infamous. Nor can a law decide whether or not people actually believe the reports of a person's misconduct.

[234] Pp. 104-105.

[235] Can. 2315.

[236] Cf. cans. 2316; 2319, § 2; 2320; 2332; 2340, § 1; 2371.

[237] Can. 2350, § 2. [238] Can. 2212, § 4.

i. Whoever, for the purpose of marriage or of satisfying lust, abducts a woman against her will either by force or violence, or abducts in any way a woman of minor age without the knowledge or without the consent of her parents or guardians, even though she herself be willing, shall be automatically excluded from the exercise of the authorized ecclesiastical acts.[239] The precise crime being punished in canon 2353 is abduction; and the penalty is incurred even if, for some reason, the marriage or the immoral acts do not follow upon the abduction. A great deal has been written about abduction, but it is possible to treat it here only in a very summary fashion. The crime of abduction involves two elements: 1) the transportation of the woman from one place to another,[240] and 2) the intention of impeding the free exercise of the rights which the woman has over her own actions, or the rights which the parents or guardians have over the actions of daughters or wards of minor age. In the present case the purpose of the abduction must be the contracting of marriage or the satisfying of lust; if the purpose of abduction is ransom, the penalty listed in canon 2353 is not incurred. If a woman of minor age freely accompanied the man for immoral purposes and her parents or guardians were so depraved as to consent to the action, the delict of abduction would not be committed. A woman is a minor till she has completed her twenty-first year.[241] The consent of both parents is ordinarily required for the marriage of a minor. If the parents disagree, however, the will of the father is to prevail, because he is the head of the family. If the daughter is under the authority not of the

[239] Can. 2353.

[240] Abduction as an impediment to marriage (can. 1074) does not require transportation of the woman from one place to another; forceful detention in a place whither she freely went, suffices. For the delict of abduction, however, there is postulated the transportation of the woman from one place to another; cf. Cappello, *Tractatus Canonico-Moralis* (5 vols., Vols. I & II, 5. ed.; Vol. III & IV, 3. ed.; Vol. V, 6. ed., Romae: Marietti, 1943-1951), V (*De Matrimonio*), 453 (hereafter cited *De Sacramentis*).

[241] Can. 88, § 1.

father but of the mother, the consent of the mother alone is required.[242] If the parents or guardians have granted independence to the girl who is still in her minority, it can be presumed that they do not object to her marrying. If a minor daughter has married, she is freed from the authority of her parents, and their consent would not be needed for a subsequent marriage of the daughter after the death of her husband, even should the girl be still a minor. If a man and a woman of minor age fled to the ordinary to seek his permission to marry, against the will of the girl's parents, the delict of abduction would not be committed, for such an act is not an unlawful circumvention of the parents' authority.[243] Only the abduction of a *woman* is punished through the law enacted in canon 2353.[244]

j. A lay person who has been legitimately condemned for the crime of homicide, or of abduction of a person of either sex who has not attained the age of puberty, or of selling a human being for slavery or some other evil purpose, or of usury, or of robbery, or of qualified theft, or of non-qualified theft of a notable amount, or of arson, or of malicious destruction of property in a very notable amount, or of grave mutilation, or of wounding, or of violence, is automatically excluded from the exercise of the authorized ecclesiastical acts and from any function he may have in the Church.[245]

Homicide is the deliberate (though not necessarily premeditated) and unjust taking of a human life. Abortion is homicide, but that crime is separately punished (with excommunication) in canon 2350, § 1. The abduction of a person below the age of puberty need not be for the purpose of satisfying the abductor's lust; any unlawful purpose will suffice for the incurring of the penalty. Sale of a human

[242] The daughter could be under the sole care of the mother because the father has died, or because, in a legitimate decree of separation, the care and education of the children has been entrusted to the mother; cf. can. 1132.

[243] Cf. can. 1034.

[244] Cf. can. 2354.

[245] Can. 2354, § 1.

being is the exchange of a human person for anything of temporal value. Usury is the charging of unjust interest on money loaned. Robbery is the unjust taking of the property of another by force; theft is the unjust taking of the property by stealth. Qualified theft is theft accompanied with a circumstance which changes the moral species of that act, as, for example, the theft of a sacred object (sacrilege). The Code of Canon Law has not defined what is to be considered as a notable amount in relation to theft. The estimation of a "notable amount" will vary with time and place. The civil law distinction between theft as a misdemeanor and theft as a felony could, perhaps, be used as a norm for judging what is to be considered theft of a notable amount in a particular locality. The same norm could be used for judging the notableness of the amount of property maliciously destroyed. Serious mutilation would include any permanent impairment of faculties or serious disfigurement. Wounding includes any serious physical harm, whether or not a weapon is used, and whether or not the injury is permanent. Violence is any attack which inflicts or seeks to inflict serious bodily harm.

"Lay person" in paragraph 1 of canon 2354 should be taken in the strict sense as not including lay religious or lay members of communities of the common life. They should be included rather under paragraph 2 of this canon, for they enjoy the privileges of clerics in the matter of trials.[246]

The punishment for the crimes described in canon 2354, § 1, could be inflicted by either the ecclesiastical court or the civil court, since these crimes constitute matters relating to a mixed forum, that is, the perpetrators of these crimes are held answerable to either of the two courts.[247] Condemnation by either court is a *legal condemnation* and, therefore, condemnation by either court results in the incurring of the penalties described in canon 2354, § 1. If a person were tried but not condemned, or not tried at all, he would

[246] Cf. cans. 614; 680.

[247] Cf. cans. 2198; 1553, § 2.

not incur these penalties, even though he committed one of the crimes.

k. Lay persons who have committed the delict of public adultery, or who publicly live in concubinage, or who have been legally condemned for other crimes against the sixth commandment, are to be excluded from the exercise of the authorized ecclesiastical acts until they show signs of true repentance.[248]

Adultery is sexual intercourse between a man and a woman who are not husband and wife, but of whom at least one is bound by a marriage bond. To commit the delict of adultery, knowledge of the existence of the marriage bond is necessary; otherwise, the sin is one of fornication, not one of adultery. The usual case of public adultery will be "marriage" between two parties one or both of whom have obtained a civil divorce.

The delict of concubinage presupposes that two unmarried persons live together as husband and wife in a more or less stable union *(ad instar matrimonii)*. The usual case of public concubinage occurs when a Catholic attempts marriage before either a civil magistrate or a non-Catholic minister. When a Catholic is involved, such "marriage" ceremonies are absolutely meaningless with reference to juridical effects.[249]

The delict of adultery and the delict of concubinage must be public before they will induce the penalty enacted in canon 2357, § 2. "Public" according to canon 2197, n. 1, means that the delict is already divulged or that, as can be seen from the circumstances, it will readily become divulged. If two persons lived together as husband and wife and were believed to be such, they would not be liable for this penalty.

[248] Can. 2357, § 2.

[249] Such ceremonies do not provide sufficient grounds for the subsequent union as a putative marriage, even if the non-Catholic party is in good faith; cf. *AAS*, XLI (1949), 158. The Church does not deign to dignify a civil ceremony involving a Catholic, with the designation of "invalid marriage"; cf. *AAS*, XXI (1929), 170; Cappello, *De Sacramentis*, V, 515-516.

If a lay person is guilty of some sin against the sixth commandment other than adultery and public concubinage, and he is legally condemned for it by either the ecclesiastical court or the civil court,[250] he is to be excluded from voting.

The penalty of canon 2357, § 2, is not incurred automatically but is to be inflicted by way of a sentence. It seems strange that a sentence should be required, but the use of the passive subjunctive in the canon leaves no room for any other interpretation. This penalty continues till the person shows true signs of repentance. True repentance requires mainly that the person desist from his crime, and that he return to the sacraments. Vermeersch-Creusen state that it remains for the ordinary to judge the sufficiency of the signs of repentance.[251] This is, no doubt, correct when there is question about the sufficiency of the signs, but when the sufficiency of the signs is obvious, there is no need of a decision by the ordinary. The canon does not indicate the need of any such decision, and therefore none should be required.

1. Catholics who dare to enter a mixed marriage, even a valid one, without the granting of a dispensation by the Church are automatically excluded from the exercise of the authorized ecclesiastical acts till they shall have obtained a dispensation from the ordinary.[252]

A mixed marriage is a marriage between a Catholic (whether baptized as a Catholic or converted to the faith after having been validly baptized as a non-Catholic) and a baptized non-Catholic.[253] Canon 2375 deals only with marriages duly celebrated according to the form prescribed by the Church; for, as explained above,[254] any other ceremony does not have even the appearance of marriage when a Catholic is involved. A Catholic could commit the delict mentioned in canon 2375 by concealing the fact that his (or

[250] This is a matter of mixed forum; cf. cans. 1553, § 2; 2198.
[251] *Epitome*, III, 352.
[252] Can. 2375.
[253] Can. 1060.
[254] P. 155.

her) partner in the marriage was not a Catholic.[255] Another instance would be the case in which the parties obtained a dispensation but gave insincere guarantees, because in this case the dispensation would be invalid.[256] Since the penalty described in canon 2375 is incurred automatically and since the canon contains the words *"ausi fuerint,"* any diminution of imputability will excuse a person from incurring the penalty.[257] The penalty ceases automatically when a valid dispensation is obtained. If a dispensation has been obtained by means of false guarantees and the non-Catholic party refuses to make sincere guarantees, the ordinary can dispense from this penalty if the Catholic party promises to do everything in his (or her) power to see that the substance of the guarantees is carried out.

m. Electoral colleges, chapters *(conventus)*, and all others concerned, who admit an elected, presented, or nominated person to an ecclesiastical benefice, office, or dignity before he has shown his letter of confirmation or appointment are automatically suspended from the right of voting, nominating or presenting until the Holy See dispenses them.[258] *"Conventus,"* in its specific pre-Code meaning, signified a chapter of religious, but it was also used interchangeably with "chapter" in a wider sense.[259] Admitting anyone to an office (or benefice, or dignity) would be signified by such acts as the electoral college's handing over of the instruments of the office (keys, books, seals), and the

[255] If the deception was not detected the marriage would be valid, since the impediment of mixed religion is only of a prohibitory and not of a diriment character.

[256] Cf. cans. 1061; 40. For an account of some cases in which dispensation (from disparity of cult) were declared invalid by reason of the insincerity of the guarantees, cf. Bouscaren-O'Connor, *1953 Supplement* to Bouscaren, *The Canon Law Digest*, ad canon 1071.

[257] Can. 2229, § 2.

[258] Cf. can. 2394, n. 3.

[259] "Capitulum seu conventus quae duo in iure summuntur promiscue . . . quamvis in praxi Capitulum vocari soleat Congregatio, seu Collegium Clericorum saecularium, et Conventus Congregatio Religiosorum."—Pichler, Lib. I, tit. VI, n. 19.

taking of an oath of obedience to the chosen candidate as the recognized superior. "Admitting an elected person before confirmation" includes admitting a *postulated* person before his postulation has been admitted.[260] "Office" must be taken in a strict sense, because there is question here of a penalty.[261] Canon 2394, n. 3, enacts the penalty for the whole electoral body. This is a change from the pre-Code legislation, in which only the guilty members were punished and the exclusive right of voting then devolved upon the innocent members.[262] The reason for the change may have been that the Holy See did not wish an election to be conducted by a minority of the electors. The admitting of the candidate to the office must be an act of the collegiate person, that is, a majority of the members must concur in the act. If the majority objected to the intrusion, the collegiate body would not incur the penalty. The canon does not *take away* the right of electing, but only suspends it. Those who have incurred this penalty could vote validly, but it is not likely that they would presume to use their right while under this prohibition. The cancelling out of the penalty is reserved to the Holy See.[263] This reservation may seem unusual, but it is indicative of the careful watch which the Holy See maintains against the rise of abuses in the filling of ecclesiastical offices and benefices.

[260] Cf. *Normae* of 1901, nn. 235, 236; also n. 238, where the *re-election* of a Superioress General who has already served for twelve years, is said to require *confirmation* by the Holy See. This, obviously, is a case of postulation. In the legislation of the Decretals persons who admitted a candidate before the admission of his postulation were deprived of their voting rights; cf. c. 23, X, *de electione et electi potestate*, I, 6.

[261] Cf. cans. 145; 2219.

[262] C. 23, X, *de electione et electi potestate*, I, 6.

[263] The special mentioning of this reservation shows that the penalty is only prohibitory and not invalidating. If it were invalidating there would be no need to mention the reservation, since canon 2237, § 1, n. 3, has already reserved electoral disqualifications to the Holy See.

ARTICLE VIII. EXPULSION FROM AN ELECTION

Expulsion of a person from an election has an element which is substantial and an element which is purely administrative. The substantial element is the decision to exclude a person. The administrative element is the execution of the expulsion. The decision to exclude or not to exclude belongs to the electoral body, whereas the execution belongs to the president of the electoral body.[264] The "decision" to exclude or not to exclude should be taken in a restricted sense to mean the resolving of *doubtful* cases, that is, cases in which the person has at least the appearance of a right to be admitted to the election. When it is obvious that the person has no right to be present, no decision by the electoral college would be required. Thus, if a stranger wanders into an election by mistake, the president can ask him to leave without asking the whole college for a decision. When a decision by the college is needed, it is to be obtained by way of a majority vote.[265] In making their decision the electors are to resolve this question: Is it morally certain that this person does not have a right to be present at this election? If he is not morally certain, an elector may not vote for the person's expulsion. The reason for this is that in a case of doubt a person is to be left in the possession of his rights.[266] The electors' votes are not to express mere opinion, that is, probable judgment, about the excluding of the person, but moral certitude. If the vote ends in a tie, the person must be left in possession of his right. There is not a conflict here between the common good and the good of the individ-

[264] The relation of the president and the electoral college is similar to the relation between the "*praeses*" and the collegiate tribunal. The *praeses* acts alone in purely administrative matters, such as the issuing of citations, the appointing of notaries, the admitting of proxies; but the tribunal must act collegiately in matters affecting the substance of the trial. Cf. can. 1577, § 1; Torré, *Processus Matrimonialis* (Neapoli: M. D'Auria, 1947), pp. 20-22.

[265] Can. 101, § 1, n. 1.

[266] "In pari delicto et causa potior est causa conditio possidentis." —Reg. 65, R. J., in VI°.

ual. The community will not necessarily suffer harm because a person with a doubtful right has been admitted for voting. The person with the doubtful right may be quite capable of voting wisely. If it is doubtful whether or not the person is capable of voting sensibly,[267] he should be persuaded not to make use of his right. If he does not agree, however, he may not be excluded from the election. The common good will hardly be jeopardized by his one vote. Even when several doubtfully qualified electors are admitted the common good can be protected by means other than their expulsion. Thus, if an obviously unfit candidate was selected, the other electors could still appeal to the competent superior to nullify the election.

If a person is laboring under a doubtful disqualification from which the Church usually dispenses, a dispensation could be sought for safety's sake. Thus, if after the election was over it was discovered that the doubtfully qualified person was in fact not qualified, there would be no need to investigate to learn whether or not his vote had decided the election and no need, if his vote did decide the election, to hold a new election.

If an elector feels that he has been expelled from the election unjustly, he may have recourse to the competent superior to have the election annulled and to have a new election summoned, at which he could be present. The Code of Canon Law does not actually mention this right, but canon 162, § 2, which grants this right of appeal to the elector who was not summoned to the election, may be applied by way of analogy.[268] It is only equitable that an elector who is deprived of his voting rights by being unjustly expelled, should have the same right to have his rights restored as has the elector who is deprived of his voting rights in consequence of not having been summoned. If the appeal is to be made, it must

[267] A person in a state of intoxication, for example would be doubtfully qualified to vote if he was doubtfully capable of placing a human act (cf. can. 167, § 1, n. 1).

[268] Cf. can. 20.

be done within three available days *(tempus utile)* after the expulsion.[269]

If the electors admit one whom they know with certainty to be disqualified, or prohibited from voting, they may be punished by the ordinary. Admitting a disqualified or a prohibited person to an election is certainly a violation of the substantial form of election, and can be punished in virtue of canon 2391, § 2.[270]

Article IX. Absent Voters

After the convocation has been lawfully issued, the right of electing belongs to those electors who are present on the day stated in the summons, the right of voting by letter or proxy being excluded unless the particular law specifies otherwise.[271] Absence is not so much a disqualification as the lack of a required condition. It is not a defect in the elector himself. Only in a very loose sense can he be said to be disqualified, inasmuch as he is one who cannot vote.

The prohibition of voting by proxy was introduced by the Code of Canon Law, though the prohibition of voting by letter dates from the time of Pope Boniface VIII (1294-1303).[272] If a particular law permits voting by proxy, it could happen that an elector would have the right of casting two votes, one his own, and one the absent voter's. Canon 164 forbids a person to vote twice in his own name, but it does not forbid him to vote twice if one of the votes is cast in the name of someone else.

If an elector is present in the house where the election is to take place but he is unable to attend because of illness, his written vote shall be taken by the tellers, unless this is against particular laws or customs.[273] It must be noted that the voter must be in the house where the election is taking place, and the reason for his absence must be illness.

[269] Cf. can. 162, § 2.
[270] Cf. Coronata, *Institutiones*, IV, 667.
[271] Can. 163.
[272] Cf. *supra*, p. 13.
[273] Can. 168.

If these conditions are not fulfilled, then a potential elector who is not present in the room where the election takes place, may not vote.

Article X. Renunciation of Electoral Rights

Occasionally a person could renounce his right of voting and thereby cease to be qualified as an elector. In any consideration relative to the renunciation of voting rights, one must look directly to the nature of the right itself. The right of voting may be a privilege pure and simple.[274] In that event the person is free to renounce his right even without giving a reason.[275] The renunciation would become effective upon acceptance by the competent superior, that is, by the who who granted the privilege or by his superior.[276] The right of voting, however, as generally enjoyed, is not only a privilege; it is also a duty. The right is given primarily for the good of the community and not (primarily) for the good of the individual who possesses the right. In this case the right cannot be renounced, neither by an individual elector nor by an electoral college as a whole.[277] When voting is a duty as well as a privilege an electoral college may not renounce the right of voting either perpetually or for a single instance. There are, of course, reasons which justify one in not *using* his right, but not using one's right is not the same as renouncing it.

[274] The Holy See, for example, could grant a lay person the privilege of voting in an ecclesiastical election.

[275] Can. 72, § 2.

[276] Can. 72, § 1.

[277] Cf. can. 72, §§ 3 & 4. If the particular law permits the renunciation of the right, that law may be followed. Usually, however, the particular law is very intolerant of the renunciation of one's voting rights. The particular often stresses the duty to vote.

CHAPTER IX

THE CESSATION OF DISQUALIFICATIONS AND PROHIBITIONS

Different disqualifications will cease in different ways, depending on their natures. Thus, natural disqualifications will cease in one way, legal disqualifications in another; penal disqualifications will require conditions for their cessation which are not required for the cessation of non-penal disqualifications. Censures cease differently from vindictive penalties. This chapter, then, will be divided according to the natures of the various disqualifications and prohibitions. Preceding the treatment of the cessation of disqualifications and prohibitions themselves, there will be a short discussion of a matter closely allied, namely, the cessation of the *obligation to observe* either the penalty of disqualification or the hindrance arising through some specific prohibition.

ARTICLE I. CESSATION OF THE OBLIGATION TO OBSERVE A DISQUALIFICATION OR A PROHIBITION

Natural disqualifications must always be observed; there is no possibility for a person's being excused from their observance. The non-observance of non-penal disqualifications is not treated in the Code of Canon Law, for it could scarcely happen that a situation would arise which would justify the non-observance of a non-penal disqualification. In regard to penal disqualifications and prohibitions, however, there could easily arise a situation wherein equity would require that a person be excused from observing the penalty. Canon 2232, § 1, states, therefore: "*Latae sententiae* penalties, whether medicinal or vindictive, automatically bind the delinquent, if he is conscious of his delict, in both forums; before a declaratory sentence, however, the delinquent is excused from observing the penalty whenever he cannot observe it without incurring infamy, and no one can demand the observance of the penalty in the external forum unless the penalty is notorious. . . ." This concession is granted only in connection with *latae sententiae* incurred penalties, and then only before the rendering of any sentence. The reason for not extending this concession to persons laboring under a penalty either imposed or confirmed by a sentence is that such persons are not deserving of this favor precisely in view of their great obstinacy. When there is danger of infamy no one can demand that a person laboring under a non-notorious *latae sententiae* penalty, as long as a sentence has not intervened, observe the penalty in the external forum. Before expelling a person from an election, therefore, the electoral body must consider the possibility of the emergence of infamy for the expelled person. If there is a reasonable probability of the person's being defamed as a result of his expulsion, and provided that there has been no sentence, the collegiate body has no right to expel the person. An individual member of the college, before bringing up an objection against a fellow member, should consider whether or not the person might not be validly and licitly exercising his right to vote in virtue of canon 2232, § 1. He should be slow to bring objections lest the fellow member be unjustly defamed among the other members of the electoral body.

A second way in which the obligation to observe a penal disqualification or prohibition can be suspended is described in canon 2290, § 1. The canon states that in very urgent occult cases, if through the observance of a *latae sententiae* vindictive penalty the guilty person would betray himself, with infamy and scandal resulting, any confessor may in the sacramental forum suspend the obligation of observing the penalty, but he must impose upon the offender the obligation of having recourse at least within a month by letter and through the confessor, if this is possible without serious inconvenience, and without the use of names, to the Sacred Penitentiary or to a bishop endowed with the necessary faculty, and of abiding by the mandates received. A case is urgent if there is a reasonable probability that infamy or scandal will occur if the person is obliged to observe the penalty and if there is not a reasonably adequate amount of time to approach the competent superior in order to obtain a dispensation. The case must be occult, that is, either the delict itself must be unknown and not readily susceptible to becoming known (material occultness), or the moral imputability of the delictual fact must be unrecognized and not apt easily to be recognized (formal occultness).[1] Canon 2290, § 1, is wider in scope than canon 2232, § 1, inasmuch as the favorable ruling of the latter canon is applicable only if there has been no declaratory sentence, whereas the faculty granted by the former canon can be used even after a declaratory sentence, provided the case remains occult.[2] The suspension dealt with in canon 2290 differs from the suspension mentioned in canon 2232 also in this, that the former suspension, once given, holds for all cases, even when there is no danger of infamy or scandal, whereas the latter suspension holds only for those instances wherein there is danger of infamy or scandal. The one suspension operates as something continuous or habitual, the other, *per modum actus*. Any confessor can use the faculty granted in canon 2290, but the confessor must have jurisdiction to hear this particular person's confession, since the faculty can be used only in the sacramental forum. The period of one month allotted for the recourse is usable time. If the recourse cannot be made without grave inconvenience, it need not be made. If the confessor can foresee at the time of the granting of the dispensation that recourse will be gravely inconvenient for a period exceeding a month, he can dispense entirely from the penalty, without imposing any obligation of having recourse to a higher superior. When recourse is necessary, the suspension of the effect of the penalty lasts till the penitent receives a reply from the superior. If the penitent culpably fails to have recourse within the specified time, the suspension lapses with the lapse of the month of usable time. The recourse need not be made through the confessor or by means of a letter; the phrase "*per epistolam et con-*

[1] Can. 2197, nn. 1 & 4.

[2] A sentence renders a case *notorious* (with notoriety of law) but not necessarily *public* (non-occult); cf. can. 2197.

fessarium" is to be taken as requiring simply the minimum. The penitent could write the letter himself, or he could go personally to the proper authority. When recourse is made to the Holy See the petition is to be sent to the Sacred Penitentiary, since the matter pertains to the sacramental forum.[3] Canon 2290, § 1, allows recourse to be made to the bishop, but not to other ordinaries.[4] If a confessor should doubt whether or not the case is really urgent, or whether there is any danger of infamy or scandal, he may validly and licitly suspend the sentence in virtue of canon 209.

Before closing this article, it may be noted that ignorance does not excuse from the effect of a disqualification.[5] Ignorance may excuse one from *incurring* a disqualification, but once the disqualification has been incurred, ignorance will not excuse from the effect of the disqualification.

Article II. Cessation of Non-Penal Disqualifications and Prohibitions

Section 1. Natural Disqualifications

When a person is incapable of performing human acts, he is incapable of voting. This disqualification, obviously, cannot be dispensed from; no positive human law or dispensation can change the fact that a person cannot act humanly. This disability for voting ceases only when the disability for acting humanly has ceased. Thus, for example, an insane elector ceases to be disqualified when he regains his sanity. The disqualification ceases automatically upon a

[3] Can. 258, § 1.

[4] One may wonder why the canon prescribes that the recourse be made only to the bishop and not to other ordinaries, but in view of the wording of the canon there is no alternative but to exclude ordinaries and other superiors who are not bishops. The exclusion of superiors who are not bishops must have been deliberate, for canons 2252 and 2254, § 1, which treat of similar cases in regard to censures, very clearly include, besides bishops, all other superiors who have the faculty of absolving from the censure. The difference in the wording of canon 2290 and canons 2252 and 2254 must indicate a difference in meaning.

[5] Can. 16, § 1.

person's obtaining or recovering his ability to act humanly. Sometimes, however, a person must prove that the impediment has ceased. A person who is habitually insane, for instance, must prove that he is enjoying a lucid interval before he can be allowed to vote, since the presumption is against his being sane at any given time. More often, however, no proof is required. Everyone, for example, is incapable of human acts in early infancy, but one does not have to prove the cessation of this impediment; its cessation is presumed by law after the completion of the seventh year of life.[6] Again, sleep renders a person incapable (temporarily) of performing human acts, but, since it is generally quite obvious whether or not a person is sleeping, no one will be asked to prove that he is not asleep.

SECTION 2. LEGAL DISQUALIFICATIONS

Non-penal disqualifications established by law cease automatically when the cause of the disqualification ceases; they can cease also by acquisition of a privilege or by way of a dispensation. An example of the automatic cessation of a disability would be the cessation of the disqualification of an exclaustrated religious upon his return to his religious community. The disqualification of the lack of the legally required age ceases upon one's attaining the required age. Cessation of the disqualification of non-membership occurs by one's becoming a member of the body in the usual way.

A privilege, which is a private law that confers on some person (or persons) a special favor contrary to or outside of the law, can point a way to the cessation of disqualifications enacted by the Code of Canon Law or by the constitutions of the various bodies in the Church. Thus, religious who have taken only their temporary vows, persons below

[6] Can. 88, § 3. A legal presumption could, of course, be overthrown by contrary factual evidence. If the factual evidence contrary to the presumption is sufficient to give moral certainty, factual evidence sufficient to destroy that moral certitude must be brought in support of the presumption; otherwise the presumption must yield to the contrary facts.

the age of puberty, non-members, and even lay persons can obtain the privilege of participating in an ecclesiastical election. A privilege can remove a disqualification directly or indirectly. The removal of the disability is direct when the disqualified person himself receives the privilege of sharing in the election; the removal is indirect when the electing body receives the privilege of admitting the disqualified person to the election. Privileges can be obtained through a direct grant of the competent superior, through the juridical agency of legal prescription, in consequence of an entrenched laudable custom, and by way of associated participation *(communicatio)* in *forma accessoria.*[7] The authority competent to grant privileges contrary to a law is the legislator who enacted the law or his superior. A privilege granting voting rights contrary to the universal law of the Code of Canon Law can be given, therefore, only by the Holy See. The juridical agency of legal prescription provides a method for obtaining voting privileges which are contrary to the particular law. It does not avail for obtaining privileges contrary to the universal law of the Code of Canon Law, however, since such privileges can be granted only by the Holy See and, hence, are not subject to the juridical agency of legal prescription.[8] Associated participation in *forma accessoria* is a manner of acquiring privileges in which the privileges enjoyed by an Order of Regulars are accorded automatically to the nuns of the same Order. There is a remote possibility that such an associated participation could serve as a means of lifting a disqualification. If, for example, the religious with temporary vows in an Order of Regulars were to receive the privilege of voting in the chapter, the religious with temporary vows in the communities of nuns of the same Order would automatically receive the same privilege. The possibility at the present time of anyone obtaining the right of voting in consequence of an established customary usage is very slight. There is little chance that a disqualified person will be re-

[7] Cf. cans. 63, § 1; 64; 65; 613.

[8] Can. 1509, n. 2.

peatedly admitted to the elections during a period of forty uninterrupted years, the length of time necessary for a practice to become a true legal custom,[9] without interference from the proper superiors. An individaul person cannot acquire voting rights by way of customary usage, since only a community capable of receiving a law is capable of inducing a custom.[10] A community could obtain by way of custom the privilege of admitting disqualified persons to its elections, or it could obtain the privilege of voting in the elections conducted by another electoral body (this latter possibility being highly improbable). In no case could a community of lay persons (that is, lay persons who are neither clerics nor religious) obtain the right to vote in elections conducted by a body of clerics or religious. Such an intrusion would be considered as a violation of the freedom of the Church, and any custom allowing such a practice would be unreasonable, and, therefore, incapable of obtaining the force of law.[11]

Dispensation provides a more frequent way for the ceasing of a disqualification. Dispensation is a relaxation of the law in a special case, made by the lawful authority for a just and reasonable cause.[12] The competent superior for a dispensation will be determined by the source of the disqualification. The disqualifications established in the universal law can be dispensed from ordinarily only by the Holy See, or by one to whom the Holy See has granted the power either explicitly or implicitly.[13] In the case of a doubt of fact about a disqualification the ordinary can dispense, provided it is a case in which the Holy See usually dispenses, even though the disqualification is one established in the universal law.[14] Every ordinary, not just the ordinary of

[9] Can. 28.
[10] Can. 26.
[11] Cf. cans. 27, § 1; 2390, § 2; Beste, *Introductio in Codicem,* p. 95; c. 56, X, *de electione et electi potestate,* I, 6.
[12] Cf. cans. 80 & 84.
[13] Can. 81.
[14] Can. 15.

the place, has this power for his own subjects.[15] The ordinary can dispense also in cases wherein recourse to the Holy See is difficult and for lack of, or through a delay in, the granting of the needed dispensation there arises the danger of great harm, provided it is a case in which the Apostolic See usually grants the dispensation.[16] Only non-penal disqualifications are being treated in this article, however, and it is difficult to visualize a situation wherein great harm could result from the observance of such a disqualification.

Disqualifications established by all authorities subordinate to the Holy Father can be dispensed from by the Holy See, by the one who established the disqualification, and by anyone to whom either of the foregoing has granted the faculties of dispensing. The Holy See has the power of dispensing because of its immediate and supreme authority over all persons in the Church. The one who established the disability can, of course, relax his own law. The power of dispensing may be delegated to a subordinate through a special act of delegation, or it may be granted in the law itself. Canon 291, § 2, for instance, grants the ordinary of the place the power of dispensing for a just cause and in a particular case from decrees of plenary and provincial councils. Thus, if a provincial council should establish certain disqualifications for electors in associations of the faithful in the province, the ordinary of the place could on occasion dispense an individual from such a disability. Chapters in religious communities sometimes establish disqualifications. The proper superior for the granting of a dispensation from such disqualifications is the chapter itself or the specific superior designated by the chapter.

SECTION 3. NON-PENAL PROHIBITIONS

Since infamy of fact is not a penalty,[17] the exclusion of those who labor under infamy of fact must be considered

[15] Can. 198, § 1.

[16] Can. 81.

[17] Cf. *supra*, p. 150.

as a non-penal prohibition. It is the only non-penal prohibition in the Code of Canon Law. Infamy of fact ceases when in the judgment of the ordinary, in view of the circumstances and especially of a long-continued amendment of life, the culprit has regained his good repute in the eyes of upright and serious members of the faithful.[18] Infamy of fact binds only in the place where it is incurred; in places where the culprit's delict is unknown the culprit is not impeded in the exercise of his rights. The question may be raised: "Is a declaration by the ordinary always necessary for the cessation of infamy of fact in the place where it was incurred?" In the opinion of this writer a declaration is needed only in cases in which there is doubt as to its cessation.[19] It would seem inequitable for the Code to demand a declaration from the ordinary when the person has obviously regained his good reputation among the people of the community. It would also put an unnecessary hardship on a person to require that he petition the ordinary for a declaration when the period of amendment has continued for such a long time that the ordinary himself has probably forgotten the whole affair. Then, too, the prohibition would usually amount to a permanent prohibition simply because the ordinary usually forgets to give a declaration and the culprit is usually too embarrassed to petition for a declaration.[20] It is advisable for the ordinary to prescribe, at the time of the declaration of the infamy of fact, the period of

[18] Can. 2295.

[19] It may seem that the writer is inconsistent in requiring a declaration by the ordinary in all cases wherein there is question of the incurring of infamy of fact (cf. *supra*, p. 150), but not in all cases wherein there is question of the cessation of the infamy. The apparent inconsistency disappears, however, when it is seen that he is using the more benign interpretation (can. 2219, § 1) in both cases. Cf. Coronata, *Institutiones*, IV, 269.

[20] Even if a declaration by the ordinary were required in all cases, a person could use *epikeia* to excuse himself in cases wherein observance of the impediment would result in the loss of his good name. If no declaration is required, then, once the person has recovered his good repute he is free to vote even in cases wherein his abstention from voting would not result in the loss of his good name.

time—depending on the seriousness and the notoriety of the delict—necessary for the regaining of the culprit's good reputation. By way of analogy with canon 672, three years of amendment is usually considered as a long period of amendment.[21] This may set some sort of standard, but it cannot be used as a uniform rule. Some delicts are more easily forgotten and amended, some less easily, depending on the nature of the delict and the identity of the persons involved. A shorter period of amendment, therefore, will be required for some crimes, a longer period for other crimes.

ARTICLE III. CESSATION OF PENAL DISQUALIFICATIONS AND PROHIBITIONS

The remission of penalties, whether by way of absolution in regard to censures or by way of dispensation in regard to vindictive penalties, can be granted only by him who inflicted the penalty, by his successor, by his competent superior, or by one to whom he has granted this power.[22] Canon 2236, § 1, sets out the general principle of competency in the matter of the removal of penalties. This general canon is developed in greater detail in subsequent canons. "The one who inflicted *(tulit)* the penalty" is to be understood to include both the one who established the penalty and the one who actually imposed it.[23] The general rule of the reserva-

[21] Woywod, *A Practical Commentary on the Code of Canon Law,* II, 504-505; Coronata, *Institutiones,* IV, 269.

[22] Can. 2236, § 1.

[23] There is some dispute whether the remission of penalties is reserved to the one who instituted them or whether they may be removed also by the one who inflicted them; cf. Christ, *Dispensation from Vindicative Penalties,* The Catholic University of America Canon Law Studies, n. 174 (Washington, D.C.: The Catholic University of America Press, 1943) pp. 77-86. Since the Code of Canon Law uses the verb *ferre* in the meaning of "establish" and also in the meaning of "impose" (cf., e.g., can. 13, § 1; 2217, § 1, n. 3; 2247, § 1), it seems to be an arbitrary restriction to limit it to the meaning of "establish." Further, paragraph 3 of canon 2236 states that a judge may not remove a penalty which was established by a superior even though the judge himself has imposed the penalty. If the removal of a penalty is already reserved by the first paragraph of the canon

tion of penalties is greatly relaxed by later canons.[24]

Anyone who can dispense from a law can remit the penalties attached to the violation of that law.[25] This rule applies whether one has the power of dispensing from the law in his own name, or whether one has the power from another. Some may not wish to concede the power of dispensing from the penalty attached to the law to those who can dispense from the law only in virtue of *delegated* authority. Since canon 2236, § 2, however, makes no distinction between those who dispense in their own name and those who dispense in virtue of authority delegated from another, no distinction should be made. Further, one who dispenses in his own name is either the lawgiver or his superior. The power of dispensing which these persons have, however, is already affirmed in the first paragraph of canon 2236. If the second paragraph is not to be a meaningless repetition, it must refer to all who have the power of dispensing, inclusive of those who receive this power from another. A consideration of the composition of a penal law will also support the view that one who can dispense from the law, even by virtue of delegated power, can remit the penalty attached to the violation of that law. A penal law has two parts: the one reflects the prescriptive order, and the other points to the penalty attached to the violation of that order. The obligation to obey the prescriptive order and the obligation to observe the penalty stem from the same source, namely, the law. If one has the power to release from the whole law, one can release also from a part of the law, that is, from the penalty attached to the violation of the law.[26] The legislator could indeed have restricted the power of the delegated person so that he could release

to the superior who established the penalty, this third paragraph would be a useless repetition. It is clear that the third paragraph is intended as an exception to the general rule enacted in the first paragraph.

[24] Cf., e.g., cans. 2237; 2245, § 4.

[25] Can. 2236, §2.

[26] Cf. Christ, *Dispensation from Vindicative Penalties*, pp. 68-70.

from the prescriptive order of the law, but not from the penalty. Nevertheless, he did not choose to do so.

A judge who in virtue of his office inflicts a penalty established by his superior, cannot remit the penalty once he has applied it.[27]

The remission of a penalty extorted by means of force or through the duress of grave fear is automatically invalid.[28]

The remission of a penalty can be granted not only to a person who is present but also to one who is absent. It can be granted absolutely or conditionally; it can be granted in the external forum or simply in the internal forum. It can also be granted orally, but if the penalty was imposed in writing, it is wise to remit the penalty in writing also.[29]

SECTION 1. ABSOLUTION FROM CENSURES

A censure, when once contracted, can be removed only by means of an absolution.[30] Absolution, in this matter, is an act of the virtue of justice by which the legitimate superior frees a culprit who has receded from his contumacy from the bond of a censure.[31] Unlike the dispensation from vindictive penalties, which is a favor, the absolution from censures is an act of justice; the delinquent has a right to absolution as soon as he recedes from his contumacy.[32] A person is considered as having desisted from his contumacy when he has truly repented of his delict, and has at the same time made proper satisfaction, or at least sincerely promised to make satisfaction, for the damages and scandal he has caused.[33]

Once a censure has been removed it does not revive except in the case wherein an obligation has been imposed under

[27] Can. 2236, § 3.

[28] Can. 2238.

[29] Can. 2239, §§ 1 & 2.

[30] Can. 2248, § 1; cf. can. 2241, § 1.

[31] Cf. Coronata, *Institutiones*, IV, 176.

[32] Can. 2248, § 2.

[33] Can. 2242, § 3.

the penalty of relapse into the censure if the obligation remains unfulfilled.[34] The censure "revives" in the sense that a new censure of the same species is incurred for the nonobservance of the obligation imposed. The new censure is numerically distinct from the old one. Imposing an obligation with the threat of an automatic relapse into the censure is equivalent to the imposing of a precept under threat of censure, and can be imposed, therefore, only by a person who has jurisdiction over the delinquent in the external forum.[35]

A person seeking absolution from censures must indicate all the cases; otherwise the absolution is valid only for the case he has mentioned. If the granted absolution is of a general character, then it is valid also for those cases, with exception of those cases which are reserved to the Holy See in a most special way, which in good faith were left unmentioned, even though the petition for absolution contemplated simply a particular case. The general absolution is not valid for those cases which were left unmentioned in bad faith.[36] Canon 2249, § 2, is to be interpreted in the sense that the general absolution is valid for all those censures which were concealed in good faith provided the one granting the absolution has the power of absolving from them.[37] It seems also that the delinquent need mention only those censures from which the particular superior or confessor can absolve in order to gain the benefit which canon 2249, § 2, accords.[38]

[34] Can. 2248, § 3. For examples, cf. cans. 2252; 2254, § 1.

[35] Cf. Vermeersch-Creusen, *Epitome*, III, 267; Woywod, *A Practical Commentary on the Code of Canon Law*, II, 478.

[36] Can. 2249, § 2.

[37] Vermeersch-Creusen, *Epitome*, III, 267; cf. Stadalnikas, *Reservation of Censures*, The Catholic University of America Canon Law Studies, n. 208 (Washington, D.C.: The Catholic University of America Press, 1944), pp. 112-116.

[38] It seems to this writer that a person is acting in good faith if he is doing everything that is here and now possible for being restored to the good graces of Holy Mother Church. Good faith requires, then, that the delinquent indicate all the censures from which

If absolution is given in the external forum it is valid also for the internal forum; if the absolution is given in the internal forum the penitent can, provided there is no scandal, conduct himself as absolved also in the external forum. Unless, however, the grant of the absolution in the internal forum can be proved or at least legitimately presumed in the external forum, the censure can be enforced by the proper superiors of the external forum, and the delinquent must obey until absolution is obtained in the external forum.[39]

An *ab homine* incurred censure is reserved to the one who inflicted the censure or pronounced the sentence, to his competent superior, to his own successor, or to his delegate.[40] A *ferendae sententiae* censure imposed by a condemnatory sentence is considered as deriving *ab homine*,[41] and, hence, is reserved. A *latae sententiae* censure is not reserved unless the law or the precept expressly mentions the reservation, and in doubt, whether of law or fact, the reservation does not hold.[42]

this particular superior can absolve him; it does not require that the delinquent mention those censures from which this superior cannot absolve anyway.

[39] Can. 2251.

[40] Can. 2245, § 2.

[41] Can. 2217, § 1, n. 3.

[42] Can. 2245, § 4. There is quite a controversy among canonists whether a penalty when established by way of a particular precept and then incurred automatically, is or is not to be considered as reserved. Some regard it as an *ab homine* incurred penalty, and, therefore, reserved; others consider it as deriving *tamquam a iure*, the equivalent of a *latae sententiae* penalty, and, therefore, not reserved unless it is explicitly so stated in the precept. Cf. Roberti, *De Delictis et Poenis*, I, Pars II, pp. 338-344; Stadalnikas, *Reservation of Censures*, pp. 85-105; Vermeersch-Creusen, *Epitome*, III, 239-240, 263; Christ, *Dispensation from Vindicative Penalties*, pp. 59-65; Moriarity, *The Extraordinary Absolution from Censures*, The Catholic University of America Canon Law Studies, n. 113 (Washington, D.C.: The Catholic University of America, 1938), pp. 93-106. The writer of this dissertation, following the opinion of Roberti (loc. cit.), holds that a *latae sententiae* penalty established by a particular precept is to be considered as deriving not *ab homine*, but *tamquam a*

A censure that is reserved in a particular territory is not reserved beyond the limits of that territory, even if the person under censure leaves the territory for the express purpose of obtaining absolution.[43] The person can obtain absolution even if a similar reservation is in force in the diocese to which he goes. The reservation imposed in his own diocese does not hold, for the reason namely that he has left the territory. Nor does the reservation of the second diocese hold, since strangers are not bound by the particular

iure. The reasons for holding this opinion are: 1) the norm for deciding whether or not a penalty derives *ab homine* seems to be the *immediate* source of the penalty in regard to its infliction. In a *latae sententiae* penalty, however, when established by way of a particular precept, the immediate source is not a person but the precept itself. Therefore, the penalty should be considered not as coming from a person (*ab homine*) but as deriving from a precept which is similar to a law (*tamquam a iure*). 2) Canon 2245 is a canon giving the most general rules on the reservation and non-reservation of censures. In determining which censures are reserved and which are not, it should, in order to preclude all confusion, employ principles of division which are mutually exclusive and do not overlap. If one considers *latae sententiae* censures that are constituted by way of a particular precept as deriving *tamquam a iure*, then the application of this rule obtains, for then no *latae sententiae* censure would derive *ab homine*, and vice versa. If on the other hand the *latae sententiate* censure, when established by way of a particular precept is considered as deriving *ab homine*, one does not have the same clear division, for this censure would then be both a penalty of a *latae sententiae* character and also a penalty that derives *ab homine*. 3) When canon 2245, § 4, states that *latae sententiae* censures when established by way of a precept are not reserved unless the precept indicates it, it did not limit the censures to those which are established by a *general* precept, as it could easily have done. It must be presumed, then, that the legislator did not wish to limit the canon in that way, but wished to include all censures established by precept, whether the precept be general in character or particular in character.

A practical solution of the problem is not difficult. There is sufficient intrinsic and extrinsic probability attaching to the opinion that holds for the "*tamquam a iure*" theory to establish a doubt of law, and, therefore, the reservation of *latae sententiae* censures that are established by way of a particular precept does not hold unless the reservation is stated in the precept.

[43] Can. 2247, § 2.

laws of that diocese.[44] An *ab homine* incurred censure is, however, reserved everywhere, so that the person under censure cannot be absolved anywhere without the proper faculties.[45] An *ab homine* incurred censure can be absolved only by the one who inflicted it, even when the culprit has transferred to another domicile or quasi-domicile.[46]

Having considered the general principles regarding the absolution from censures, one may now consider the various superiors and other persons who enjoy the faculty of absolving.

I. *The Holy See.* In virtue of his primacy the Holy Father can absolve from any censure, no matter by whom instituted, or inflicted.[47] The Holy Father seldom exercises personally his power of absolving;[48] ordinarily he exercises his power through the Tribunal of the Sacred Penitentiary and the various Congregations. In the internal forum, including the internal non-sacramental forum, the Sacred Penitentiary is competent for all cases, except those that are reserved to the Holy Father personally.[49] Even, however, when the case is reserved to the Holy Father personally, the petition for absolution is to be sent through the Sacred Penitentiary. During the vacancy of the Holy See the Sacred Penitentiary can absolve in the internal forum in urgent cases even from those censures that are reserved to

[44] Can. 14.

[45] Can. 2247, § 2.

[46] Can. 2253, n. 2.

[47] The Holy Father cannot abrogate the natural or the positive divine law, but there are no censures deriving from either of these laws.

[48] The Holy Father has reserved to himself the absolution of 1) the excommunication attached to delicts committed in connection with the election of the Roman Pontiff, 2) the excommunication attached to violations of secrets of the Holy Office, and 3) the excommunication attached to violations of secrecy in the causes of beatification and canonization; cf. Pius XII, const. *Vacantis Apostolicae Sedis*, 8 dec. 1945, nn. 41, 60-62, 80, 92-95, 100—*AAS*, XXXVIII (1946), 65. Cf. Moriarity, *Extraordinary Absolution from Censures*, p. 178.

[49] Cf. can. 258, § 1.

the Holy Father personally.[50] In the external forum the nature of the delict and the persons involved will determine the competent Congregation for the granting of the absolution. The Sacred Congregation of the Holy Office is competent for all cases involving delicts against the doctrine regarding faith or morals,[51] and its competency in these matters supersedes the competency of all other Congregations. The Sacred Congregation for the Propagation of the Faith is competent to absolve the censures incurred by persons living in the mission territories of the Church.[52] The Sacred Congregation of the Council handles those cases which involve the secular clergy and the laity.[53] The Sacred Congregation for Religious exercises the power of absolving from censures incurred by religious, clerical or lay.[54] The Sacred Congregation is competent for cases involving persons of the Oriental rites.[55] The absolution from *ab homine* incurred censures which have been imposed upon the persons named in canon 1557 are always reserved to the Holy See, for the simple reason that *ab homine* penalties are reserved to the one who inflicts them, and the Holy See alone is competent to inflict or declare penalties in regard to these persons.[56]

II. *Ordinaries.* No ordinary below the Holy Father can dispense from any of the universal laws of the Church unless the Code of Canon Law or the Holy See gives them the power to do so.[57] In *public* cases the Code of Canon Law grants ordinaries the power of absolving from all *latae sententiae* censures enacted in the Code, except in the cases which have been brought to the contentious forum as crimi-

[50] Pius XI, const. *Quae divinitus,* 25 mart. 1935, n. 12—*AAS,* XXVII (1935), 112; Pius XII, const. *Vacantis Apostolicae Sedis,* 8 dec. 1945, n. 17—*AAS,* XXXVIII (1946), 72.

[51] Can. 247.

[52] Can. 252.

[53] Can. 250.

[54] Can. 251.

[55] Can. 257.

[56] Can. 2227, § 1.

[57] Can. 81.

nal suits or as civil suits and the cases which have been reserved to the Apostolic See.[58] If the case is being tried in the ordinary's own court as a penal action, he can drop the case and grant absolution to the culprit.[59] All cases reserved to the Holy See, whether reserved in a most special way, or in a special way, or even in a simple way, are outside the ordinary's competence when the case is public. The Code of Canon Law makes one exception to this rule; it grants the ordinary the power of absolving from the excommunication that is reserved to the Holy See in a special way when it attaches to the delicts of apostasy, schism, and heresy, whenever the case is brought to the external forum.[60] In *occult* cases the Code of Canon Law grants ordinaries the power of absolving personally or through another, from *latae sententiae* censures that are not reserved or that are reserved to the Holy See in a simple way.[61] An ordinary of the place can absolve, besides his own subjects, also strangers; other ordinaries can absolve only their own subjects.[62] Local ordinaries cannot absolve from censures established by a plenary or a provincial council except in particular cases.[63] A just cause is required for the validity of the absolution whenever an ordinary absolves from a censure established by the Holy See or by a plenary or a provincial council.[64] The repentance of the delinquent is a sufficient cause. In cases of doubt regarding the sufficiency of the cause, the absolution can be given.[65] A censure imposed by the ordinary can be absolved by his superior. The superior of the local ordinary is not the metropolitan, but the Holy See. The superior of a religious ordinary would be determined by the constitutions of the community, except for the fact that the Holy See is always the highest

[58] Can. 2237, § 1, nn. 1 & 2; 2210. Cf. also can. 1725, nn. 1 & 2.
[59] Cf. Coronata, *Instittuiones*, IV, 143.
[60] Can. 2314, § 2.
[61] Can. 2237, § 2.
[62] Can. 2253, n. 3; cf. can. 198, §§ 1 & 2.
[63] Can. 291, § 2.
[64] Cans. 84, § 1; 291, § 2.
[65] Can. 84, § 2.

superior. The ranking of superiors is usually reflected in the following sequence: provincial superior, provincial chapter, superior general, general chapter. The constitutions may demand that the superior act with the consent or the advice of his council in serious penal matters. The successors of the local ordinary who can absolve censures include, besides the succeeding bishop, the cathedral chapter (or the board of diocesan consultors) and the vicar capitular (or diocesan administrator) who rule over the see during its vacancy.[66] The power of the vicar general to absolve without a special mandate from censures imposed by the bishop or the court is disputed.[67]

[66] Cf. cans. 391, § 1; 423; 427; 431, § 1; 432, § 1; 435, § 1.

[67] Cf., e.g., Christ, *Dispensation from Vindicative Penalties*, pp. 97-100, who holds that the vicar general cannot absolve without a special mandate. Those who say a special mandate is required argue that since a vicar general cannot impose a penalty without a special mandate (cf. can. 2220, § 2), he cannot absolve without a special mandate. In answer to this argument it must be said that the inability to absolve from a censure does not follow as a necessary and logical consequence from the inability to impose a censure. The Code of Canon Law accords to confessors the power of absolving from certain censures (cf. can. 2253, n. 1), though it does not give them the power to impose any; it could, therefore, grant also to vicars general the power of absolving from censures, although it denies them the power of inflicting them (without a special mandate). It is quite consonant with the benign spirit of the Code of Canon Law in penal matters (cf. can. 2219, § 1) to be more restrictive regarding the imposition of censures than regarding their absolution. In support of the view that a special mandate is not needed the following arguments can be adduced: 1) The person who inflicts a censure can also absolve from it (can. 2236, § 1). This authoritative individual, however, becomes properly identified not through his physical person but through his juridical personality (that is, through his office). Now, the vicar general and the bishop have a juridical identity; the vicar general acts with vicarious (though ordinary) power as an *alter ego* of the bishop. If the vicar general, then, absolves from a censure imposed by the bishop, it is juridically the same person who inflicted the penalty and who absolved from it. 2) Canon 368, § 1, states that the vicar general has all the powers in temporal and spiritual matters which the bishop has as an ordinary, except for those matters which the bishop has reserved to himself, or which by

III. *Others Enjoying Jurisdiction in the External Forum.* Since minor superiors in communities of exempt clerical religious have not only domestic power but real jurisdiction over their subjects,[68] they can absolve their subjects from non-reserved censures in the external forum.[69]

IV. *Confessors.* The confessor's power of absolving from censures varies with certain circumstances.

a. *Ordinary Cases.* In ordinary circumstances a confessor can absolve only from non-reserved censures, and this only in the sacramental forum.[70] If a confessor, not knowing of the reservation, absolves from a reserved censure, the absolution is valid as long as it is not a case of a censure incurred *ab homine,* or of a censure reserved to the Holy See in a most special way.[71] This faculty is given for the benefit of the penitent, and therefore it does not matter, as far as the validity of the absolution is concerned, what the reason may be for the confessor's ignorance. The ignorance may be crass or even affected, or it may result from inadvertence. A confessor who has faculties from the local ordinary can absolve a religious from censures reserved in the community to which the penitent belongs.[72] This holds true even though the confessor himself belongs to the same religious community.

b. *Extraordinary Cases.* In certain extraordinary circumstances confessors are given special powers of absolving from censures.

1) *In danger of death.* If the penitent is in danger of death the confessor, even though he enjoys no special faculties, can absolve from all censures, even censures incurred

law require a special mandate. Nowhere in the Code of Canon Law is a special mandate required for the vicar general to enable him to absolve from a censure; therefore, none is needed.

68 Cf. can. 501, § 1. This canon does not limit the possession of jurisdiction to major superiors, so there is no reason to exclude minor superiors.

69 Cf. can. 2253, n. 1.

70 Can. 2253, n. 1.

71 Can. 2247, § 3.

72 Can. 519.

ab homine and censures most specially reserved to the Holy See. In the case of absolution from *ab homine* incurred censures or from censures most specially reserved to the Holy See, the penitent, should he recover, is bound, under penalty of relapsing into the censure, to have recourse, in the case of the *ab homine* incurred censure, to the one who inflicted the censure or, in the case of a censure most specially reserved to the Holy See, to the Sacred Penitentiary, or to a bishop or to anyone else endowed with the necessary faculties, and he must be prepared to obey their mandates.[73] "Danger of death" has not the restrictive meaning that attaches to the phrase "*articulus mortis.*" It means any danger of death which is reasonably proximate, arising from any cause whether interior or exterior to the penitent. Danger is reasonably proximate if there is a reasonable chance that the person will not have another occasion of going to confession before death. Thus, a person who is in danger of losing his sanity can be said to be in danger of death even though there is no probability that he will die in the foreseeable future. Soldiers in a state of mobilization for war are in danger of death.[74] In cases of doubt the confessor can absolve validly and licitly.[75] Since canon 2252 does not limit the censures from which the confessor can absolve in danger of death, even censures which do not impede the reception of the sacraments, as for example suspensions, can be absolved. The confessor is not bound to inform the penitent of his obligation of having recourse if he can foresee that the penitent will surely die, or if he thinks that the admonition will disturb the dying person's peace of soul. When recourse is necessary it must be made

[73] Can. 2252. If a priest in danger of death is absolved from the censure incurred for attempting marriage, and if a separation is not possible, then upon his recovery he is obliged to have recourse to the Sacred Penitentiary, even though the censure is reserved to the Holy See in a simple way; cf. *AAS*, XXVIII (1936), 242; can. 2388, § 1.

[74] *AAS*, VII (1915), 282.

[75] Cans. 2245, § 4; 209.

within a month after convalescence.[76] The month is to be computed, of course, as a usable time. There is some question whether or not the mandates, once they have been received, must be obeyed under pain of relapsing into the censure. Canon 2252 seems to connect the newly emerging penalty solely with the neglect to institute the recourse. There is a doubt of law, and therefore, in practice, the penitent would not relapse into the censure for failing to observe the mandates.[77]

2) *In urgent cases.* In urgent cases, namely, when the censures cannot be observed externally without danger of grave scandal or infamy, or when it is burdensome for the penitent to remain in the state of grave sin for such time as would be necessary on the part of the competent superior to make due provision, then any confessor can, in the sacramental forum, absolve from *latae sententiae* censures, no matter how they are reserved. He must, however, impose upon the penitent the obligation, under pain of relapsing into the censure, of having recourse within a month, at least by letter and through the confessor, if it can be done without grave inconvenience, without mentioning the penitent's name, to the Sacred Penitentiary or to a bishop or other superior who has the faculty for absolving, and of fulfilling the latter's injunctions.[78] It will be noted that this faculty can be used only in regard to *latae sententiae* censures, and not in regard to *ab homine* incurred censures.[79] It seems that the legislator thought that anyone who was so contumacious that he did not recede from his contumacy when admonished, but permitted himself to be sentenced, was not deserving of the favor extended in canon 2254.[80]

[76] Cans. 2252; 2254, § 1.

[77] Cf. can. 2219, § 1. For a fuller discussion of the problem cf. Moriarity, *Extraordinary Absolution from Censures*, pp. 132-139.

[78] Can. 2254, § 1.

[79] Nor can it be used to absolve from the censure automatically incurred by a priest who has attempted marriage and who is now unable to separate from his consort; cf. *AAS*, XXIX (1937), 283.

[80] Moriarity (*Extraordinary Absolution from Censures*, p. 188) thinks that this canon can, in virtue of canon 20, be applied also to

To use canon 2254, one must have the faculties to hear confessions, since the canon in no way implies the bestowal of jurisdiction in the sacramental forum. In using canon 2254, there is nothing amiss in deliberately stirring up the penitent's conscience so that he will feel that it is burdensome for him to remain in grave sin, since it is part of the confessor's task to make his penitent hate sin. Suspension can be absolved by the confessor in virtue of canon 2254 to forestall scandal or infamy, but inasmuch as it does not prohibit the reception of the sacraments it could not be absolved on the grounds of freeing the penitent from the great burden of sin.

When absolution is given in virtue of canon 2254, recourse must be made regardless of how the censure is reserved. If in some extraordinary case the recourse is morally impossible, the confessor himself can, except in the case of the absolution from the censure mentioned in canon 2367, give absolution without imposing the obligation of recourse, but he must impose a suitable penance and require suitable satisfaction for the scandal given. If the penitent fails to observe the penance and to make the satisfaction within a suitable time determined by the confessor, he shall fall back into the censure.[81] Recourse is morally impossible when it cannot be made without serious inconvenience. This is usually the case when either the penitent or the confessor will not, or probably will not, return to the place where the confession was made. In this case the confessor cannot make the recourse for the penitent, and the penitent himself is, usually, *impar scribendi,* that is, incapable of drawing up the petition in the proper form. Recourse is morally im-

ab homine incurred censures. To the writer this does not seem correct. The legislator must have had some purpose for inserting the words "*latae sententiae*" into the canon. He must have intended deliberately to exclude *ab homine* incurred censures, otherwise he would simply have omitted the phrase.

[81] Can. 2254, § 3. The censure mentioned in canon 2367 is the excommunication most specially reserved to the Holy See and incurred for the crime of "*absolutio complicis.*"

possible also when there is danger that the letter of petition will be opened by unauthorized persons. Recourse is usually considered morally impossible if the impossibility lasts for a period of a month.[82] The penitent does not fall back into the censure unless his failure to make recourse was gravely culpable. Falling back into a censure is tantamount to incurring a new censure and, therefore, presupposes serious sin.

Nothing prevents the penitent, even after he has received absolution in the manner above indicated, or even after he has had recourse to the superior, from going to another confessor who has the special faculties needed for his case, and, after repeating the confession or at least the crime to which the censure is attached, obtaining absolution. When he has received absolution, he shall accept the injunctions of the confessor and shall not afterwards be obliged to observe the injunctions given by the superior to whom he has had recourse.[83]

SECTION 2. RELEASE FROM VINDICTIVE PENALTIES

The legislation on the cessation of vindictive penalties is much simpler than the legislation on the cessation of censures. The reason for this is that vindictive penalties do not exclude one from the reception of the sacraments as some censures do, and, therefore, there is not the same urgent need to provide for their expeditious removal. Also, censures seek to break the contumacy of the delinquent, and they should be quickly removed once they have accomplished their purpose. Vindictive penalties, however, are meant to repair the harm done to the public order, and this is usually a slow and gradual process.

[82] The Code of Canon Law does not state this, but the norm is borrowed from the first paragraph of canon 2254. The canon implies that a period longer than a month is an unreasonable length of time for putting off the recourse, and so it is concluded that it would be unreasonable also to require that a person be forced to make his recourse after such a period of time has passed.

[83] Can. 2254, § 2.

Release from a vindictive penalty can result from a change in the law. If a penal law, or at least the penalty attached to the law, is abrogated, those who have incurred the penalty are freed from it, provided that the penalty is a vindictive penalty and not a censure.[84] The more common way for vindictive penalties to cease, however, is either through expiation or by way of a dispensation.[85] Expiation looks to the lapse of the time period for which the penalty was imposed or to the fulfillment of some other condition requisite for the cessation of the penalty.[86] Dispensation, in this matter, is an act of favor by which a competent superior releases a person *post factum* from the penal bond of a law. It is necessary to go somewhat more into detail concerning those who have the power of dispensing from vindictive penalties.

I. *The General Rule.* The general rule for dispensations is contained in canon 2236. This canon states that dispensation from vindictive penalties can be granted only by the person who inflicted the penalty, by his competent superior or successor, or by one to whom the power has been granted.[87] Further, anyone who can dispense from a law can dispense from the penalty attached to it.[88] A judge who *ex officio* inflicts a penalty cannot dispense from it once it has been imposed.[89] The vicar general's power of dispensing is disputed but in the opinion of this writer he shares the bishop's power of dispensing, except for those cases which the bishop has reserved to himself.[90]

II. *Special Powers of Dispensing Granted to Ordinaries.*[91]

[84] Cf. can. 2226, § 3.

[85] Can. 2289.

[86] For an example of a condition other than the passage of time requisite for the cessation of a vindictive penalty cf. can. 2375.

[87] Can. 2236, § 1.

[88] Can. 2236, § 2.

[89] Can. 2236, § 3.

[90] Cf. *supra*, pp. 181-182, footnote n. 67. What was said there concerning the vicar general's power of absolving from censures applies with equal force to his power of dispensing from vindictive penalties.

[91] For those included under the term "ordinary" cf. can. 198.

Various canons in the Code of Canon Law give the ordinary special powers of dispensing over and above those granted in canon 2236. When using these special powers the ordinary needs, for the validity of the dispensation, a just and reasonable cause.[92] The repentance of the culprit is not always a sufficient reason for the granting of a dispensation. The reparation of the scandal caused must also be considered. In cases of doubt regarding the sufficiency of the cause the ordinary can validly and licitly dispense.[93]

a. *Special Power of Dispensing from Vindictive Penalties Imposed by Particular Law.* In particular cases and for a just reason the ordinary may dispense from vindictive penalties imposed by a decree of a plenary or a provincial council.[94] This is the only special power that ordinaries have regarding the dispensing of vindictive penalties imposed by the particular law.

b. *Special Power of Dispensing from Vindictive Penalties Imposed by the Universal Law.* The ordinary's power of dispensing from vindictive penalties imposed by the universal law of the Code is contained in canons 2237, 81, and 15.

1) *In Public Cases.* In public cases the ordinary can dispense from *latae sententiae* vindictive penalties established in the universal law, except for those cases which have been brought to the contentious forum[95] and also with reference to the following individual penalties: penalties involving ineligibility to or deprivation of, benefices, offices, committed assignments in the Church, and active and passive voting rights; perpetual suspension; infamy of law; deprivation of the right of patronage; and deprivation of privileges or favors granted by the Apostolic See.[96]

[92] Cf. cans. 84; 209.

[93] Can. 84, § 2.

[94] Cf. can. 291, § 2.

[95] Can. 2237, § 1, n. 1. This restriction of the ordinary's power of dispensing continues not just during the trial but, if the person is found guilty and is sentenced, even afterwards; cf. Coronata, *Institutiones*, IV, 142-143.

[96] Can. 2237, § 1, n. 3.

2) *In Occult Cases.* In occult cases the ordinary can dispense from all *latae sententiae* vindictive penalties enacted in the universal law.[97]

3) *In Urgent Cases.* In cases wherein there is danger of great harm in delay, and if it is a case from which the Holy See usually dispenses, the ordinary can, in a particular case, give a dispensation.[98] This provision of canon 81 holds good, not only for dispensing from the law in its entirety, but also for dispensing from a penalty attached to a law, for canon 2236, § 2, which states that anyone who has the power of dispensing from a law can dispense also from the penalty attached to it, in no way implies that the person must have an ordinary or a habitual power of dispensing from the law in order to qualify him for dispensing from the penalty attached to it. Any power of dispensing from the law, even such as is given for special circumstances as in canon 81, will suffice to entitle the person to dispense from the penalty attached to it.[99] The ordinary's power of dispensing in virtue of canon 81 extends even to those cases which are ordinarily excluded from his faculties by canon 2237, § 1. His power does not extend, however, to vindictive penalties imposed by way of a condemnatory sentence, since canon 81 authorizes him to dispense only from penalties imposed by the universal law, and not from those imposed by a particular sentence.

4) *In Doubtful Cases.* In cases of doubt whether or not a person has actually incurred a disqualification enacted in the universal law the ordinary can dispense, provided it

[97] Can. 2237, § 2. It should be noted that in occult cases the ordinary can dispense even if the *latae sententiae* penalty has been confirmed by a declaratory sentence; paragraph two of canon 2237 does not exclude cases which have been brought to the contentious forum.

[98] Can. 81.

[99] Cf. also *supra*, pp. 173-174, where it was pointed out that a dispensation from a penalty is a dispensation in the true sense. Since it is a true dispensation the canons concerning dispensations (cans. 80-86) should be applicable to it.

is a case wherein the Holy See usually dispenses.[100]

III. *Special Powers of Dispensing Granted to Confessors.* Ordinarily a confessor has no power of dispensing from vindictive penalties. In certain urgent cases, however, canon 2290 grants him special powers. When there is danger of scandal or infamy and when recourse to the proper superior is not possible any confessor can, in occult cases, dispense in the sacramental forum from *latae sententiae* vindictive penalties. He must, however, impose upon the penitent a suitable penance and must require suitable reparation for any scandal given. If the penitent fails to observe the penance and to make reparation within a reasonable time determined by the confessor, he shall relapse into the penalty.[101]

Article IV. Admission to the Election in Favor of Electors Who Become Qualified After the Election Has Begun

It may happen that a person who is not qualified to vote at the time the vacancy occurs may become qualified within the period of time granted by the law for the holding of the election. If the person is not qualified at the time set by the superior for the holding of the election he is not to be admitted, nor is there any obligation to postpone the election in any way in order to enable the disqualified elector to become qualified.[102] If it is possible for a disqualified elector to become qualified in time to take part in an election, he is to be summoned, so that he may take steps to become qualified. If an elector becomes qualified after the election has begun but before anyone has been elected to the office, he is to be admitted to the election. The only reason that could be alleged for excluding him is his lateness, but lateness is not given by the Code of Canon Law as one of the

[100] Can. 15.

[101] Cf. cans. 2290, § 2; 2254, § 3. Paragraph 1 of canon 2290 authorizes the confessor only to *suspend* the obligation of observing the penalty, and was treated above, pp. 164-166.

[102] Pirhing, Lib. I, tit. VI, n. 13.

reasons for barring an elector from an election. To justify the admission of an elector who is late a directive norm may, unless there is a particular law of the electoral college to the contrary, be borrowed from the rules governing papal elections. In the election of the Pope any Cardinal is admitted to the election if he comes after the election has begun but before a Pope has been elected.[103] Electors who are late in other elections, therefore, should also be admitted, even if their reason for being late is that they could not previously be admitted because of a then existing disqualification.[104]

[103] Pius XII, const. *Vacantis Apostolicae Sedis*, 8 dec. 1945, n. 38. —*AAS*, XXXVIII (1946), 77.

[104] Someone might contend that, if the election is prolonged over several days, those who seek admission after the first day are not to be admitted, since canon 163 says that the right of electing belongs to those who are present on the *day* (*dies*) set in the summons. To this it must be answered that the Latin word *dies* does not mean only "day" but also time in general. Canon 163 does not mean the right of electing belongs only to those who are present on the *day* set by the summons for the beginning of the election; it means that the right belongs to those who are present at the *time* of the election, excluding the absent. Since this is a law restricting one's right to vote, it should be interpreted in a restrictive sense (cf. can. 19). Those who are excluded from voting by canon 263, therefore, should be limited to those who are absent during the entire time of the election; they should not include also those who are absent during only the first day of it.

CONCLUSIONS

1. The pre-Code laws excluding certain persons from elections were true laws of disqualification in the fullest sense, and not merely prohibitory laws. A person laboring under a disqualification lacked the capacity of voting validly. Ignorance of the disability did not excuse from the nullifying effect. (pp. 3-5).

2. No one has the power of disqualifying an elector unless he has received this power, at least remotely, from the Holy See or the local ordinary. The power may come proximately from the particular laws which have been approved by the Holy See or by the local ordinary. (pp. 71-77).

3. *Collegium* in canon 165 means the electoral body as such, not the larger parent group of which the electoral body is a part. Anyone not belonging to the electoral body, even though he belongs to the parent group, is an *extraneus*. This interpretation is in keeping with the historical concept of *collegium*. (pp. 80-83).

4. According to canon 167, § 1, n. 3, *all* censures imposed or confirmed by way of a sentence disqualify. This holds true not only for excommunication, particular personal interdict, and general suspension imposed on an individual, but also for general personal interdict and general suspension imposed on a community, for interdict from entry into a church, and for a particular suspension imposed on an individual. These latter penalties, if imposed as *vindictive penalties, do not disqualify*. (pp. 100-101; 102-103).

5. If there has not been a sentence a person branded with infamy of law does not lose his right to vote (in this regard canon 167, § 1, n. 3, must be considered as an exception to canon 2294, § 1), nor is he barred from exercising his right. (pp. 104-105, 151).

6. The heretical sects as noted in canon 167, § 1, n. 4, include not only the non-Catholic Christian sects, but all sects which teach any doctrine contrary to the teaching of the Church. (pp. 110-111).

7. A candidate is "unworthy" of being elected, presented, or nominated if he lacks any of the qualities required by the law for his valid or licit election. *Indignus* and *non-idoneus* have the same specific meaning in this matter. (pp. 131-134).

8. To learn whether or not the vote of a disqualified elector has determined the outcome of an election, the election can be "reconstructed," without the participation of the disqualified voter(s), by means of a secret poll. (p. 145).

9. Expulsion of a disqualified voter, if it evinces a purely administrative act, is to be executed by the president of the electoral body. If it is a substantial act, however, it is to be performed by the whole college. (p. 159).

BIBLIOGRAPHY

Sources

Acta Apostolicae Sedis, Commentarium Officiale, Romae, 1909—

Bouscaren, T. Lincoln, *The Canon Law Digest*, 3 vols. through 1953, Milwaukee: Bruce Publishing Co., Vol. I, 1934, Vol. II, 1943, Vol. III, 1954 (Annual Supplements by Bouscaren, T. Lincoln-O'Connor, James I.).

Bullarum Diplomatum et Privilegiorum Sanctorum Romanorum Pontificum Taurinensis Editio, 24 vols. et appendix, Augustae Taurinorum, 1857-1872.

Bullarium Pontificium Sacrae Congregationis de Propaganda Fide, 2. ed., 5 vols., Romae, 1839, cum Appendice ad *Bullarium*, 2 vols., Romae, 1858; Index Analyticus, Romae, 1868.

Canones et Decretae Concilii Tridentini ex Editione Romana a 1834 Repetiti, accedunt S. Cong. Card. Conc. Trid. Interpretum Declarationes ac Resolutiones ex ipso Resolutionum Thesauro et Constitutiones Pontificiae Recensiores ad Ius Commune Spectantes e Bullario Romano selectae, Neapoli, 1859.

Codex Iuris Canonici Pii X Pontifiicis Maximi iussu digestus, Benedicti Papae XV Auctoritate promulgatus, Romae: Typus Polyglottis Vaticanis, 1917.

Codex Regularium Monasticarum et Canonicarum, 6 vols., ed. L. Holstenius, ed. altera, cura M. Brockie, Augustae Vindelicorum, 1759.

Codicis Iuris Canonici Fontes, cura Emi Petri Card. Gasparri editi, 9 vols., Romae (postea Civitate Vaticana): Typis Polyglottis Vaticanis, 1923-1939. (Vols. VII-IX ed. cura et studio Emi Iustiniani Card. Serédi).

Collectanea in Usum Secretariae Congregationis Episcoporum et Regularium, 2. ed., cura A. Bizzari Archiepiscopi Philippensis Secretarii edita, Romae: ex Typographia Polyglotta S. C. de Propaganda Fide, 1885.

Corpus Iuris Canonici, editio Lipsiensis secunda, post Aemilii Richteri curas . . . instruxit Aemilius Friedberg, 2 vols., 1879-1881. Editio anastice repetita, Lipsiae: Tauchnitz, 1928.

Corpus Iuris Civilis, 3 vols., Vol. I, Institutiones, recognovit Paulus Krueger, 15. ed.; Vol. II, Codex Iustinianus, recognovit et retractavit Paulus Krueger, 10. ed.; Vol. III, Novellae, recognovit Rudolfus Schoell, absolvit Guilelmus Kroll, 5. ed., Berolini: Apud Weidmannos, 1928-1929.

Decretales D. Gregorii Papae IX, una cum glossis restitutae, cum privilegio Gregorii XIII, Pont. Max. et Aliorum Principum, 2 vols., Romae, 1582.

Decretum Gratiani emendatum et notationibus illustratum una cum glossis Gregorii XIII Pont. Max. iussu editum, 2 vols., Romae, 1582.

Denziger, Henricus, *Enchiridion Symbolorum, Definitionum et Declarationum de Rebus Fidei et Morum*, 28. ed. augment., post Clementem Bannwart et Iohannem B. Umberg denuo edidit Carolus Rahner, Friburgi Brisgoviae: Herder, 1952.

Gregorii I Papae Registrum Epistolarum, 2 vols. in 5, ed. P. Ewald et L. M. Hartmann, Berolini, 1891-1899.

Hardouin, Jean, *Acta Conciliorum et Epistolae Decretales ac Constitutiones Summorum Pontificum*, 12 vols., Parisiis, 1714-1715.

Jaffé, Philippus, *Regesta Pontificum Romanorum ab condita Ecclesia ad annum post Christum natum MCXCVIII*, 2. ed. correctam et auctam auspiciis Guilelmi Wattenbach curaverunt F. Kaltenbrunner, P. Ewald, S. Loewenfeld, 2 vols., Lipsiae, 1885-1888.

Labbeus, Philippus, et Cossartibus, Gabrielis, *Sacrosancta Concilia, cum duobus apparatibus*, 17 vols. in 18, Parisiis, 1672.

Liber Sextus Decretalium D. Bonifatii Papae VIII, Clementis Papae V Constitutiones, Extravagantes tum vigenti D. Ioannis Papae XXII tum Communes, haec omnia cum suis glossis suae integritati restituta, 2 vols., Augustae Taurinorum, 1588.

Mansi, Ioannes, *Sacrorum Conciliorum Nova et Amplissima Collectio*, 53 vols. in 60, Parisiis, Arnheim, Leipzig, 1901-1927.

Normae secundum quas Sacra Congregatio Episcoporum et Regularium in novis religiosis congregationibus approbandis procedere solet, Romae, 1901.

Sacrosanctum Oecumenicum Concilium Tridentinum Additis Declarationibus Cardinalium, ex ultima recognitione Ioannis Gallemart necnon remissionibus Augustini Barbosae et annotationibus practicis Cardinalis De Luca cum variis Rotae Romanae decisionibus, editio novissima, Matriti, 1762.

Authors

Abbo, John A.-Hannan, Jerome D., *The Sacred Canons*, 2 vols., St. Louis: B. Herder Book Co., 1952.

Andreae, Ioannes, *In Titulum de Regulis Iuris Novella Commentaria*, Venetiis, 1581.

Augustine, Charles, *A Commentary on the New Code of Canon Law*, 8 vols., St. Louis: Herder, 1918-1922.

Baldus (Baldo degli Ubaldi), *Super Decretalibus*, Lugduni, 1547.

Beste, Udalricus, *Introductio in Codicem*, 3. ed., Collegeville, Minn.: St. John's Abbey Press, 1946.

Brockhaus, Thomas Aquinas, *Religious Who Are Known as Conversi*, The Catholic University of America Canon Law Studies,

n. 225, Washington, D.C.: The Catholic University of America Press, 1946.

Cappello, Felix, *Summa Iuris Canonici*, 3 vols., Vols. I & II, 4. ed., Vol. III, 3. ed., Romae: Apud Aedes Universitatis Gregorianae, 1945-1948.

———, *Tractatus Canonico-Moralis de Sacramentis*, 5 vols., Vols. I & II, 5. ed., Vols. III & IV, 3. ed., Vol. V, 6. ed., 1943-1951.

Castellini, Lucas, *De Electione et Confirmatione Canonica Praelatorum Quorumcumque Praesertim Regularium*, Romae, 1625.

Christ, Joseph James, *Dispensation from Vindicative Penalties*, The Catholic University of America Canon Law Studies, n. 174, Washington, D.C.: The Catholic University of America Press, 1943.

Cicognani, Amleto Giovanni, *Canon Law*, authorized English version by J. O'Hara and F. Brennan, 2. revised ed., Westminster, Maryland: The Newman Press, 1949.

Constitutions of the Congregation of the Missionaries of Mariannhill, Mariannhill (South Africa): Mariannhill Mission Press, 1950.

Coronata, Matthaeus Conte a, *Institutiones Iuris Canonici*, 5 vols., Vols. I, II, III, & V, 2. ed., Vol. IV, 3. ed., Taurini: Marietti, 1939-1948.

———, *Ius Publicum Ecclesiasticum*, 3. ed., Taurini: Marietti, 1948.

Creusen, Joseph, *Religious Men and Women in the Code*, 1. English trans. by Edward F. Garesché, 4. English ed., revised and edited to conform with the 5. French ed., Milwaukee: Bruce, 1942.

Crnica, Antonius, *Commentarium Theoretico-Practicum Codicis Iuris Canonici*, 2 vols., Sibenik: Kačić, 1940.

De Baysio (Bayso, Baisio), Guido, *Rosarium seu in Decretorum Volumen Commentaria*, Venetiis, 1587.

Dontaus, Hyacinthus, *Rerum Regularium Quadrapartita Praxis Resolutoria*, 2 vols., Neapoli, 1652.

Esswein, Anthony Albert, *Extrajudicial Penal Powers of Ecclesiastical Superiors*, The Catholic University of America Canon Law Studies, n. 127, Washington, D.C.: The Catholic University of America Press, 1941.

Fagnanus, Prosper, *Commentaria in Quinque Libros Decretalium*, 5 vols. in 4, Venetiis, 1709.

Haring, Johann B., *Grundzüge des katholischen Kirchenrechts*, 3. ed., 2 vols., Graz: Ulrich Mosers Buchhandlung, 1924.

Hefele, Carolus-Leclercq, Henricus, *Histoire des Conciles*, 11 vols. in 21, Paris: Letouzey et Ané, 1901-1952.

Hervé, J. M., *Manuale Theologiae Dogmaticae*, 4 vols., Vol. I, 46 ed.,

Vols. II, III & IV, 42. ed., Parisiis: Berche et Pagis, 1949-1952.

Hinschius, Paulus, *System in katholischen Kirchenrechts mit besonderer Ruecksicht auf Deutschland,* 4 vols., Berlin, 1869-1888.

Hostiensis, Cardinalis (Henricus de Segusio), *In Libros Decretalium Commentaria,* 6 vols. in 4, Venetiis, 1581.

———, *In Sextum Decretalium Commentaria,* post *In Libros Decretalium Commentaria* addita, Venetiis, 1581.

———, *Summa Aurea,* Venetiis, 1570.

Innocentius IV (Sinibaldus de' Fieschi), *In V Libros Decretalium Commentaria,* Venetiis, 1570.

Jone, Heribertus, *Commentarium in Codicem Iuris Canonici,* 3 vols., Paderborn: Officina Libraria F. Schöningh, 1950-1955.

Maroto, Philippus, *Institutiones Iuris Canonici,* 2 vols., Romae: Apud Commentarium pro Religiosis, Vol. I, 3. ed., 1921.

Migne, P. J., *Patrologiae Cursus Completus, Series Latina,* 221 vols., Parisiis, 1844-1864.

Moriarity, Francis E., *The Extraordinary Form of Absolution from Censures,* The Catholic University of America Canon Law Studies, n. 113, Washington, D.C.: The Catholic University of America, 1938.

Nervegna, Joseph, *De Institutis Votorum Simplicium Religiosorum et Monalium,* Romae: E Cooperativa Polygraphica Editrice, 1904.

Noval, I., *Commentarium Codicis Iuris Canonici,* Lib. IV, *De Processibus,* Pars I, *De Iudiciis,* Romae: Marietti, 1920.

Oesterle, G., *Praelectiones Iuris Canonici,* Vol. I, Romae: Collegio S. Anselmi, 1931.

Ojetti, Benedictus, *Synopsis Rerum Moralium et Iuris Pontificii,* 3. ed. emendata et aucta, 4 vols., Romae: Ex Officina Polygraphica Editrice, 1909-1914.

Ottaviani, Alaphridus, *Institutiones Iuris Publici Ecclesiastici,* 2 vols., Vol. I, 3. ed., Vol. II, 2. ed., Civitate Vaticana: Typis Polyglottis Vaticanis, 1936-1947.

Panormitanus, Abbas (Nicolaus de Tudeschis), *Omnia quae extant Commentaria,* 8 vols., Venetiis, 1588.

Parsons, Anscar, *Canonical Elections,* The Catholic University of America Canon Law Studies, n. 118, Washington, D.C.: The Catholic University of America Press, 1939.

Passerini, Petrus Maria de Sextula, *Tractatus de Electione Canonica,* Romae, 1693.

Pichler, Vitus, *Ius Canonicum secundum Quinque Decretalium Titulos Gregorii Papae IX Explicatum,* 2 vols., Ravennae, 1741.

Pignatelli, Jacobus, *Consultationes canonicae,* 11 vols. in 6, 1700, plus 2 vols. in 1, 1711, Colloniae Allobrogum.

Pirhing, E., *Ius Canonicum in Quinque Libros Decretalium Distributum*, Dillingae, 1722.

Rainer, Eligius George, *Suspension of Clerics*, The Catholic University of America Canon Law Studies, n. 111, Washington, D.C.: The Catholic University of America, 1937.

Reiffenstuel, Anacletus, *Ius Canonicum Universum*, 4 vols., Venetiis, 1735.

Roberti, Franciscus, *De Delictis et Poenis*, Vol. I, Pars I, 1930, et Pars II, 1938, Romae: Appolinaris.

Samuelli, Franciscus M., *Disputationum Controversiae de Canonica Electione in regularibus Praelatis atque cathedralium ecclesiarum canonicis eligendis*, Venetiis, 1644.

Schaefer, Timotheus, *De Religiosis ad Normam Codicis Iuris Canonici*, 4. ed. aucta et emendata, Romae: Editrice "Apostolato Cattolico," 1947.

Schmalzgrueber, Franciscus, *Ius Ecclesiasticum Universum*, 5 vols. in 12, Romae, 1843-1845.

Schroeder, H. J., *Disciplinary Decrees of the General Councils*, St. Louis: B. Herder, 1937.

Stadalnikas, Casimir J., *Reservation of Censures*, The Catholic University of America Canon Law Studies, n. 208, Washington, D.C.: The Catholic University of America Press, 1944.

Tatarczuk, Vincent A., *Infamy of Law*, The Catholic University of America Canon Law Studies, n. 357, Washington, D.C.: The Catholic University of America Press, 1954.

Torre, Joannes, *Processus Matrimoniales*, Neapoli: M. D'Auria, 1947.

VanderVeldt, James H.-Odenwald, Robert R., *Psychiatry and Catholicism*, New York: McGraw-Hill, 1952.

Vermeersch, A.-Creusen, J., *Epitome Iuris Canonici*, 3 vols., Vol. I, 7. ed., 1949, Vol. II, 6. ed., 1940, Vol. III, 6. ed., 1946, Mechliniae-Romae: H. Dessain.

Wernz, Franciscus X., *Ius Decretalium*, 6 vols. in 10, Vol. I, 3. ed., Prati, 1913, Vol. II, 3. ed., Prati, 1915, Vol. III, 2. ed., Romae, 1908, Vol. IV, 2. ed., Romae, Pars I, 1911, Pars II, 1912, Vol. V, 3. ed., Prati, 1914, Vol. VI, 3. ed., Prati, 1913.

Wernz, Franciscus-Vidal, Petrus, *Ius Canonicum ad Codicis Normam Exactum*, 7 vols. in 8, Vol. I, 2. ed., 1952, Vol. II, 3. ed. a Aguirre recognita, 1943, Vol. III, 1. ed., 1933, Vol. IV, 1. ed., Tom. I, 1934, Tom. II, 1935, Vol. V, 3. ed. a Aguirre recognita, 1946, Vol. VI, 2. ed. a Cappelo recognita, 1951, Romae: Apud Aedes Universitatis Gregorianae.

Woywod, Stanislaus, *A Practical Commentary on the Code of Canon Law*, revised by Callistus Smith, 2 vols. in 1, New York: Joseph F. Wagner, 1952.

Articles

Larraona, Arcadius, "Commentarium Codicis," *CpRM*, XVI (1935), 429-432.

———, "De Electionibus Religiosorum," *CpR*, IX (1928), 335-336.

Roelker, Edward, "Acquired Rights and the Retroactivity of Laws," *The Jurist*, IV (1944), 491-521.

Periodicals

Archiv fuer katholisches Kirchenrecht, Innsbruck, 1857-1861; Mainz, 1862—

Commentarium pro Religiosis (from 1935, *Commentarium pro Religiosis et Missionariis*), Romae, 1920—

Jurist, The, Washington, D.C., 1941—

BIOGRAPHICAL NOTE

Timothy Mock was born in Aberdeen, South Dakota, on August 6, 1926. He received his elementary education at St. Mary's School in Aberdeen. In the fall of 1940 he entered St. Bernard's Seminary at Sioux Falls, South Dakota. He was admitted to the novitiate of the Congregation of Mariannhill Missionaries at Brighton, Michigan, in August, 1945, and was professed a year later. After studying Philosophy for two years at St. Benedict's Seminary at Brighton, Michigan, he was sent by his superiors to St. Meinrad Major Seminary, St. Meinrad, Indiana, for one year of theological study. He completed his final three years of theological study at St. Benedict's Seminary, Brighton, Michigan. He was ordained to the priesthood on May 25, 1952. In September, 1952, he entered the School of Canon Law at the Catholic University of America. He received the degree of Bachelor in Canon Law in June, 1953, and the degree of Licentiate in Canon Law in June, 1954.

ABBREVIATIONS

AAS—*Acta Apostolicae Sedis.*

Bizzarri—*Collectanea in Usum Secretariae Congregationis Episcoporum et Regularium.*

Bull. Rom. Taur.—*Bullarium Romanum,* Taurienesis Editio.

c.—canon seu caput.

can.—canon.

C.—Causa seu *Codex Iustinianus.*

Commentaria Novella—*In Titulum de Regulis Iuris Novella Commentaria.*

Conc. Trident.—Concilium Tridentinum.

CpR(M)—*Commentarium pro Religiosis (et Missionariis).*

D.—*Digestum Iustiniani* seu Distinctio.

D. B.—Denziger-Bannwart.

Hardouin—*Acta Conciliorum et Epistolae Decretales ac Constitutiones Summorum Pontificum.*

In Clem.—Panormitanus, *Commentarium in Clementinas Epistolas et earum Glossas.*

Inst.—*Institutiones.*

Mansi—*Sacrorum Conciliorum Nova et Amplissima Collectio.*

MPL—(*Migne, Patrologia Latina*), Migne, Jacques Paul, *Patrologiae Cursus Completus,* Series Latina.

Pont. Com. ad Cod. auth. Interp.—Pontifical Commission for the Authentic Interpretation of the Code.

Rosarium—De Baysio, Guido, *Rosarium seu in Decretorum Volumen Commentaria.*

S. C. C.—Sacra Congregatio Concilii.

S. C. Ep. et Reg.—Sacra Congregatio Episcoporum et Regularium.

S. C. super Statu Regularium—Sacra Congregatio super Statu Regularium.

S. C. de Religiosis—Sacra Congregatio de Religiosis.

s. v.—sub verbo; sub verbis.

ALPHABETICAL INDEX

CANON LAW STUDIES*

358. Sesto, Rev. Gennaro J., S.D.B., A.B., S.T.L., J.C.L., Guardians of the mentally ill in ecclesiastical trials.
359. Carroll, Rev. James J., A.B., J.C.L., The bishop's quinquennial report.
360. Curtin, Rev. William Thomas, A.B., J.C.L., The plaint of nullity against the sentence.
361. Ganter, Rev. Bernard J., J.C.L., Clerical attire.
362. Goertz, Rev. Victor M., J.C.L., The judicial summons.
363. Heintschel, Rev. Donald E., A.B., J.C.L., The medieval concept of an eccclesiatical office.
364. Kelliher, Rev. Jeremiah Francis, S.A., A.B., S.T.L., Loss of privileges.
365. Mock, Rev. Timothy, C.M.M., J.C.L., Disqualification of electors in ecclesiastical elections.
366. Smyer, Rev. Francis Anthony, A.B., J.C.L., Canonical regulations regarding exposition of the Blessed Sacrament accord- to canons 1274 and 1275.
367. Wiggins, Rev. Urban C., A.B., J.C.L., Property laws of the state of Ohio affecting the Church.

* For a complete list of the available numbers of this series apply to the Catholic University of America Press, 620 Michigan Ave., N.E., Washington (17), D.C., for a general catalogue.

www.ingramcontent.com/pod-product-compliance
Lightning Source LLC
LaVergne TN
LVHW050243080826
844660LV00012B/591

* 9 7 8 0 8 1 3 2 2 5 3 1 9 *